William Ferguson Beatson Laurie

Sketches of Some Distinguished Anglo-Indians

With an Account of Anglo-Indian Periodical Literature

William Ferguson Beatson Laurie

Sketches of Some Distinguished Anglo-Indians
With an Account of Anglo-Indian Periodical Literature

ISBN/EAN: 9783337060435

Printed in Europe, USA, Canada, Australia, Japan

Cover: Foto ©ninafisch / pixelio.de

More available books at **www.hansebooks.com**

SKETCHES OF SOME

DISTINGUISHED ANGLO-INDIANS.

WITH AN ACCOUNT OF

ANGLO-INDIAN PERIODICAL LITERATURE.

BY

COLONEL W. F. B. LAURIE,

RETIRED ROYAL (MADRAS) ARTILLERY;

Author of " Orissa, and the Temple of Jagannáth," "Our Burmese Wars and Relations with Burma," "Second Burmese War," &c.

" L'honneur acquis est un caution de celui qu'on doit acquérir."
            Rochefoucault.

" Insidet quædam in optimo quoque virtus, quæ noctes ac dies animum gloriæ stimulis concitat atque admonet, non cum vitæ tempore esse dimittendam commemoratorem nominis nostri, sed cum posteritatis adæquandam."

CICERO, *Pro Archia Poeta, cap. ii.*

LONDON:
PRINTED AND PUBLISHED BY JOHN B. DAY,
"SAVOY STEAM PRESS," SAVOY STREET, STRAND.

1875.

TO THE MEMORY OF

MY FATHER,

THIS LITTLE BOOK

IS AFFECTIONATELY INSCRIBED.

PREFACE.

DR. JOHNSON remarks on the difficulty of the first address on any new occasion; and it would be well if an Anglo-Indian author could find some easy and successful method of introducing his last performance to the British public. My direct appeal, through a prospectus, not only to Anglo-Indians, but to the reading world in general, for patronage to this little work, having met with a fair share of success, it would seem only desirable to send it forth without any further prefatory remark than "I am much obliged." But, conceiving it to be necessary, as it is also a time-honoured custom, to say something regarding the contents, I shall, endeavouring to be brief, commence by alluding to the fact of even a larger number of names of Anglo-Indians, and others, appearing together in these pages, than was at first contemplated. They are more or less distinguished; but there is certainly a goodly array; and my humble attempt to do justice to some of them (Anglo-Indians) is apt to remind one of the famous lines at the conclusion of Shakspeare's " King Henry V."—in which the liberty is now taken of putting one line in italics, and altering " This star of England," to suit the occasion :—

>" Thus far, with rough, and all unable pen,
>   Our bending author has pursued the story ;
> *In little room confining mighty men,*
>   Mangling by starts the full course of their glory.
> Small time, but, in that small, most-greatly liv'd "
>   These *stars* of India !

Several additional stars, among the departed as well as the living, might, perhaps, have been introduced with advantage. Doubtless, when the time comes, some more able pen will do such luminaries—who, through force of character, for their hour became " lords of the ascendant " —ample justice. However, it may not be out of place to remark that, besides the great name of Lawrence, others appear among the rulers of the Punjab who have deserved well of their country—Sir Robert Montgomery, (now a Member of the Council of India), Sir Donald Macleod, and Sir Henry Durand. Following India's severest trial, it would have been pleasing to record the many good actions which distinguished the lives of three such Lieutenant-Governors; and the violent and sudden deaths of the latter two would have thrown around the sketches a melancholy halo of interest. Sir Henry Durand alone would furnish an interesting volume. As a Lieutenant of the Bengal Engineers, with the force under General Sir John (afterwards Lord) Keane, he blew open the great gate of the fortress of Ghuzni, firing the fuze with his own hand. By this fearless act he was first distinguished.* In September, 1844, he relieved the gallant Major Broadfoot (who fell at Ferozshah) in the Commissionership of the Tenasserim Provinces, taking up the difficult question of the revenue assessments. Timber in the Thoongeen forests next occupied his attention; and, in spite of great hostility from the trade, Captain Durand traversed these picturesque, yet lonely, haunts of Chin-India, and made himself acquainted, by local examination and inquiry, with everything regarding them, with a view to improvement; evincing the same admirable spirit of inquiry which, nearly thirty years after, led Sir Henry Durand, ruler of the Punjab, to leave the camp, and visit the outpost garden and town of Tank. Having inspected the outpost on foot, Sir Henry proceeded on one of the camp elephants in a howdah with the Nawab of Tank, whose son was in advance on horseback to show the way. On another elephant were several British officers of rank, the whole forming a striking, though not uncommon, Oriental picture. At the entrance of the town are two gateways, one (the outer) of sufficient height to allow an elephant and howdah to pass; the second, considerably

* The historian of the War in Afghanistan records this successful military operation:—"Captain Thomson, of the Bengal Engineers, directed the movements of the explosion party; and with him were his two sub-alterns, *Durand* and Macleod, and Captain Peat of the Bombay Corps. Lieutenant Durand was obliged to scrape the hose with his finger ends, finding the powder failed to ignite on the first application of the portfire."

lower. From outer to inner gateway the ground rises. The Lieutenant-Governor's elephant passed the outer gateway with ease; but the second appeared too low. The officers did not think Sir Henry would pass through it. Those who have been in India know well the rapid pace of some elephants, which seems to quicken (as if the animal had an increasing sense of his importance) on entering a town on any great occasion. Although there was a short pause after passing through the first gateway, it was just preparatory to a more rapid sweep through the second. The elephant proceeded; and, before warning could be given, the crash of a breaking howdah was heard, and a highly useful, as well as brilliant, career was over. *

The other sad event, which happened in London, is of too recent occurrence to require mention here. And now we turn to the living. There is Sir Douglas Forsyth, who has explored hitherto unknown countries in Central Asia, and has given an impetus to trade in that fickle region hardly experienced before. Mr. Forsyth's visit to Yarkund dates as far back as April, 1870, reminding one of the useful work of exploration through which Sir Alexander Burnes and other Anglo-Indians first rose to distinction.

In December, 1870, we find T. D. Forsyth, Esq., C.B., on special duty, writing to the Secretary of the Punjab Government, that "when Mirza Mohamed Shedee, Envoy from the Atalik Ghazee, ruler of Kashgar, and the country known as Eastern Turkestan, had an interview with the Viceroy of India at Calcutta, on the 28th March, 1870, he preferred a request, on behalf of his master, that a British officer might be sent back with him, on a friendly visit to the Court of the Atalik Ghazee, as an evidence of the friendship existing between the two Governments, and with a view to strengthen and cement it." Mr. Forsyth's in-

* The officers on the second elephant got down, and found Sir Henry on the ground, just beyond the inner gateway, lying on his face. This melancholy accident to a distinguished Anglo-Indian happened on the evening of the 31st December, 1871. Sir Henry Durand breathed his last on the evening of the 1st January, 1872, to the sincere grief of the Government of India, and his numerous friends and admirers.—(From letter from T. H. Thornton, Esq., D.C.L., Secretary to Government of the Punjab). Sir Henry (as Colonel and C.B.) was a Member of the Council of India, under the Right Honourable Sir Charles Wood, Bart., G.C.B., M.P., in 1860.

structions were to go to Yarkund merely on a friendly visit to the Atalik Ghazee, and for the purpose of "opening up and giving impulse to the trade with that country." The expedition, under Mr. Forsyth, among other useful personages, included Mr. R. B. Shaw, "the first Englishman who ever went to Yarkund, and who may be called the pioneer of Central Asian trade with India;" Dr. Henderson, medical and scientific officer, subordinate to whom were Native Doctor Mohamed Yasseen, one bird collector and one plant collector; Mir Akbar Ali Khan Bahadoor, C.S.I., of Abyssinian celebrity, acted as Native Secretary. The Report consists of 214 pages, with valuable trade statistics, and information on routes in the appendix.*

With similar laudable efforts on the part of the Indian Government, the Anglo-Indian has a chance of being utilised in the East, and, consequently, of becoming distinguished, which he has seldom had before. The Iron Duke says in his Despatches that the affairs of America "will always hang upon the skirts of Great Britain." So will those of India, as a matter of course; but, in the latter case, more must be effected. They must not only hang on the skirts of Britannia, but be woven into her dress, becoming, as it were, a part and parcel of herself, by a process which Manchester ingenuity may yet devise!

Among other distinguished living Anglo-Indians, we have the Right Honourable Sir Bartle Frere, Sir Henry Rawlinson, Sir George Clerk, Sir Erskine Perry, Sir William Grey, and Sir George Campbell; the latter well-known Bengal civilian† forming one, under the Viceroy, Lord Northbrook, and Sir Richard Temple (erst-while a Calcutta reviewer) another, of the grand energetic triumvirate who did so much to crush the Bengal famine of 1874. Such well timed energy cannot but command intense admiration. With even the twelve or more names already mentioned, a most interesting volume of sketches could be produced.

It is curious to notice how the all-important science of

---

* See also Appendix v., "Action in Eastern Asia." The Yarkund Envoy paid a state visit to the Viceroy, January 19th, 1875, and had left Calcutta for Bombay.

† Now of the Council of India.

geography is mixed up with Anglo-Indians at the present time. Sir Henry Rawlinson, K.C.B., Member of the Council of India, and now V.P.R.G.S., succeeded the late Sir Roderick Impey Murchison as President of the Royal Geographical Society, and was himself succeeded in that post by Sir Bartle Frere, G.C.S.I., K.C.B., also a Member of the Indian Council. We may also mention that Mr. Clements Markham, C.B., Assistant-Secretary, Revenue Department, India Office, is Secretary to the above learned body. We have just heard that slavery has been abolished on the West coast of Africa; and this brings to mind how, in the middle of 1873, her Majesty called Sir Bartle Frere to her Privy Council as a recognition of his services towards extinguishing slavery on the East coast. The Anglo-Indian everywhere is becoming a man of the time. It is pleasing to note that energy and intellect have not only distinguished him in India and the East; but, at home, he has recently come forward in a remarkable degree to discuss great principles in social science, and to aid the grand lever of civilisation at the present day—education. A celebrated Anglo-Indian, a former Viceroy of India (Lord Lawrence), has not long left the seat at the London School Board he so worthily occupied; and a late popular and energetic Governor of Madras, who did so much for that Presidency— and who for the work he did there, and from the interest he takes in the country, may be almost styled an Anglo-Indian—Lord Napier and Ettrick—turning from the most important questions of social science, is now a member of the School Board; and, perhaps, a more zealous worker in the cause of popular elementary education has never appeared before. But Anglo-Indians of every degree, at home, are, as a rule, anxious to work if they can only find employment; and if a "bad liver" is occasionally to be found among them it is generally coupled with a good heart! We may expect in future years to see the Anglo-Indian utilised at home to an extent hitherto unknown. When such a wished-for consummation arrives, it will be no small pleasure also to note that English indifference to Indian affairs has vanished, and that "personal and social sympathy," recently alluded to by Sir George Campbell *

* At a meeting of the "National India Association," Dec. 1874.

as wanting to our rule in India, has become more general.

The actions of distinguished men detailed in this little volume, it is to be hoped will assist the judgment of those anxious to form an opinion on some of them, but who have no time to peruse larger works, and the fame the actors have gained certainly affords every hope of a bright future; or, to give a translation of the French motto on the title-page:—

> "Honour acquired, is a guarantee
> That, as the past, so shall the future be." *

Three of the principal sketches are almost, if not entirely, new—Mr. John Colvin, General Beatson, and Sir John Kaye. In some of the others a repetition of expression will occasionally be found, which long intervals between their production, and a desire not to spoil their entirety, may readily excuse. I must ask the indulgence of the public for introducing among the lighter papers, "Falcieri: An India Office Sketch;" but I trust the reasons for so doing are sufficiently explained. There are people who think little about India, but who care a vast deal about any novel incident in the life of one who "lived as a separate spirit"—Lord Byron;† and after reading my brief paper on "Tita," they may feel inclined to look into the purely Anglo-Indian sketches, when if they should gain even a slight knowledge of what they did not know before, the writer's labours will not have been in vain. The sketch of Anglo-Indian Periodical Literature, and the paper on Sir Henry Lawrence, originally appeared in a London magazine, at first (as its name held forth) an Oxford *star*, which, although it had pecuniary and literary support from its well-wishers—among them two of England's most distinguished writers—after uncertain twinklings for a year or two, suddenly disappeared from the literary firmament, leaving no sign! Some good judges, and a few of the London journals, having done me the honour to think well of

---

* Translated by the late Major-General P. J. Begbie, a worthy if not a distinguished Anglo-Indian, who translated some valuable works on Artillery, from the French, and wrote a History of the Coast (Madras) Artillery.

† See also note at end of Appendix—"Lord Byron and India."

my *Dark Blue* contributions, the most important of them are here reproduced. The "Periodical" sketch—perhaps the only thing of the kind existing—may form some relief to the heavier fare provided for my readers.

With regard to the spelling of Indian words, I should remark that as far as possible, uniformity has been attempted; but where a writer of distinction is quoted, his own spelling is generally given. I have made use of what I conceive to be the most correct and approved forms of spelling; and I now trust that the word *Burma* will never again be written with an *h* at the end, to which it is no more entitled than China or Russia.*

The portrait of Sir John Kaye, represented in his diplomatic uniform, with the Knight's collar and star of the much coveted Order of the Star of India (of which the Viceroy is Grand Master, and "Heaven's Light our Guide" the appropriate motto), and which is an admirable likeness, will doubtless please the friends of that distinguished Anglo-Indian, as well as the reading public who have admired his writings. By such men, if we may again quote Cicero, we are reminded of what we should leave to posterity:—"An statuas et imagines, non animorum simulacra, sed corporum, studiose multi summi homines reliquerunt: consiliorum relinquere ac virtutum nostrarum effigiem non multo malle debemus suimus ingeniis expressam et politam?" †

It may be stated, in concluding this somewhat rambling preface, that pains have been taken in the all-important matter (for a good record) of correct dates, with the view to being useful as well as entertaining.

---

* Introducing the general use of the Roman character into India for the vernacular languages—so ably brought forward by Mr. Frederick Drew, and admirably commented on by Sir Charles Trevelyan (President) at the Conference of the Society of Arts, February 12th—although we are loath to part with the Oriental characters, would no doubt aid in producing uniformity in the spelling of Indian words.

† CICERO, Pro Archia, cap. 12.—The motto from Cicero on the title-page is thus translated by a learned friend :—"There resides a kind of virtue in every good man, which, night and day, stimulates his mind with the incentives of glory, and suggests that the record of our name is not to be obliterated with the time of our life, but is to be handed down to posterity."

So now, apologising for unavoidable delay in its production, I cast my little book upon the waters, trusting that it may be deemed at least a healthy contribution to Anglo-Indian literature, and, for the present, respectfully bidding my kind friends and patrons—farewell!

W. F. B. L.

"TORRE LEIGH," OXFORD GARDENS,
NOTTING HILL, W., *March 8th*, 1875.

CONTENTS.

	Page
I.—SIR ALEXANDER BURNES, C.B.	3
II.—JAMES BURNES, K.H., LL.D., F.R.S.	15
III.—SIR HENRY LAWRENCE, K.C.B.	28
IV.—JOHN RUSSELL COLVIN, B.C.S. (Lieutenant-Governor of Agra, 1857)	44
V.—BRIGADIER-GENERAL JAMES GEORGE NEILL	68
VI.—MAJOR-GENERAL WILLIAM FERGUSON BEATSON	25
VII.—COLONEL WILLIAM HENRY SYKES, M.P., F.R.S.	106
VIII.—MAJOR-GENERAL WILLIAM HENRY MILLER, C.B.	112
IX.—MAJOR-GENERAL ALBERT FYTCHE, C.S.I.	112
X.—SIR ARTHUR PURVES PHAYRE, K.C.S.I. (the new Governor of Mauritius)	135
XI.—SIR JOHN WILLIAM KAYE, K.C.S.I., F.R.S.	149
LINES SUGGESTED BY THE FUNERAL OF SIR GEORGE POLLOCK	163
FALCIERI: AN INDIA OFFICE SKETCH	165
ANGLO-INDIAN PERIODICAL LITERATURE	174
SPORTING LITERATURE IN INDIA	225

APPENDIX.

I.—LORD PALMERSTON AND SIR ALEXANDER BURNES	231
II.—DR. BURNES' VISIT TO THE COURT OF SIND	234
III.—SIR JAMES OUTRAM, G.C.B., K.S.I.	238
IV.—FIELD-MARSHAL SIR GEORGE POLLOCK, G.C.B., G.C.S.I.	246
V.—ACTION IN EASTERN ASIA	249
Note.—LORD BYRON AND INDIA	257

SKETCHES OF
SOME DISTINGUISHED ANGLO-INDIANS.

THE- BROTHERS BURNES.

INTRODUCTORY.

"THE old East India House, in Leadenhall Street, is rapidly disappearing, and nothing remains to shew of it except the portico, and this will be levelled to the ground in the course of a few days." Such was the announcement made in the London journals about the middle of September, 1862. Warehouses and chambers were soon to cover the site of the once palace of London merchants, of the Company founded in the year 1600, under the denomination of " The Governor and Company of Merchants trading to the East Indies," which had risen to such great eminence in the commercial and political world.

Here was a grand theme for reflection ! The disappearance of the relic of what has been well styled the most celebrated association of ancient or modern times, which extended its sway over the entire Mogul Empire ;— what an interesting subject for the student of history !

The merchants first transacted business in the Nag's Head Inn, Bishopsgate Street. The old East India House, I learn, was erected after 1726, and completed and enlarged in 1798—99. What a number of celebrated men had stood under the portico, now about to be swept away !* No more were we to gaze on that stately entrance, on that tympanum containing figures such as

*[What a contrast the old House forms with the palatial India Office in St. James' Park, recently presided over by the Duke of Argyll, and now (1874) by the Marquis of Salisbury !]

Mercury, attended by Navigation, followed by tritons and sea-horses—emblems of commerce—introducing Asia to Britannia, before whom she spreads her productions.

But we might continue to think of those architects of their own fortunes—nearly all of them belonging to the middle classes—who had given such imperishable lustre to Indian history. In selecting for the following pictures the Traveller and the Physician, as connected with the Indian service, I will not presume to say that the greatest example of each class has been presented. The sketches must speak for themselves.

After the spirit of mercantile enterprise, to those who have laboured like the above two actors in the great drama, India owes much of her prosperity. To go back; we have the traveller and "political," Sir Thomas Roe, who, after exploring the Amazon, in America, first travelled to the Court of the Great Mogul; we have Boughton, the surgeon and diplomatist, who cured the Mogul's beautiful daughter, and, as a recompense, was allowed to found British trade in Bengal.

Hindustan has since then passed through many trials. The demand for cotton, it is to be hoped, will now do much for Bombay and Madras; and, whatever may be thought of amalgamation, let us, as calm observers, accept as prophetic truth, what was eloquently uttered by Her Majesty's Secretary of State (July 17th, 1862), that there is "a future of great prosperity in store for India."

LONDON, *October* 23*rd*, 1862.

THE BROTHERS BURNES.

I.

SIR ALEXANDER BURNES, C.B.

"L'immense et courageux voyage de M. Burnes."
Baron Humboldt.
"Vous avez tracé sur la portion peut être la plus obscure de l'Asie une ligne lumineuse."
Royal Asiatic Society of Paris to Sir Alex. Burnes.

THE unexpected death of a man possessing so many great qualities as Dr. James Burnes, I am sure caused a deep sensation of heartfelt sorrow in Western India, as it did to many in this country. The circumstances attending the feeling of grief differed widely from those which accompanied the loss of his distinguished brother, Sir Alexander. No fearful tragedy at Cabool, or elsewhere, brought about his end. He died in one of our chief cities of industry, in our own glorious land—the physician at length the chief sufferer in a domestic scene of sorrow—far away from the "splendour and havoc of the east."

It has struck me that brief sketches of the careers of the two most distinguished of the family may not be unacceptable to many readers at the present time: standing forth, as the brothers do, in the picture gallery from India, as brilliant examples of energy and goodness, worthy of imitation by all about to enter Her Majesty's Indian Service.

Sir Alexander was born at Montrose, in Scotland, on the 16th of May, 1805. After a rather brilliant academical career, the youth, whose great grandfather was brother to the father of Scotland's immortal bard, was appointed a cadet in the Bombay army, and arrived at that Presidency on the 31st October, 1821. In India, before he had reached his twentieth year, his superior talents, industry, and zeal, had fully attracted the attention of the authorities; and he soon commenced his career of greatness as Persian interpreter to a force of 8,000 men, assembled for the invasion of Sinde. In 1826 he was appointed a Deputy-Assistant Quartermaster General; and at this period he drew up a valuable statistical paper on Wagur, which gained him the thanks of Government, a handsome pecuniary reward, and the high favour of the celebrated Bombay Governor and Indian politician, Mountstuart Elphinstone.

His labours thus approved by those who knew well in what real excellence consisted, afforded proofs of a disposition to combine "the advancement of general knowledge with the exemplary discharge of his official duties."

At the age of twenty-three, his memoir on the eastern mouth of the Indus contributed more information than had ever before been given on that subject; his industry was untiring; and his abilities and exertions, in 1829, drew forth the admiration of the gifted political writer and energetic governor, Sir John Malcolm. The impressions which Sir John had early received of the character of the enterprising and highly-qualified young officer, Lieutenant Burnes, were soon fully confirmed; and when youths at home were just leaving college, the young Indian traveller and politician had already gone a long way in the path to fame.

Passing over many of his early travels and researches—chiefly of a general and geographical character, in some of which he was assisted by Lieutenant James Holland,* a talented and enterprising officer—we come to early in the year 1830, when a present of horses from the King of England to the Maharajah Runjeet Singh, arrived at Bombay. On Burnes' appointment to the political assistancy at Cutch, he had been transferred from the Quartermaster General's department. Along with the royal present, came a letter of compliments from Lord Ellenborough, the Minister for India, to the Sikh Chief. The Supreme Government, at the recommendation of Sir John Malcolm, nominated Lieutenant Burnes to proceed to Lahore with the horses and

* [Colonel James Holland, *late* Quarter-Master General, Bombay Army.]

letter—" the authorities, both in England and India, conceiving that much information might be derived from such a journey." It was desirable to obtain knowledge regarding everything pertaining to the geography of the Indus. He took with him also presents to the Ameers of Sinde, whose jealousy, shortly after the expedition had moved forth, in January, 1831, began to manifest itself in annoying delays and obstructions. But out of evil came good; for these very vexations afforded the enterprising traveller time to make a full survey of all the mouths of the Indus, with maps illustrating the river's course and its various localities. Burnes' reception at Hyderabad, the capital of the Ameers, was hearty and cordial. No small portion of the personal regard with which he was received was owing to the obligation which his skilful and humane brother, Dr. Burnes, had conferred on the Ameer, in curing him of a disease some years before.* A full account of his reception at the Sikh capital of Lahore, where the mission arrived on the 18th July, will be found in "Burnes' Travels into Bokhara," one of the most fascinating books of travel ever published—full of graphic description, and valuable geographical and statistical information—having for its motto the following lines from Horace:—

> " Per syrtes iter æstuosas,
> ,, ... per inhospitalem
> Caucasum, vel quæ loca fabulosus
> Lambit Hydaspes."

At Loodianah, Burnes had met the Ameer of Cabool for the first time; and his views regarding our future ally, Shah Soojah-ool-Moolkh, and Afghan politics in general, began to be formed.

In December, our unwearied traveller visited Kurnaul and Delhi, when he was presented to the Great Mogul, the fifteenth descendant from Timour. If then, how much more now, is the Mogul harmless, "realmless, and a prince

---

* See Burnes' Travels, and *Narrative of a Visit to the Court of Sinde*, by Dr. James Burnes, K.H.—The former have on the title-page, "By Lieutenant Alexander Burnes, F.R.S., of the India Company's Service."

without the shadow of power!"* Central Asia having to be explored, the sanction of the Governor-General (Lord William Bentinck) gained, the journey was commenced on the 2nd January, 1832. The route taken was that along the line of the Sutlej, till the river is joined by the Beas or Hydaspes. But, leaving the consideration of such matters to the readers of his famous book of travels, let us proceed to June, 1833, when Burnes received orders to proceed to England as the bearer of his own despatches. The fame of his adventures had long preceded him. The Montrose youth had done wonders in an incredibly short space of time. Lord William Bentinck wrote to the Court of Directors, that "the Government of India considered the information of Lieutenant Burnes as to the state of the countries betwixt India and Russia of such primary importance, that it should be communicated direct to the home authorities by that gentleman himself." He arrived in London early in October, after a few months' voyage round the Cape.

Ambition seemed satisfied. By the India House and by the Board of Control, he was most cordially received as a true British son from the East, who had done real service to his country. At Court he received marked consideration, and afterwards the special acknowledgments of William the Fourth, for the "unpublished map and memoir which he had presented to his Majesty." Eventually, Burnes' manuscripts passed into the hands of the far-famed John Murray, the publisher, whose *dictum*, that "every man has a book in him," was of peculiar value in the case of the great Oriental traveller. Such a book of travels had not appeared for many a day. Nearly nine hundred copies were sold off in a single day; and the publisher gave the author eight hundred pounds for the copyright of the first edition. Mr. Lockhart (editor of the *Quarterly*, and the tasteful producer of the Spanish ballads) called on Lieutenant Burnes, and told him that it surpassed, in interest, any book of travels he had ever read. It was trans-

---

* When this sketch had gone to press, I learned that the last of the Great Moguls, the King of Delhi, died at Rangoon on the 11th November (1862), and was buried the same day—the Mahomedans in the town heedless of the event.

lated into German and French. The critic's art was impartially exercised in every influential quarter; and, in addition to his qualifications as a very keen traveller, it was added, with reference to governing the affairs of an Indian Empire, that one had appeared " in every respect well qualified to tread in the steps of our Malcolms and Elphinstones."

Burnes was now elected a member of the Royal Asiatic Society, when all the honours were heaped upon him which that brilliant association could bestow. The Bombay lieutenant was the lion of the day. The Earl of Munster, President of the above Society, so appreciated the value of his work that he reviewed it in the *United Service Journal*, where it is remarked that "the reflection that Mr. Burnes is the first European, for twenty-one centuries, who has sailed the whole length of the Indus, naturally excites inquiry as to existing traditions of its first great navigator." He was complimented by Baron Humboldt, by the Institute of France, and by the Royal Asiatic Society of Paris, and had the silver medal of the French Geographical Society bestowed upon him. He was already a member, and had received the gold medal of the Royal Geographical Society of London.

From Paris he writes to his brother:—"The French critics give me even greater praise than the English. Is it not curious ? I have been reviewed in France, Germany, Russia, and England, and not yet in my native country " (Scotland, alluding to the *Edinburgh Review*). *

Louis Philippe, hearing he was in Paris, sent the ever indefatigable Lord Brougham in search of him, that he might confer on him the decoration of the Legion of Honour, which his Majesty desired to do with his own hands. Still, some of the critics were *at* him for certain trifling defects ; but we find him in good humour—as he might well be—declaring in the sincerity of his heart, " In all truth, I have got enough praise."

The great traveller, geographer, and commercial statist, at the age of twenty-nine, was waited on by some of the

* Almost simultaneously with the Bokhara travels, appeared the short memoir of the journey of 1829, into the Desert between Cutch and the Indus.

most distinguished men at that time in London. The Marquis of Lansdowne held out his hand to him; and not long before his departure for India, gave a farewell party, where Lords Howick, Morpeth, Auckland, the present Earl Russell, and the witty Sidney Smith, were among the guests. Lord Brougham—the ever steady friend of progress—thought highly of the opinion entertained of him by the philosophers of France. Burnes became, too, the lion of the hour at the literary soirées of Holland House. Such attention no lieutenant in any age had ever received before. It was enough to turn the head of any ordinary mortal; but the subaltern was *extra ordinary*, and survived it.

After declining Lord Ellenborough's offer of the Secretaryship to the Legation to the Court of Persia (eventually to become British Minister at the Court of Teheran), he laughs at Persia and her politics, and declares—"What are a colonelcy and a K.L.S. to me? I look far higher, and shall either die or be so." India was his chosen field of action. Of Sir John M'Neill (afterwards Ambassador at Teheran) he says, before leaving England, "He is an able fellow, and by far the fittest person in England for the situation." Burnes left London, with a "flaming despatch" from the Court of Directors in his pocket, on the 5th April, 1835, reaching India on the 1st June, by France, Egypt, and the Red Sea. On his arrival in Bombay he resumed his duties of assistant to the Resident at Cutch, Colonel (afterwards Sir Henry) Pottinger. Truly, the Governor-General (Lord Auckland) thought that Captain Burnes' abilities were wasted in such a situation. He was placed under the orders of the Supreme Government with a view to his future progress. A line of policy, it was determined in August, 1836, beyond the Indus was to be pursued. The young captain was appointed the head of a mission, the object of which was negociation with the Ameers of Sinde for the protection of the free navigation of the Indus. From Hyderabad* he was to proceed through the Punjab, by Attock and Cashmere, to Cabool, and (the mission being a purely commercial one) to enter into commercial arrangements with Dost Mahomed. Events

* Reached 18th January, 1837.

on the Persian frontier soon changed the character of the mission. Sir John M'Neill and Captain Burnes became in close communication with each other. Enquiries as to the state of trade were soon to give place to the question of how to be prepared for war! Burnes was satisfied that could the Persians succeed against Herat, Candahar would be at their mercy. But other matters of greater importance to the rising political were about to occur. With the view of interposing the mediation of the Indian Government betwixt Dost Mahomed and Runjeet Singh, in order to extend commerce and avert a war, Captain Burnes was instructed to proceed to Cabool. The mission entered the Khyber Pass on the 3rd September, 1837; and, on the 20th, Burnes entered Cabool escorted by Mahomed Akbar Khan, the favourite son of Dost Mahomed.

The remaining events in Burnes' life may be said to be matters of history. On the 1st October, 1838, Lord Auckland issued his famous proclamation of war. In November, the Ruler of the Punjab and the Governor-General had long interviews together at Ferozepoor; but the Envoy for Cabool was to be Sir William MacNaghten and not Captain Burnes. There can be no doubt that Burnes was in every way qualified for such a post. We were about to invade strange countries which *he* knew well, and to impose an obnoxious sovereign on a fierce and determined people. While Burnes was arranging for the reception of the army at Shikarpore, he received a copy of the Government *Gazette*, in which he found himself knighted and advanced to the rank of Lieutenant-Colonel in the army. He was also made Companion of the Bath.

It is curious to notice that, while Burnes was on a political mission in Beloochistan about this time, making arrangements connected with the expedition, the Khan of Khelat remarked to him that it was easy to get our armies into the country, but *how were we ever to get them out again?* On the final restoration of the Shah Shoojah, in September, 1839, Burnes was appointed political resident at Cabool; and he continued to act along with the Envoy there till the hour of his death.

Dr. Buist, who compiled the best memoir of Sir Alexander from printed books and papers, says forcibly :—" The

Cabool tragedy opened with the murder of Sir Alexander Burnes, it has closed by the anuihilation of a force which, including camp followers, amounted to from 12,000 to 15,000 men." Sir Alexander repeatedly warned the Government of the approaching crisis, and the catastrophe which proved fatal to him and so many of his countrymen; "and was amongst the first who fell in the Ghilzie insurrection, in November,* 1843; his younger brother, Lieutenant Charles Burnes, perishing along with him." Truly we may say with the French reviewer†—"Comment ne pas envier à l'Angleterre ces agens intrépides, qu'elle trouve toujours prêts à se dévouer à son service!"—And so here I conclude this brief sketch of Sir Alexander Burnes, in the words of his learned and esteemed biographer; ‡ "carried off in the prime of life—'only thirty-six years old, so young, yet so much already done for immortality;' so much time remaining, as it appeared to us short-sighted mortals, to maintain and to extend his fame." In my humble judgment, it may be added, he shines as a great geographer and useful traveller more than as a great politician. Objections may be taken to some actions of his policy—what public servant escapes them? But who will dare not to admire the British traveller who first beheld "the scenes of Alexander's wars, of the rude and savage inroads of Jenghiz and Timour, as well as of the campaigns and revelries of Baber, as given in the delightful and glowing language of his commentaries?" "In the journey to the coast," writes Sir Alexander, "we had marched on the very line of route by which Alexander had pursued Darius; while the voyage to India took us on the Coast of Mekran and the track of his admiral Nearchus."‖

* On the 2nd.   † Revue de Paris, Octobre, 1844.
‡ George Buist, Esq., LL.D.—1842.

‖ [The omissions in the foregoing sketch, of a most distinguished Anglo-Indian, will be partly supplied by citing the following interesting passages illustrating the esteem in which he was held, and exhibiting some distinctive points in the character of Sir Alexander Burnes.]

NOTES CHARACTERISTIC OF SIR ALEXANDER BURNES.

THE ATHENÆUM CLUB.

On his return to London from Paris, the Athenæum Club admitted him as a member without ballot, and the following notice of this is given in a letter dated January, 1835 :—
"The Athenæum Club has elected me over the heads of 1,130 candidates as a member, on account, as they are pleased to say, of my 'distinguished eminence.' I took my place yesterday, and you will judge of the Club when I name the first men I met—Hallam, Sir G. Staunton, Sidney Smith, D'Israeli, Crawford of Java, &c."

ESTEEMED BY EMINENT MILITARY OFFICERS AND MERCHANTS.

It may here be not inaptly remarked how completely the clear judgment, energy, and decision of character of Sir Alexander Burnes won the confidence and esteem of all the most eminent military officers with whom, during his career in India, he was associated. Sir David Leighton, Sir Thomas Bradford, Sir John Malcolm, Lord William Bentinck, the Earl of Dalhousie, Sir Henry Fane, and Lord Keane—admired and appreciated qualities in him which had rendered themselves among the most distinguished of their noble profession. The celerity with which he prepared himself for his exertions in the cause of geographical science is one of the most conspicuous characteristics of his earlier career. Of the various commercial reports drawn up by him, and laid from time to time before the Bombay Government, it was remarked by the merchants who examined them that they were written as if by one who had been a trader, and nothing but a trader from his youth. His controversy with the missionary Wolfe indicated a knowledge of theology, and dexterity in polemics not frequently found amongst military men.

DISTINCTION.

To these high qualities for the attainment of distinction he added a deep-seated and indomitable ambition which no difficulties could damp or subdue. He had determined on achieving greatness, and he appeared to have the means within his reach when it pleased Providence to cut short his earthly career. He was judicious and eminently fortunate in his selection of coadjutors, and had the happy faculty of attaching those who had laboured along with him most fervently to his person. He was simple in his manners, and for the most part sprightly and playful in his conversation, with alternating fits of absence and abstraction. His friendships were warm, enduring, and sincere. Not easily soured by disappointment, he submitted with the cheerful alacrity of a well-conditioned mind to the annoyances which came in his way. He was one of the kindest of brothers and most dutiful and affectionate of sons. Had he not been cut off in the flower of his age, at the very time when he had reason to believe that his deferred hopes of enjoying the highest position in Afghanistan were about to be realized, he might have looked forward to the attainment of honours such as those conferred on a Malcolm and an Elphinstone, with whose names his own had been so often associated, and in whose estimation he so early held a distinguished place.

BURNES WELL IN HARNESS.

"On the Indus, 5th July, 1837.—I am literally overwhelmed with business. I came to look after commerce, to superintend surveys, and examine passes of mountains, and likewise certainly to see into affairs to judge of what was to be done hereafter, but the hereafter has already arrived, and I have all but deserted my ledger for treaties and politics; my proceedings up to Shikarpore you are aware of. As I approached Cabool war broke out with the Afghans and Sikhs, and my position became embarrassing; I was even ordered by express to pause, and while hanging on my oars another express still cries—pause, but places a vast latitude in my hands, and 'forward' is my motto; forward to the scene of carnage, where, instead of embarrassing my Government, I feel myself in a situation to do good. It is this latitude throughout life that has made me what I am, if I am anything, and I can hardly say how grateful I feel to Lord Auckland. I have not as yet got the replies to my recommendations on our line of policy in Cabool consequent on a discovered intrigue of Russia, and on the Cabool chief throwing himself in despair on Perso-Russian arms. I have at last something to do, and I hope to do it well."

BURNES AND DOST MAHOMED.*

"CABOOL, 30th October, 1837.—Here a hundred things are passing of the highest interest. I arrived here on the 24th of last month, and have had a very cordial reception. Dost Mahomed Khan has fallen into all our views, and in so doing has either thought for himself or followed my counsel, but for doing the former I give him every credit, and things now stand so that I think we are on the threshold of a negotiation with King Runjeet, the basis of which will be his withdrawal from Peshawur, and a Barukzye receiving it as a tributary of Lahore, the Chief of Cabool sending his son to ask pardon. What say you to this after all that has been urged of Dost Mahomed Khan's putting forth extravagant pretensions? Runjeet will accede to the plan I am certain, but Wade is a great little man, if you comprehend what I mean, and while he is looking to the horizon (to use his own words) of politics and considering, events crowd on, and spoil his speculations. I have, on behalf of Government, agreed to stand as mediator between the parties, and Dost Mahomed has cut asunder all his connection with Russia and Persia, and refused to receive the ambassador from the Shah now at Candahar; his brothers at that city have, however, caressed the Persian Elchee all the more for this, and I have sent them such a Junius as I believe will astonish them. I had indeed reason to act promptly, for they have a son setting out for Teheran with presents to the Shah and the Russian Ambassador, and I hope I shall be in time to explain our hostility to such conduct. Everything here has indeed run well, and but for our deputation at the time it happened, the house we occupy would have been tenanted by a Russian Agent and a Persian Elchee. I hardly know what the Government of India will think of my measures, for my line of conduct is only indicated by them, not marked out. Yet I am inspirited by their free use of laudatory adjectives regarding my proceedings hitherto; . . . . I am in a very critical position, and so they tell me—*totidem verbis;* —but I like difficulties, they are my brandy."

* [This and the following extract will be of interest at the present time, or after the Ameer of Caubul was said to have imprisoned his eldest son, Yakoob Khan, for his inclination to give over Herat to the Persians.]

HERAT AND THE CZAR.

"I HAVE found out all the ramifications of the Czar's emissaries, and an explanation of his coveting Herat. His Majesty sees that that is the entrepôt of Persia, India, Cabool, and Toorkistan, and as his fairs in southern Persia progress to maturity, he looks to increasing the facilities of communication, and from Herat to Bokhara and Nijni Novogorod there are no intervening mountains. In pushing on Persia to Herat he but insinuates his own power in the very direction he desires. All this view of things was gravely propounded at Bokhara the year after I left it, for the Russians took alarm at what we were about, and reduced their duties to keep the traders with them. Is not this something to have been effected by two weary travellers plodding their way into Tartary!"—From "Memoir" by Dr. Buist; in "Notes on His Name and Family," by Dr. James Burnes. 1851.—[For correspondence with Lord Palmerston, see Appendix I.]

II.

JAMES BURNES, K.H., F.R.S.*

"He finds 'mid foreign crowds a friend,
A home 'neath every sky."—D. L. R.

BORN at Montrose, February 12, 1801, Dr. Burnes was educated at the University of Edinburgh, and Guy's and Saint Thomas's Hospitals in London, and arrived at Bombay in the Company's service, with his brother, the late Sir Alexander, on the 31st October, 1821.

The early career of Dr. Burnes can be traced from an official report drawn up under the orders of the Commander-in-Chief at Bombay, and which was subsequently submitted to his Majesty King William the Fourth. After having been successively attached to the artillery at Matoonga; the Convalescent Hospital at Severndroog; the 5th regiment Madras Native Infantry at Malligaum—the three previous Medical Officers of which had died of cholera; and the 24th regiment Bombay N.I. at Bassadore; he was posted in February, 1823, to the 18th regiment N.I. stationed at Bombay, where he was also selected to superintend the institution for the check of cholera. In 1824, the honourable appointment of surgeon to the Residency in Cutch having been offered by Mr. Elphinstone for competition, as a reward to medical officers who would pass in the native language, Dr. Burnes was the one of the five candidates who was successful. On his quitting the 18th regiment, we find him commended in orders for "his professional abilities, humanity, and feeling towards the sick, and his constant and unwearied attention to his duties." †

* The chief portion of this sketch is abridged from the "Memoir," by W. A. Laurie, Esq. (March, 1850), who wrote it while Dr. Burnes was on his return to his native land. The brief record was extracted from Indian periodicals, and "Memoirs" on the same subject, by Drs. Grant, of Calcutta, and Buist, of Bombay.

† Regimental Order, November 18th, 1824.

As a volunteer, he accompanied, in 1825, the field force and detachments which expelled the Sindians and other plunderers who had invaded and devastated Cutch, forcing the British Brigade to retire to the Hill-fort of Bhooj. In 1827, the Ameers of Sinde, between whom and our Government a very uncordial feeling had subsisted for years, unexpectedly solicited his services, and sent an Envoy to invite him to their capital, where he remained some months under circumstances which will be best explained by the following extract of an official dispatch from the Resident in Cutch, Sir Henry Pottinger, to Government (Political Department, No. 19 of 1828):—"The Honourable the Governor-in-Council will perceive that Mr. Burnes was only finally allowed, by the Ameers of Sinde to come away under a promise of his early return; and although the unsettled state of that country has since led to their Highnesses requesting him to postpone his visit; yet, from the terms in which they speak of Dr. Burnes (who, they say, is not only the most skilful of all Physicians, but their best friend, and the cementer of the bonds of amity between the two governments) it is pretty certain they will again invite him to their Court. . . . It is due to their Highnesses to mention that they have treated Mr. Burnes, during his sojourn at Hyderabad, with the most marked distinction and kindness, both as a professional gentleman to whom they were indebted for advice, and as an officer of the British Government deputed in that capacity, at their special request. In the latter light they received him, on his first arrival, in a State Durbar, with every honour and formality, and afterwards made him welcome at all times, with a degree of cordiality and politeness which, as the Native agent justly observes in his letter to me, 'they have never before evinced towards any gentleman.'"

The Government sanctioned Dr. Burnes' acceptance of liberal presents from the Ameers, and also presented him with a handsome pecuniary donation on his return to Bhooj. He was likewise complimented, in strong terms, on the zeal and ability he had displayed at Hyderabad, and received the thanks of the Government for the highly interesting narrative of his visit, which, under the orders of the Resident in Cutch, he had submitted for its information. The Governor personally intimated that but for the good use he had made of his time, much that was important would have remained unknown and unnoticed. The Commander-in-Chief pronounced the narrative a most valuable addition to the geography of India; and the Governor of Bombay directed it to be presented to the Royal Asiatic Society through Sir John Malcolm, circulated to public servants, and printed at the expense of the State. The "Narrative of a Visit to Sinde" drew from the Geographical Society of France a declaration that Dr. Burnes had deserved well of Geography.* It was published in England in 1830, and has gone through successive editions, both in India and in Europe; being the best account of the country we yet possess.

Dr. Burnes' invitation by the Ameers, and his visit to their Court, were evidently the first link in the chain of those great events which took place in reference to the Indus; and it is not at all improbable that had the request of those rulers to retain him, which has been referred to in the official dispatch above quoted, been complied with, much of the trouble and expense which were incurred, might have been spared. But it did not suit the policy of the day; and it was not till two years afterwards that his brother was deputed again to open a negotiation with the Ameers, and to ascend the Indus. Those who are familiar with that officer's travels, will recollect that the Ameers stated that he was doubly welcome as the brother of Dr. James Burnes. Sir Alexander Burnes' visit was followed by Sir Henry Pottinger's Embassy in 1832-3, for the purpose of demanding the free navigation of the Indus to British merchants, and the great events to the west, with which we are familiar.

In 1829, Dr. Burnes married Sophia, daughter of the late Major-General Sir George Holmes, K.C.B.

* M. Alexandre Burnes, Lieutenant d'Infanterie de la compagnie Anglaise des Indes, est frère de M. James Burnes Chirurgien-Major à Bhoudj dans le Cotch. Ce dernier fut appelé en 1827, à Haiderabad, pour donner ses soins, à un des Emirs. Il a publié une relation de son voyage. Ainsi les deux frères ont bien mérité de la géographie, en nous donnant des détails sur des pays peu connus." —Bulletin of the Geographical Society of France, 1833.

C

In 1830, the same reputation in the north-west frontier, which had induced the Ameers of Sinde to invite and welcome Dr. Burnes to their capital, led to the Cutch Regency bringing his conduct and services specially to the notice of Government, with a request that they might have the power to remunerate them. He had now been nearly five years in that lately conquered and distracted country; and such was the feeling towards him, that the Resident reported, in the words of the Cutch government, that "there was no one of any class or rank who would not, if sick, reckon upon his services at midnight."* The reply of the Bombay government is in the following terms: —"The Governor-in-Council directs me to signify to you his concurrence in the proposal of the Durbar to remunerate the professional services of Dr. Burnes, and requests that, in making this communication to the Durbar, you will suggest the mode in which the object in view can be effected with most attention to the feelings of the Prince and his family, and to those of Mr. Burnes, whose kind and unwearied attention, which the honourable the Governor (Sir John Malcolm) has had full opportunity of learning, has, the Governor-in-Council is aware, created the most lively sentiments of gratitude, while it has established, in the strongest manner, his claims to the approbation of Government."

Nearly of the same date is a Government letter to the Resident at Bhooj, acknowledging Dr. Burnes' "History of Cutch," which has since been published, along with his Narrative, and may be found in a compressed form in the last edition of the "Encyclopædia Britannica."

In December, 1831, we find Sir Henry Pottinger, on his departure as Envoy to Scinde, reporting to Government that, in "consideration of the long connection which has subsisted between Dr. Burnes and himself, he will be excused from bearing testimony to his merits and claims, and strongly recommending him to favourable notice." And in April following, there is a dispatch from the new Resident, Colonel Bagnold, which acknowledges that "in conducting the important duties of the frontier," he has "derived the most valuable assistance from his exertions,

* Letter to Government, Political Department, January 27th, 1830.

talents, and information, afforded by him gratuitously, and to the benefit of the public service, in a department distinct from his own, and consequently the more highly to be appreciated." At the end of the same year, Dr. Burnes' services were again brought to notice as having, in the political department, "amply evinced the greatest zeal and ability for the public service." Other quotations might be made from the papers we have referred to, but enough has been given to satisfy the reader that these services were neither few nor unacknowledged by his superiors.

In October, 1833, Dr. Burnes was forced to quit Cutch, on sick certificate, after having struggled with the fever of the country for many years. In the February following, he embarked for Europe by the overland route, and an interesting account of the journey (at that time attended with some difficulty), extracted from his letters, was published in the Bombay newspapers. He took the route of Malta, Sicily, Naples, Rome, Florence, Venice, Geneva, and Paris. While at home, amongst other honours conferred on him, he was created a Doctor of Laws by the University of Glasgow, and elected a Fellow of the Royal Society of London, and of the Royal College of Physicians of Edinburgh. He was also presented at Court by his friend the late Earl of Dalhousie (who had then returned from the command of the army of India), and received the honour of the Guelphic Knighthood from the sovereign.

On again returning to Edinburgh to make preparations for his departure to India, a public entertainment was given to him, Lord Ramsay* in the chair, when he received the present of a magnificent silver vase, bearing, besides a Masonic inscription, an intimation that it was a token of "regard and esteem for him as a gentleman." The committee for its presentation consisted of the Marquis of Dalhousie, Admiral Sir David Milne, G.C.B., Sir George Ballingall, Professor of Military Surgery in the University, Sir Reginald Macdonald Seton, better known as the hospitable " Staffa," and other individuals. Before quitting Edinburgh, he devoted a few leisure hours to his sketch of the History of the Knights Templars, having been encouraged

* Afterwards the Marquis of Dalhousie, Governor General of India.

to undertake the work by offers of valuable documents in the possession of old and noble families, and especially requested to leave amongst his friends some such token of remembrance. The book was brought out in a very elegant form; but only a few copies, besides those for distribution amongst private friends, were printed. It contains illustrations of the curious fact mentioned in "Mills's Chivalry," that the Order of the Templars has descended to our own days; and traces the history of these Knights, and of those of St. John of Jerusalem, in Scotland. A great portion of his stay in Europe was devoted to visiting the countries on the continent, and we believe that he had seen and communicated with more of the eminent men of the present day than any other individual from India.

On the 24th December, 1837, Dr. Burnes returned to Bombay; and Sir James Carnac conferred on him, unsolicited, the first vacant medical staff appointment in his gift, namely, the Garrison Surgeoncy of Bombay. In Calcutta, as in Bombay, Dr. Burnes was received as the best friend of masonry, of which nothing need be said here.

In a memoir drawn up in the City of Palaces, Dr. Grant writes—"Dr. Burnes has seen much of the world, and his manners and conversation at once give the impression of one who had observed well and benefited by what he had seen and learned; being pleasing, winning, and of a reflective cast. It has been truly said of old, that a good countenance is a perpetual letter of recommendation; and no one who has once seen Dr. Burnes can deny that he bears this enviable missive with him wherever he goes. A family resemblance may be traced in features and occasional turns of expression and manners between himself and his distinguished brother Sir Alexander, but there are, nevertheless, characteristic points of difference. Sir Alexander, when we had the pleasure of seeing him, looked spare and thin, compared with his brother; not that Dr. Burnes is exactly anything approaching to a 'stout gentleman,' but he has less angularity of feature and frame, than the enterprising traveller and keen politician. The one is sharp, quick, and rapidly decisive, expressive, and penetrating. The other, though full of energy in any matter he engages in, is more subdued in manner and expression, and his bearing more fraught with amenity. Sir Alexander, for instance, in an argument, uses a sword-like logic that he thrusts at once, and with a masculine hand, to the point. The argumentative weapon of the other too, is 'of the ice-brook's temper,' and of a perfect point and polish, but is like that of Harmodius wreathed with flowers. Both have a marked frankness of address.

"That Dr. Burnes is a person of singularly attractive manners and disposition, no one who has ever enjoyed the pleasure of his acquaintance can question for an instant; and a more triumphant proof of this cannot be appealed to than the warmth of his reception by not only the Masonic body of Calcutta, but society at large, so far as he could become known to it during his short stay among us. It has appeared to us that a portion of this attractiveness is hereditary; for the full dark eye, the well arched brow, expressive mouth, and, in a word, the whole countenance, when lighted up in the brilliance of congenial social intercourse, have often reminded us of the best portraits, graphic and biographic, of his great kinsman the poet."

Dr. Burnes returned from Calcutta* early in 1841, having been requested by Sir James Carnac, then Governor of Bombay, to undertake the office of Secretary to the Medical Board, a post in which it was thought he would be able to afford much benefit to his own department. In that year he presided at the St. Andrew's dinner; but, owing to the deplorable Cabool catastrophe, in which his brothers lost their lives, he remained for some time afterwards in retirement. His next prominent appearance was on the occasion of his laying the foundation-stone of the Jamsetjee Jeejeebhoy Hospital, which ceremony created a great sensation at Bombay in January, 1843. In December, 1844, he established the Lodge "Rising Star," for the admission of natives, and a beautiful medal, cut by Wyon, was struck by them in consequence. † In August, 1844,

* From a visit paid in 1840.

† The Hindus paying this honour to Burnes reminds one of the Duchess of Devonshire's beautiful lines on Sir W. Jones :—

"Admired and valued in a distant land—
His gentle manners all affection won;
The prostrate Hindu owned his fostering hand,
And science owned him as her favourite son."

he presided at the dinner given to Sir Henry Pottinger. In July, 1846, he was promoted to be Superintending Surgeon, and a piece of plate was voted to him by his brother officers, "in manifestation of their esteem, and the sense they entertain of his accelerating promotion, and of the uniform urbanity which he, in his official position, evinced on all occasions in his intercourse with all ranks." On quitting the Medical Board Office, the Board brought to the notice of Government the "distinguished zeal and ability" with which he had performed his duty for five and a half years; and in handing up this testimonial, the Commander-in-Chief added from himself, that " for several years he had had constant opportunities of having officially under his own notice the untiring zeal and great ability with which Dr. Burnes performed his varied duties in the most stirring times ever known at this Presidency in the Medical Branch, and in all the Military Departments."

In February, 1847, Dr. Burnes was transferred to the Poona Division, where he remained until his promotion to the Medical Board in September, 1848. Shortly after his arrival at Bombay, he was appointed a Member of the Board of Education; and the interest he took in its business is best shown by his addresses at the Grant College; by his successful efforts for the student apprentices; and by the Board having, on his departure, recorded "its deep regret at the loss of his valuable services, particularly in the department of Native Medical Education, to which he has devoted so much attention, and wherein his rare talents and extensive experience have enabled him to act with such marked efficiency;" a regret in which the Government expressed its entire participation. The Medical Board also intimated to Government their deep regret that ill health was about to deprive the Medical Service of an officer who had been "so long its pride and ornament, and of whose honourable career and eminent merits the public records bore such ample testimony."

He was one of the Trustees of the Oriental Bank, and a warm promoter of the schemes for the promotion and encouragement of arts and manufactures, in an improved form, among the natives. He was also President of the Medical and Physical Society, and Vice-President of the

Bombay Branch of the Royal Asiatic Society. It may be added, that, before his departure the Geographical Society of Bombay elected him an Honorary Office-Bearer for life, "in testimony of their appreciation of his services to the cause of Geographical Science."

Though Dr. Burnes rarely appeared before the world as an author, his tastes were eminently refined and literary, and his mind abundantly stored with general knowledge. The account of his visit to the Court of Hyderabad sufficiently shows what might have been looked for from his pen had he found leisure or inclination to write for publication. He ever took an active share in the promotion of all intellectual pursuits, and was one of the most elegant and most attractive members of general society in Western India. Fond of company, in which he was always the favourite, and where he eminently shone, he was the person most generally fixed upon to preside at public meetings and do the honours where entertainments were given to distinguished strangers or members of the community; and his address, on the occasion of a public dinner being given to Sir H. Pottinger on his way from China, was so marked for elegance and aptitude, as to be reprinted in all the leading journals of Europe. The eminent official position he so long enjoyed in the service, to which he was an honour, was always employed by him in endeavouring to advance merit and promote unpretending worth—to assist the necessitous and soothe those heats and irritations which will occasionally arise in the best regulated communities, and which tend so grievously to impair the comfort of public men and to interfere with the interests of the service. As a private friend he was ever warm, constant, and sincere in his attachments. Though generally to be met with in every scene of harmless merriment, gaiety, or festivity, no man more frequently approached the couch of sickness or chamber of suffering—none could strive more to soothe the pangs of sorrow or anguish of affliction. He left India almost without an enemy, and with scarcely an acquaintance who was not also an admirer and a friend.

In G. O., by the Right Hon. the Governor-in-Council (19th Nov., 1849), allowing him to retire, * his eminently

* As Physician-General of the Bombay Army.

useful services were brought forward, announcing that his services extended beyond the line of his own profession; and the same zealous devotion to the public interests was apparent in those which "distinguished him throughout his meritorious career in the medical department." *

Since 1850, Dr. Burnes chiefly resided in London, making occasional visits to his native town of Montrose. He was a magistrate for the counties of Middlesex and Forfar. With regard to his native county, Lord Brougham had inscribed his name in the roll of Justices—a remarkable compliment, at a time when no new commission was issued, to a visitor from India, who possessed no property in the shire. The compliment had been continued since the accession of Her Majesty.

In 1851, he drew up an elegant little work, entitled "Notes on his Name and Family," printed for private circulation. On the title-page figures the crest which he obtained from the Herald Office, in allusion to the devotion to their country shown by his two brothers. Out of a mural crown—the rim inscribed CABOOL—a demi-eagle is displayed transfixed by a javelin; and round the whole is the appropriate motto: OB PATRIAM VULNERA PASSI.

In addition to being an able writer,† Dr. Burnes was an eloquent and impressive speaker; but, on his return home, he seldom appeared in public. At the influential meeting held on the 5th of March, 1861, to do honour to that distinguished soldier and statesman, Sir James Outram, he made a most eloquent speech, from which I take the following remarks on the career of the Bayard of the East:—

"I am possibly in a somewhat different position from other speakers, inasmuch as I have passed the best days of my life in the same public service with him, and in daily observation of him. And having watched his career throughout—the truthfulness of his character and indomitable courage, that early brought him into notice—the energy and tenderness with which he brought to God and man, while yet a youth, the wild Bheels of the jungle (in my opinion the noblest of his achievements)—his wondrous pursuit of the Afghan Ameer, Dost Mahomed, and perilous escape afterwards from Khelat through hostile tribes to

* Here ends abridgement of "Memoir." † [See Appendix II.]

the sea-coast—the heroic part he took in the defence of the Hyderabad Residency—with the other varied incidents of his stirring life, all showing abnegation of self, with an uncompromising resolve to do his duty—up to the time he startled Europe, though not so much India, by his magnanimity in making place for an illustrious comrade —an act which reminds us of some of those recorded of the great Condé—(cheers)—and completed his military exploits at Lucknow to enter the Supreme Council—I look upon him as the model of the high-minded public servant, whether soldier or statesman—the man whom parents may urge their sons to follow, the *chevalier sans peur et sans reproche*, as happily applied to him by Sir Charles Napier, and as so completely realising the classical descriptions just given by a new and eloquent historian of another great warrior and statesman, Alexander Farnese, Prince of Parma, that the words might be inscribed on the pedestal of his statue—' UNTIRING, UNCOMPLAINING, THOUGHTFUL OF OTHERS, PRODIGAL OF SELF, GENEROUS, MODEST, BRAVE.' " (Much cheering.) *

The death of Dr. Burnes' eldest son, occasioned by a noble act of self-devotement during the Indian mutiny, brought him no common sorrow. The doctor was twice married—his brother, Alexander, never. And there was every prospect of our hero's attaining "a green old age," when he sickened and died† at Manchester, on the 19th of September, 1862, regretted by all who knew him.

" After life's fitful fever,
He sleeps well ! "——

He who was perhaps, reader, " thine own friend, and thy father's friend." Like all that is mortal, he had his faults: he was, throughout his career, too fond of distinction (by some considered a virtue); his zeal for a friend or relative, a few may think, occasionally led him too far in the business; but, take him for all in all, he was a noble specimen of humanity. And, while I pay this imperfect tribute to

* [See also Appendix III.—Sir James Outram.]
† From the effects of disease of long standing, contracted in India.

his memory, with his intelligent features beaming from a portrait before me, I think of those he endeavoured to serve, recalling to mind the beautiful poem with the line —so applicable towards the close of every year—

"Who has not lost a friend?"

ADDENDA.

DR. BURNES AS A MASON.

SOME able men, who knew him well, especially in Bombay, are inclined to think that Dr. Burnes was most distinguished as a Mason. He certainly shone as a bright, particular star, among the brethren of the "mystic tie;" and no where did he seem more in his element than when—to use the words of his kinsman the poet—"honoured with supreme command," he "presided o'er the sons of light." Masonry with him, as with too many, was not a mere name. He put his whole soul into the business, and thoroughly believed in its Godlike nature to produce good fellowship among men. If his brother, Sir Alexander, may be styled the most wonderful traveller, Dr. James' has an equal right to be considered the most energetic and brilliant Mason that ever came to India. But in whatever he undertook, the subject of the foregoing sketch proved himself to be an able and well-read man, although, from the nature of his profession debarred from the same opportunities, not so distinguished as his brother. The following passage displays no ordinary ability. It is from a speech on the "India Question," delivered at the Court of Proprietors of India Stock, 27th January, 1858 :—

A NATIVE OF INDIA.—THE SEPOYS.

"A native of India has no notion of political rights; his forefathers had none, and he cannot comprehend their being yielded to him except from a cowardly terror of himself. Such concessions, in fact, are diametrically opposed to his conception of the dignity and authority of a ruler.

'Born to be controlled,
Slave of the forward and the bold,'

what he requires from England is a well-chosen, vigorous, and benignant Governor General, armed with ample power to enforce authority, protect person and property, and administer justice promptly and efficiently to the people, and to handle Sepoys on the principle laid down by the poet ;—

> '*Tender-handed* stroke the nettle,
> And it stings you for your pains;
> *Grasp it* like a man of mettle,
> And it soft as silk remains.
> 'Tis the same with grovelling natures:
> Use them *kindly*, they rebel;
> But be *rough* as nutmeg-graters,
> And the rogues obey you well.'

" Ere long these mutinies will pass away, leaving behind them, with all their horrid recollections, a not unprofitable lesson. Nations, like men, are subject to frenzy and delirium, and within the memory of some living, the most refined and civilised people upon earth were perpetrating upon each other the most cruel atrocities. The Prætorian Guards, the Janissaries, the Mamelukes, the Sepoys, are all reproductions of the same bloody history,—the natural development which follows from rude and mercenary armies gaining a knowledge of their own power. But with this knowledge the Sepoys have also learned this great lesson, that if brute force was with them for a season, the intellect that commands force and power was with England."

SIR HENRY LAWRENCE:

A BIOGRAPHICAL STUDY.*

———◆◆◆———

DR. JOHNSON emphatically assures us that no species of writing seems more worthy of cultivation than biography, "since none can be more delightful or more useful, none can more certainly enchain the heart by irresistible interest, or more widely diffuse instruction to every diversity of condition." There is a powerful charm to be found in narratives of the lives of particular persons, to which we readily conform our minds, as containing "circumstances and kindred images" which, with not a few of us, mark "the story of our life from year to year." Keeping such ideas steadily in view, we may affirm, without hesitation, that for the earnest youth of the present generation, for a simplicity, a grandeur, a strength, a sublimity of character, which shining forth in the day of trial must ever keep up the fame of old England throughout the world, no better study can be presented than the eventful life of Sir Henry Lawrence.† To officers who can look back on a long Indian service, some of whom will recollect the energetic cadet at Addiscombe, and watched the Indian career of our "hero in the strife" till his glorious death at Lucknow, the study of such a life is intensely interesting. To Englishmen who have never visited the East, but many of whom, in these uncertain times—when beating swords into ploughshares appears to be as far distant as ever, and

---

* *Dark Blue* for January, 1873.

† "Life of Sir Henry Lawrence. By the late Major-General Sir Herbert Benjamin Edwardes, C.B., K.C.S.I., and Herman Merivale, Esq., C.B."— 1872. "Lives of Indian Officers, illustrative of the History of the Civil and Military Service of India." By John William Kaye (now Sir John Kaye, K.C.S.I.)—1869.

nation is still on the alert to rise against nation—may find themselves sooner than they reckon on in any part of the world, ready to uphold the honour of Great Britain, the careful reading of such a life will perhaps do more real good than such biographical studies as Charles the Twelfth of Sweden, " the most extraordinary man, perhaps, who ever appeared in the world," as the great Lord Clive, " the heaven-born general," or even as our loved hero of heroes, the illustrious Wellington, who " exhausted nature and exhausted glory."

The biographer of the iron King of Sweden, the King who
—"left a name at which the world grew pale,
To point a moral or adorn a tale,"

thinks that conquerors are a species between good kings and tyrants, partaking most of the latter, and have a glaring reputation. Still, we are naturally eager to know the most minute circumstances of their lives. The biography which has lately been so favourably received by the public, and especially by those who love to study the character of India's immortal roll of heroes and statesmen, in the first volume by Sir Herbert Edwardes, most successfully carries out the idea of "minute circumstances;" while, in the second, the more serious and business-like part is most admirably executed by Mr. Merivale, under whose careful eye and experienced judgment the whole of this most noble work has been ushered forth into the world. Into such a life as that of Sir Henry Lawrence we have assembled together some of the finer qualities which distinguished the foregoing immortal trio (Charles the Twelfth, Lord Clive, and Wellington); and here and there we find traits which also remind us of Nelson, Howard (Lawrence was styled "the Howard of the Punjab"), Chalmers, Havelock, and Neill; and greatest quality of all for success in life—on which Sir Fowell Buxton has laid so much stress—he had ENERGY in a wonderful degree. Although rather late in the day, to give some of the leading points in such a life may be of interest to our readers.

Before perusing the complete "Life of Sir Henry Lawrence," the student would do well to make himself master of the hundred or more pages devoted to our hero in Sir John Kaye's "Lives of Indian Officers."

These interesting and graphic sketches—drawn by a master-hand—being "illustrative of the History of the Civil and Military Service of India," and written on the principle "that the best biographies are those in which the autobiographical element is the most prominent,"* will, even in these distracting times for much reading, create a desire to go right through the larger volumes, causing the young soldier and statesman *in esse* to read, as we all should read, in the words of Shakspeare—

"As if increase of appetite had grown
By what it fed on."

Henry Montgomery Lawrence was born at Maturah, in Ceylon, on the 28th June, 1806. His father, every inch a soldier, was garrisoned in that island, after very distinguished service in the South of India, particularly at the second siege of Seringapatam, where, as Lieutenant Lawrence, under General Baird (the mighty Sir David), he commanded one of the two subalterns' parties† appointed to cover the forlorn hope at the memorable assault of that fortress (4th May, 1799). Judging from his extraordinary military career, most interesting details regarding which are furnished by Sir Herbert Edwardes, Alexander William Lawrence must indeed have been a first-rate officer, exhibiting a life well versed in the ups and downs of martial adventures. He seemed to laugh at impossibilities, and say, "It *must* be done!" on all occasions; and doubtless, "he only wanted the opportunity which rank gives to have done great things." His "God-fearing" wife appears to have been a pattern of womanly goodness; and when little Henry arrived on the stage of life, on which he was destined to play so prominent a part, the proud mother had every reason to say, as she afterwards did to a lady at Galle, "There's *my* Matura diamond."

With such parents, it was quite to be expected that a

* "Lives," p. 400.

† "Lieutenant Hill (74th)," writes Colonel Alexander Beatson, historian of the war with Tippoo Sultan, "commanded the right Subaltern's party."

rare jewel would be presented to the world. The son "achieved greatness," and so made all the setting for it himself. Henry Lawrence's career at Addiscombe forms a most interesting study, bringing forcibly out the truth of the saying that "The boy's the father of the man."

At Addiscombe, we learn that Henry was always asking the "reasons" of things, and "tracing effects to their cause." Although such inquisitive power—if it may be so called—may hinder rapid progress at school or college, still the habit is invaluable towards forming a great statesman, and, in some respects, a great soldier. The very facts of his being "best in mathematics," and fond of "making military surveys of the country round," go some way to prove how strong the desire must have been within him to ask reasons and questions; and we find this desire running all through his life, and especially during many of the gravest events of Indian history, from the first Sikh war to the glorious relief of Lucknow. Perhaps, when a brother cadet (Robert Macgregor) saved him from drowning—as Sir John Kaye remarks, "the one noticeable incident of Henry Lawrence's early life"—he was anxious to learn the hydrostatic and pneumatic principles by which such a catastrophe could have taken place.

Regarding the school and Addiscombe career of Henry Lawrence, Sir Herbert Edwardes sums up "in a few home words of the brothers and sisters," which will amply repay perusal; but the following must be cited as one of the most interesting passages in the book:—"I remember my brother Henry" (says Sir John, the present Lord Lawrence)* "one night in Lord Hardinge's camp, turning to me and saying, 'Do you think we were clever as lads? *I don't think we were!*' But it was not altogether that we were dull. We had very few advantages, had not had very good education, and were consequently backward and deficient. We were both bad in languages, and always continued so, and were not good in anything which required a technical memory; but were good in anything which required thought and judgment. We were good,

---

* In a "Conversation with the Author" For the other "home words," see vol. i., pp. 30, 31.

for instance, in history. And so far from Henry being *dull*, I can remember that I myself always considered him a fellow of power and mark; and I observed that others thought so." Thus we have the secret of the two brothers' success in life. They possessed those qualities in which the majority of public men are deficient, despite ever so much learning—tact and judgment. Perhaps, as a rule, we should call no man dull till we know him well, or opportunity brings him out. Who would ever have imagined that young Walter Scott, far from "*dux*" in his class, with a cluster of boys beside him listening to his recital of some strange tale, would have become the immortal author of "Waverley" and "Marmion?"

It has been truthfully remarked, and we have heard it from the mouth of a shrewd Indian General, who knew him in the morning of life, that none of his contemporaries predicted that our hero would live to outstrip them all. A hundred dull youths becoming great men might be cited. And on ripe manhood also we should restrain our judgment. Sir Henry Lawrence—in India great before—became immortal at Lucknow. And the famous General Neill—the avenging angel of the Sepoy rebellion —almost unknown before, became immortal in his glorious march to assist Havelock and punish the mutineers. Neill, during the second Burmese war, gave one the idea of a pleasing gentleman, but of an ordinary soldier. He was rather sparing of his remarks, but you got a telling smile from him, if no more. His manner was decidedly retired, while we marched north with the view of clearing the new conquest of Pegu of dacoits and other disturbers of the peace in the "golden" valleys of Burma.

Doubtless those who had the honour of knowing or serving under Sir Henry Lawrence, notwithstanding his hitherto brilliant career, never expected the wonderful energy and forethought displayed at Lucknow.

At length "Aunt Angel" fits out Henry; the Colonel (his father) "wouldn't hear of it;" and he takes his departure for India. He arrived in February, 1823, and joined the head-quarters of the Bengal Artillery at Dum-Dum, not far from Calcutta. And now life commences in earnest in "the nursery of captains" and of able politicals.

In eleven chapters—making twelve in all—Sir Herbert Edwardes does his utmost to produce a wonderful biographical study; and the very minuteness of the biographer's details forms, we think, the chief excellence of his volume. There is nothing of the water-colour sketch about the picture. It is a genuine portrait, on which we look with the same interest as on a picture by Reynolds, Lawrence, or Raeburn. The lights and shadows are admirably brought out. The noble rivalry between the brothers to help their parents—the influence of religious friends—the varied events of the first Burmese war, where Henry first smelt powder, concluded by a fever and the peace dictated at Ava (1826) by Sir Archibald Campbell—form the chief subjects of the second chapter. In the third, through sheer perseverance, Henry passes the examination for interpreter at Cawnpore. In the fourth, Henry marries Honoria Marshall, "a model wife," which wise act reminds us of the remark of an able Calcutta reviewer, while writing on married life in India, that "did the Court of Directors" (now Her Majesty's Secretary of State for India in Council) "but understand their real interests as well as the Athenians did theirs, they might perhaps make it imperative that their officers should, on entering the service, be provided with a wife." In India, through a good wife, men's minds are regulated, "their ideas and manners become softened, and their souls are cared for."* Mrs. Lawrence's "thoughts about death," in a letter to her husband at the end of this chapter, are very affecting.†

The fifth chapter—from 1838 to 1841—contains speculations on another war with Burma (which did not take place till 1852), and war with Nepaul—the first note of the Caubul War—Lawrence's wise resolution to write for the press the "Adventures in the Punjab," shortly after his first political appointment—concluding, after striking examples of mental energy and devotion to the service of the State, with the death of his little daughter. This is a chapter which requires especial study. The *mens æqua in arduis* becomes strongly apparent. There is also an impending duel, and a wife's beautiful remonstrance; the

* *Calcutta Review*, No. 8, p. 406, vol. iv.   † pp. 164, 165.

duel was prevented by Henry Lawrence's brother officers in the artillery, and an age was beginning to dawn when it was thought that, for an affront, there was little satisfaction in shooting a man, or in carrying out the eloquent but unruly Grattan's advice to his son, just as the Irish orator was about to leave the world, "Always be ready with the pistol!"

This affair leads Sir Herbert Edwardes to remark on the cessation of duelling in the British army, which had been slightly prevalent a quarter of a century before:— "He who would judge the error fairly must go back a quarter of a century [to just before Waterloo]. Then a duel was 'an affair of honour;' now it is a 'disgraceful affair.' To shrink from shooting your neighbour then was to be a coward for life; now we may be allowed even to shrink from being shot, and bear no cross."*

The sixth and three following chapters are pregnant with interest: and they were especially so at the time when our first Anglo-Indian Field-Marshal, the noble and gallant Sir G. Pollock, "the head of the great representatives of the old Company's army, who won and maintained our great Indian Empire," found an honoured resting-place in Westminster Abbey (Oct. 16th, 1872). Sir George, like Sir Henry Lawrence, was a Bengal artilleryman, belonging also to a family which carried out Bacon's fine expression of "achieving greatness," and Indian artillerymen were among the pall-bearers—of whom, doubtless, Sir Henry Lawrence, his brother officer, had he been spared, would have formed one—who consisted of Lieut.-Gen. Sir George Lawrence, K.C.S.I., C.B.; Major-Gen. Sir V. Eyre, K.C.S.I., C.B.; Sir J. W. Kaye, K.C.S.I.; Major-Gen. Sir George McGregor, K.C.B.; Major-Gen. Sir J. Brind, K.C.B.; and Lieut.-Gen. Sir J. Alexander, K.C.B. The Right Hon. Lord Lawrence, G.C.B., G.C.S.I., Sir Henry's brother, followed in order of procession, just before the Members of the Council of India, the Duke of Argyll and the Council having felt, with admirable taste and feeling, that the glorious old Abbey was the only fit place to receive Pollock's honoured remains.

We now return to Henry Lawrence, as great events are

* p. 195.

on the gale, and begin to think there is every chance of Mr. Hudleston's prophecy becoming true, which he made to Henry's sister, Letitia (who was unwilling to let him go), just before our hero's departure for India: "You foolish thing," he said, "Henry will distinguish himself. All your brothers will do well, I think; but Henry has such steadiness and resolution that you'll see him come back a general. *He will be Sir Henry Lawrence before he dies.*"* To the student of Indian history, the sixth chapter is invaluable. It prepares him for the great drama of the War in Afghanistan, so ably written by Sir John Kaye; and when "Alps upon Alps" of difficulties were arising in every direction, he finds Lawrence serving bravely in the midst of them. General George Pollock had been despatched with a force to the Afghan frontier. Sale and Macgregor wrote from Jellalabad, urging the immediate advance of Pollock's brigade, and Lawrence, Wild, and their gallant comrades were repulsed in an attempt to throw in supplies. The Khyber was yet to be forced, and everything was black as storm-threatening night. But after such darkness, as the German poet sings, cometh the light of morn—"suddenly the brightest light springs from the darkest day." The political services of Captain Lawrence in Afghanistan at this time were very valuable. Soon came preparations for an attack on the Khyber Pass (related in the eighth chapter), Pollock's advance and victory, Lawrence's renewed exertions; the eventual dismantling of Jellalabad and Ali Musjid; and next the return to "Home, sweet home"—the whole forming in Sir John's pages one of the saddest and most eventful histories ever written. The student, with this biography beside him, should thoroughly master it.; and, as old Colonel Lawrence said, when one of his children having finished Rollin's "Ancient History" "closed the volume with an exulting bang"—"begin it again at the beginning."† It may here be interesting to note that the "Life of Washington" made a lasting impression on Henry Lawrence's mind; and another biography read to the children, under the discipline of the Colonel, was the "Life of Sir Thomas Munro," one of the greatest soldiers

* pp. 32, vol. iv. † p. 30.

and statesmen England and India ever had, so much admired by George Canning, and whose example continued to influence the future hero of Lucknow during his brilliant career.

In the tenth, eleventh, and twelfth chapters, extending from 1842 to 1844, we have Lawrence as active as ever—Lord Ellenborough rewarding him with high appointments, and eventually making him Resident at the Court of Nepaul. Numerous most important events in the history of India follow, all of which are touched on in a most interesting manner by the gallant biographer, whose bright day of distinction was also fast drawing nigh.* The concluding or twelfth chapter describes the scenery and manner of life in Nepaul, where, as remarked in a paper on Periodical Literature in India, we found the great political watching and waiting; and, while a Sikh Invasion of British India and the Mutiny of 1857 had been foreshadowed, with great energy assisting his brother officer, Mr. Kaye (the editor and originator of this far-famed periodical), with contributions for the *Calcutta Review.*

So much, then, for the first volume of the "Life of Sir Henry Lawrence," compiled by his "dear friend and scholar in Indian Administration and Statesmanship, Sir Herbert Edwardes." Sir Herbert, who, while in England had been entrusted by the Lawrence family to write a memoir of Sir Henry, died in December, 1868, leaving chapter twelve unfinished. Mr. Merivale, Under-Secretary of State for India, now became the biographer, and, having arranged the first volume for publication, began the second from the materials left him at the point at which he took up the work. The difference of style in the two volumes has been considered remarkable; but superiority has been assigned to Mr. Merivale,† who,

* Mr. Merivale writes that "Sir Herbert's best-remembered title to the gratitude of his countrymen was gained in the three months, May to August, 1848, when, with a mere handful of men at his disposal, he kept in check the revolted Sikhs before Mooltan."—*Preface.*

† [This able and distinguished public servant died on the 8th February, 1874, and the Duke of Argyll in Council appointed Sir Louis Mallet, C.B. (one of the Council), his successor as Under-Secretary of State for India. Sir Louis is known "by reputation as jointly with Cobden the author of the French Treaty, and," continues a well-known M.P., "one of our ablest political economists and public servants."]

having more striking and recent materials to deal with, has, as a distinguished writer, produced a book worthy of the graceful American, Washington Irving, or some of our best English writers of biography, forming the brilliant half of a most interesting biographical study.

With two such admirable volumes before him, should the reader be—as Major Straith, of Addiscombe, used to recommend to the student of fortification—" thorough in his study," he will be forced to the inevitable conclusion after their perusal that the great Indian officer appears to have been eminently fitted for every post he occupied. Throughout his life he comes forth as "the right man in the right place." Whether as artillery subaltern fighting his battery; revenue surveyor; political agent; adventurous traveller; conciliator of native soldiery; philanthropist and founder of the noble asylums which bear his name; writer of elaborate essays, "gravid" with important matter on a variety of subjects, for the *Calcutta Review*, or of sketches for the newspapers; one haranguing the natives in their own language and fearlessly telling the warlike races of India that England could hold her own in the country despite whatever might happen to us elsewhere;* or as the prudent, brave, and energetic commander of troops during the crowning scene of India's "severest trial"—on every occasion he displayed extraordinary powers, forcing us to repeat what Johnson said of Addison's various ways of presenting truth—"*mille habet ornatus, mille decentur habet.*"

The second volume consists of eight chapters, with some valuable appendices. The years 1844, 1845, are about to become a critical time for India, the latter year even more so than 1842, when Lord Ellenborough succeeded Lord Auckland, and the Khyber was yet far from being forced. Henry Lawrence's literary pursuits, assisted by his admirable wife, in Nepaul, and the foundation and early history of the Lawrence Asylum, are fully detailed at the commencement of Mr. Merivale's volume. Regard-

* The author of this sketch is responsible for the incident of Lawrence thus addressing the natives. If memory serves right, it happened when the Crimean War was at its height, and an uneasy feeling existed about our success before Sebastopol.

ing his literary pursuits, we have spoken in our sketch of Anglo-Indian Periodical Literature. Sir John Kaye is the grand authority on this subject; and the later biographer remarks that this distinguished writer "was united to Sir Henry by the bonds of strong personal friendship, and also by those which exist between editor and contributor." Who would have thought that the "sweet and gentle boy," of whom his amiable sister said she could not "recall his ever telling an untruth," or the "rather tall, raw-boned youth of sixteen," at Addiscombe, "with high cheek-bones, small grey eyes, prominent brows, and long brown hair"—a "very rough Irish lad"—would ever have become a Calcutta reviewer, unless we accept the fact, not common with the critical brotherhood, that "he could, when necessary, take or give a licking with a good grace?" Mr. Merivale gives a list, which we believe not to be complete,* of Sir Henry and Lady Lawrence's contributions to the *Calcutta Review*, among them the famous essays on "Military Defence of our Indian Empire," "The Sikhs and their Country," "Indian Army," "Army Reform," and "Englishwomen in Hindustan" (by Lady Lawrence). Of Sir Henry's as well as of Sir Herbert Edwardes' style as reviewers we have given slight specimens in our sketch of Anglo-Indian Periodical Literature. But there was one point we did not touch upon—the handwriting of the Nepaul reviewer! Sir John Kaye tells us in his "Lives"† that "his handwriting was not the most legible in the world, and the copyists whom he tried only made matters worse." It was not, perhaps, quite so bad as that of the great divine, philosopher, and statesman, Dr. Chalmers, whose mother frankly declared that she always put Tom's letters in her drawer in order that he might read them to her himself when he came home; but it was certainly defective, and cost East Indian and native compositors (who do the printing business in India) much trouble. This may remind us of some remarks by Samuel Rogers, the gifted

* [A nearly complete list will be found in the April number (1874) of the *Calcutta Review*, with an article entitled "The First Twenty Years" of that periodical, by George Smith, LL.D., lately retired from the *Friend of India*, to which he has long been so bright an ornament.]

† p. 115.

and amiable author of "The Pleasures of Memory." He said it is inexcusable in anyone to write illegibly, and tells us that he got a plain hand by tracing the master's copies against the window; also that when the great Lord Clive informed his sisters by letter that he had returned them an "elephant" (at least, so they read the word), the true word was "equivalent." In the middle of 1844, the recall of Lord Ellenborough had arrived in Calcutta, and Sir Henry, afterwards Lord, Hardinge, was now Governor-General. The first Sikh war, throughout which Lawrence's knowledge of the Punjab was invaluable, and which was very highly appreciated by Lord Hardinge, together with his appointment of Resident at Lahore, form strong landmarks in our hero's career; and when at length, events having become of a more peaceful character, after the war he left India, on account of his health, for England, and was made a K.C.B. (April, 1848), returning to India the same year, he seemed to be in a fair way to exhaust glory if not nature. He was now—fulfilling Mr. Hudleston's prophecy—SIR HENRY LAWRENCE—determined to do his duty before he died! A useful rather than a glorious life seemed to be his aim. And Sir Henry appears to have been well aware of the truth conveyed in the beautiful verse:—

> "The boast of heraldry, the pomp of power,
> And all that beauty, all that wealth e'er gave,
> Await alike th' inevitable hour:
> The paths of glory lead but to the grave."

When he returned to India, Lord Dalhousie was Governor-General,* and his relations with that stern, and, as some think, greatest Indian Proconsul, are admirably told by Mr. Merivale. Of course, the annexation and the non-annexation policy could not agree for a moment. Lord Dalhousie, too, was quite unlike the amiable "old Peninsular hero," and "favourite pupil of Wellington in his greatest wars," Lord Hardinge. Sir Henry's views regarding annexation are thus summed up in his article

* His Lordship arrived in Calcutta on the 12th January, 1848, shortly before Sir Henry left for England, where he arrived in March, returning with his wife in November.

on Oudh in the *Calcutta Review*, quoted by Sir John Kaye, and which are quite in accordance with the policy we are pursuing at the present time:—"We have no right to rob a man because he spends his money badly, or even because he ill-treats his peasantry. We may protect and help the latter without putting the rents into our own pockets." He was Resident at Lahore and President of the Lahore Board after the Second Sikh War (1849), which ended in the annexation of the Punjab.

We now pass on to chapter eighteen of the work (January, 1853—March, 1857), which contains an account of Sir Henry's valuable labours as Agent in Rajpootana, where, among other humane projects, he turned himself to the abolition of widow-burning, and "the reformation of the prison discipline of the States,"—quite in keeping with his other noble efforts, such as rescuing poor European soldiers' children from the unseen wretchedness of barrack life, and giving them a comfortable asylum on the Hills—the sad death of Lady Lawrence, Lord Dalhousie's succession by Lord Canning, and Sir Henry's appointment to the Chief Commissionership of Oudh. The story of his wife's death, about which Mr. Merivale gives some striking extracts from Sir Henry's letters, is very sad, and some of his remarks after the event to his friend ("spiritual director"), Mrs. Hill, deeply interesting:—"He ' wonders why we are allowed to sin and to suffer, why some are born to bliss, and others to misery.'"

"He ' desires to be assured that he and his departed wife must hereafter dwell together.'" And yet this brave Christian soldier, with a heart brimful of charity, must have been aware of the merciful promise that the mysteries of our

—— "natures unrevealed below,
We yet shall learn and wonder as we know."

Doubtless, when his bereavement—producing what the Orientals style "sorrow devouring sorrow"—was less acutely felt, he found, like the puritan Havelock, comfort in the Divine order to "be not faithless but believing."

Our imperfect sketch, or biographical study, draws to a close, and the crowning effort of a most glorious career is nigh. The terrible mutiny of 1857 was prophesied by Sir Henry Lawrence years before it took place. In this year he was entrusted by the Governor-General with "the chief direction of military as well as of civil affairs" in Oudh, and became a brigadier-general. It may also be added that Sir Henry Lawrence, in the event of the death or the retirement of Lord Canning, was appointed Provisional Governor-General by the Home Government. "No soldier of the Company's army," writes Sir John Kaye, "had ever been so honoured." The last two chapters of Mr. Merivale's most interesting volume, Sir John's graphic pages, and the pens of other writers, have done our noble "hero in the strife" full justice; so it would be simple presumption to attempt adding anything to such vivid descriptions. Our chief object here has been to draw public attention, especially that of students—those who are preparing for India—to one of the most glorious lives which have adorned the nineteenth century—that of "a distinguished statesman and a most gallant soldier." The particulars of his death are most affecting. During his superhuman exertions at the siege of Lucknow, on the 1st of July, a shell burst in his room at the Residency, and severely shattered his thigh. Among Sir Henry's last directions, communicated to his successor, Major Banks, during great sufferings, were :—" Let every man die at his post; but never make terms. God help the poor women and children." "Spare the precious health of Europeans in every possible way from shot and shell." (Mr. Merivale has it " from shot and sun.") "Entrench—entrench —entrench. Erect traverses. Cut off enemy's fire." "Put on my tomb only this: HERE LIES HENRY LAWRENCE, WHO TRIED TO DO HIS DUTY. May God have mercy on him." He died from exhaustion on the morning of the 4th July, "and," writes Dr. Fayrer, who attended his deathbed, "his last moments were peaceful." On such an occasion one is tempted to think that

"One crowded hour of glorious life
Is worth an age without a name."

" When I think of death," says Grahame of Claverhouse to Mr. Morton, " as a thing worth thinking of, it is in the hope of pressing one day some well-fought and hard-won field of battle, and dying with the shout of victory in my ear; that would be worth dying for—and more, it would be worth having lived for!" This grand speech from the genius of Sir Walter Scott is all for glory; but Sir Henry Lawrence preferred duty, and his personal courage was quite equal to that of Claverhouse. Duty was his first aim; and of this noble Anglo-Indian it may well be said—

> "The elements
> So mix'd in him, that Nature might stand up,
> And say to all the world, 'This was a man!'"—*Shakspeare.*

So splendid a character also suggests a gem from the literature of Germany, which is from a translation* of "Words of the Heart," by J. C. Lavater, "For the Friends of Love and Faith." Such Christian philanthropy, as exhibited by the "Howard of the Punjab," and especially towards poor soldiers' children, might almost make us imagine that he had the words engraven on his heart—

> "Leave to the Dust—Dust!
> To the Earth—the Seed!—
> Those glorious with it grow up!
> So we shall behold ourselves once again Glorious!"

At the conclusion of his volume Mr. Merivale has the following striking passage, which we consider one of the finest in the whole work:—"Fourteen months after Sir Henry's death, in August, 1858, the Government of India passed, under Act of Parliament, from the hands of the East India Company to the direct control of the Crown. He was, therefore, the last of that great line of statesman soldiers—the last in the list which begins with Clive and ends with himself—who held to the end, and dignified, the simple title of 'servants of the Company;' and with him closes one of the strangest and not least glorious chapters in the history of England and of the world." Originating in a few gunners' crews and factory guards, the Company's army became a gigantic host of a nature unparalleled in ancient or modern times.

On the 22nd July, 1857, three weeks after his death,

---

* Manuscript by Mrs. Henry Westmacott.

the Court of Directors in London resolved that "Sir Henry Montgomery Lawrence, K.C.B., be appointed provisionally to succeed to the office of Governor-General of India, on the death, resignation, or coming away of Viscount Canning, pending the arrival of a successor from England." Sir Henry, had he lived, would have succeeded him provisionally. But Lord Canning—the pilot who weathered the storm—died in England (June 17th, 1862), not in India as asserted in this volume, and his successor, Lord Elgin, died in India (1863), and was succeeded by Lord Lawrence, who "was then named to hold the magnificent vice-royalty which would have been his brother's."

There is a monument to the memory of Sir Henry Lawrence in St. Paul's Cathedral; "but," writes his friend, Sir John Kaye, "the grandest monument of all is to be found in the asylums which bear his name"—the name of one, perhaps, unequalled "in the ranks of the servants of any Christian State in the latter ages of this world."*—*Age kahùn kya;* or, *ziyada kya nuheen*—what more need be said—in favour of such a biographical study?

* The latter remark is from William Russell's "Diary in India," quoted by Sir John.

NOTE.

With reference to the comparative merits of the two volumes forming this excellent biography, alluded to in our sketch, Mr. Merivale wrote to the author about a month before his death, on kindly acknowledging receipt of "the favourable notice":—"The book has been very well received, with some difference of opinion, I think, as to the merits of the respective authorships."

JOHN RUSSELL COLVIN, B.C.S.*
(LIEUT.-GOVERNOR OF AGRA, 1857.)

"One civilian only, among so many military men! What can be the reason for such a disproportion in the arrangement of some distinguished Anglo-Indians?" To this very natural question on the part of the reader, the writer would beg leave to reply, that it is not out of any want of respect for, or appreciation of, the high qualities and splendid actions of the Indian Civil Service, that he has not introduced more purely civil sketches into his pages, but from the fact of no other materials for such having come in his way; and his knowing that there are very many able writers, possessed of knowledge only to be obtained in that service—particularly of days gone by—who are ready, should the demand arise, to do the civilians of India full justice.

It is, perhaps, safer and better, therefore, that a military writer should confine himself to military men and soldier-politicals such as form the chief sketches here presented. But there is one item of knowledge in which the writer considers himself second to no man living, and that is an acquaintance with the magnificent hospitality of the Anglo-Indian civilian. He experienced it in the morning of life in Madras and Bengal, and to the close of his service, during many wanderings, and is glad to think he was never one of those who grudged the civilian his far larger salary, as, for many years, from reading and observation, he had opportunities of becoming aware of his mental attainments, his arduous duties, his vast responsibilities, his courage in facing difficulties, as well as of his social qualities. He recollects on one occasion, while on the march, meeting the collector and magistrate (the ruler in fact), of a district as large as Wales—a genuine Anglo-Indian collector of the old school—whose hospitable tent

* Written in December, 1874.

was adorned by a walking stick of colossal proportions—a *lathie* probably resembling what Dr. Johnson carried to thrash Ossian Macpherson if required—which weapon of defence had its story. It was simply that a week or so before the collector had been surrounded and attacked while engaged in his multifarious duties for the natives' welfare, and narrowly escaped serious injury. No troops were asked for, but he determined not to go abroad among his subjects without a thick stick in future. Even a little incident like this, to a soldier, naturally inspired respect for the civilian, which continued to grow stronger, and reached its acme when he heard of the numerous instances of his "pluck" in the terrible mutiny of 1857.

The following sketch is of a distinguished Bengal civilian, who died in harness, just as the light was beginning to break on "the shadows, clouds, and darkness" which had so long rested on a most awful period of our Indian history. Surely the career of a Lieutenant-Governor who died at such a crisis, of the Chief of the Agra Presidency, "the model government of India," where our overthrow was more immediate, and our disappearance more complete than elsewhere,* the ruler of a population of twenty-three millions (fifteen millions being agricultural), where everything had been done, through village schools and peasant proprietors, to raise the people to exertion "by means of their interest in the land;" surely such a career is well worthy of a brief study.†—John Russell Colvin was the second son of James Colvin, of the great mercantile house of Colvin and Co., and was born at Calcutta in May, 1807. Educated till nearly fifteen at St. Andrew's, Fifeshire, after a short time passed with a private tutor, he entered the East India College at Haileybury. He must have been a distinguished student, for he at once obtained the highest place among his contempor-

* See *Calcutta Review*, No. 66, December, 1859, p. 428—Article "Lord Dalhousie.

† This sketch of Mr. Colvin is chiefly compiled from a most interesting memoir in the *Times* (November, 1857), by a distinguished Bengal civilian, Sir Charles Trevelyan, the well-known "INDOPHILUS"—the Christian philanthropist—known also to fame as a financier, and who was for a short time Governor of Madras. The writer has also had the benefit of notes from private and other sources.

aries, and kept it throughout, his talents, energy and industry giving the promise of a valuable public servant. No one will venture to dispute that Haileybury produced many great and useful civilians; and it remains to be seen in our days of coaching and competition whether the same certain supply of energetic talent will be obtained as in days gone by.

Colvin went to India in 1826, and after passing most creditably the College of Fort William, began his career as assistant to the Register of the Sudder Court, Mr. Macnaghten, afterwards the famous Sir William, who, as the British envoy was so treacherously assasinated* in the Afghan War. In this court probably the young civilian gained his first knowledge of native character, although, perhaps, the future mighty secretary and unfortunate envoy was hardly the best man to implant such knowledge. Still here Colvin must have learned something in the way of forming his opinion of Asiatics, there being no sounder than that written twelve years after to Secretary Macnaghten, by Sir Alexander Burnes:† "You can only rely upon them when their interests are identified with the line of procedure marked out to them; and this seems now to be a doctrine pretty general in all politics." At this period we are told that although John Colvin "lived laborious days," like a sensible man, "he did not scorn those delights which belonged to his age and character." His next appointment was Assistant to the Resident at Hyderabad, Mr. William Byam Martin, remarkable for the cultivation of literary tastes during the most active period of his Indian career. In 1832 Lord William Bentinck created the office of Assistant-Secretary in each of the Government Departments at Calcutta "on the model of the English Under-Secretaryships," Colvin being selected for Assistant Secretary in the Revenue and Judicial department. He was promoted in 1836 to be Secretary to to the Board of Revenue in the Lower provinces of Bengal. The most important event in his official life took place, when, on the 4th of March, 1836, Lord Auck-

* Shot by Akbar Khan, 23rd December, 1841.
† Hussin Abdul, 2nd June, 1838.

land took his seat as Governor-General of India. His Lordship wanted "the best man" as Private Secretary, and asked those who were able to form a correct judgment on the subject. John Colvin was appointed, and how "ably and zealously" he served his master forms a grateful record by Lord Auckland, the first passage in which is:—" Mr. Colvin, has worked, I may say, rather with me than under me, during six years. He has had, and he has deserved my entire confidence. He brought to his duties an extensive and accurate knowledge of the interests of India, in its history, and in the details of its administration." There could have been no more trying period for the zealous Secretary than that shortly before the famous proclamation of war was issued (1st of October, 1838), by the Governor-General, when it is believed that the mind of Lord Auckland was so thoroughly bewildered betwixt peace and war,—the voice of Burnes and of the more experienced councillors being on the one side, "those of Captain Wade, the Resident at Loodianah, and the Secretaries Macnaghten and Colvin being on the other," that scarcely an hour elapsed without his Lordship's views alternating "from peace to war, and war to peace." It is strange that "Indophilus" does not allude to this important matter in his memoir. No more difficult position for a British statesman can be imagined than, during an impending storm in or on the confines of India, with terrific breakers ahead, to say boldly, "To be, or not to be !" The five small words, *to think is to act* contain the very quintessence of decision of character; but then, what genius it requires, at the head of such an empire, to think rightly ! A great statesman for India must be to the manner born. The Marquis Wellesley and Lord Dalhousie had the faculty of decisive, speedy action in weighty political matters, far above nearly all other Governors-General. The former, at the begining of the present century, to help on the work of consolidating the empire, at once resolved to occupy the province of Cuttack, in Orissa, which led to Pûri and the far famed temple of Jagannáth (the Lord of the World), the stronghold of Hindu idolatry, falling into our hands, but all his orders were conciliatory. Nearly fifty years after, Lord Dalhousie, to prevent another Sikh invasion of

British India, at once resolved, when aggression had been made, to fight the Sikhs "with a vengeance," leaving conciliation to follow the conquest if possible. In both cases, and in numerous others among their actions, a grand decision of character is apparent. Lord Auckland with the Russian bug-bear, and a most difficult country for warfare, in his mind's eye, became overwhelmed in a sea of indecision, and in the opinion of some good judges, almost at the bidding of his pilots, the secretaries, proclaimed one of the most disastrous wars on record. Perhaps, as this world goes, the actual decision to make war was not wrong; but in the state of Lord Auckland's mind, there should have been no final decision at all; and with the hope of conciliatory action, and the fullest preparations to resist aggression, he should, as a blow to trifling and dangerous indecision, have gone in heart and soul for peace.

We are inclined to think that the towering ambition of Sir William Macnaghten is chiefly to blame in this sad piece of business. Sir William did everything in his power to sway the councils of the Government of India. Although a famous Oriental scholar, and, in many respects, a valuable servant of Government, he knew nothing of Afghan diplomacy, as was eventually proved by the way he acted in "the Peshawur question." He lacked the accuracy of observation, the general soundness of judgment, and the valuable political views of Sir Alexander Burnes. Attentively looking at the Chief Secretary's character, he was just the man to have great weight with such a statesman as Lord Auckland. But, at the same time, it is a fact that Mr. Colvin's influence with the Governor-General was very great, and, rightly or wrongly, he is said to have identified himself with, or to a degree inspired, the policy which led to our Caubul disasters.

Mr. Colvin, like his master, was grieved at our position in the East, at a period of some humiliation on our part, with reference to Persia and Russia, and may have thought it just possible that diplomatic errors might be corrected, and British prestige restored, by letting slip "the dogs of war;" but the whole tenor of his career does not show any tendency to inculcate a war policy. As will be seen in the remainder of this sketch he was essentially a peaceful man, or, like Clive, when a youth, he might have left the Civil Service for the Army.

As we have said before, he died in harness, when the first awful cloud of the mutiny was passing away. And this leads to a very interesting question, which has not yet been fairly answered—Had the Afghan war any effect in producing that mutiny? An eminent Anglo-Indian takes a very strong view when, talking of the people of India as "far-distant, strange, and peculiar," he says that "the most stupendous crime that modern history records" was the Afghan invasion. "a crime deeply affecting that very people." And then, in a tone of indignant eloquent declamation, he remarks, "It was there that the right of England, her true might, was shivered, and the glorious prestige of our nation in Asia passed away! It was there in the perpetration of an unhallowed scheme, that the Hindustani Sepoy saw an army of his comrades under the torn banner of Britain 'melted like snow in the glance of the Lord,' and got from the Afghan resisting the invader, the first glimmering of his own power!" But many years before those words were uttered (1858), we had almost recovered our prestige by the glorious deeds of our troops under Pollock and Nott, by the gallant and chivalrous actions of Napier and Outram in Sind, and by the decisive battles which took place (an Indian Waterloo* among them), with a very strong foe, while we resisted and drove back the Sikh invaders of British India! And even in the year of the mutiny the people must have observed how well Sir John Lawrence held the Punjab, "kept back the wild tribes of Afghanistan, whose bands were mustering in Caubul for the invasion of India, and forced Wilson to the storm of Delhi."† Truly we may say that, during the Indian crisis, a kind Providence looked after us; and even enlightened Hindus and Ma-

---

* Sir Herbert Edwardes styled Ferozshah the Indian *Waterloo*.

† *Calcutta Review* (1859), No. 63, p. 248. *The Reviewer* is of opinion that Mr. Montgomery (now Sir Robert, the esteemed Member of Council), was the only other man (except Sir Henry Lawrence) who could have held the Punjab. He likewise praises the admirable conduct of Davidson and Macpherson at their respective courts.

homedans were forced to note what Shakspeare tells us, that

"There's a divinity which shapes our ends,
Rough hew them as we will."

It may be said, then, although Lord Auckland, or his secretaries, gave us the Afghan war, that war had little or nothing to do with producing the Indian Sepoy Mutiny of 1857, which chiefly arose from over confidence, and a growing want of tact and discipline—of course difficult to maintain where Brahmanic caste is so powerful—in our relations with the Bengal army! Our grand fault in the East, since Warrèn Hastings (the first Governor-General) consolidated the empire which Clive conquered, has been overconfidence. John Bull, in all his political conduct, especially in India and the neighbouring countries, from his kindly nature and knowledge of his inherent power, is too apt to confide, and too slow to prepare. Clouds on the horizon do not dismay him: they have passed away before, and will pass away again. This is hardly according to the advice of Burke, or our greatest political orators and writers, and, nearly twenty years ago, was alluded to in the *Calcutta Review:*—" Trusting overweeningly, like true Englishmen, in our intrinsic strength; confiding with more than Mahomedan infatuation in our '*ikbal;*' we leave much, sometimes all, to fortune. Such was long, very long, our practice on the North-West Frontier." We now return to Mr. Colvin. He came home with Lord Auckland in 1842, to enjoy that "chief nourisher" in an Anglo-Indian career, a furlough. Both mind and body were refreshed after three years' comparative leisure. He returned to India in 1845, and for a year held the appointment of Resident in Nepaul, after which he was transferred (1846) to the Commissionership of the Tenasserim Provinces, where, in a difficult position his administration gave much satisfaction to the Government as well as to the public. He had left the land of Vishnu and Siva to sojourn in the entirely different region of Gaudama. Here his measures, says "Indophilus," regarding the timber trade —for the community of Moulmein, although energetic and enterprising, may be literally styled a *wooden* one— "were held to be particularly useful, and he did much good by framing an uniform code of procedure for the native judges." In 1848 (if we recollect right) Mr. Colvin was promoted to the Sudder Court, Calcutta, where "he became *facile princeps*, so much so that it was commonly said that the pleaders had sometimes to be reminded that they ought to address the Court and not Mr. Colvin." This is very remarkable when we consider that he had no regular judicial training. All his knowledge of law was gained by hard study, and his becoming chief in a learned Court may be justly deemed "a proof of his intellectual superiority." As Sudder Judge, he may be said to have made his *best* score. The Court at the time was in little repute, and he pulled it up effectively. While on the Bench, he remonstrated with Lord Dalhousie for appointing a junior to the Foreign Office. His Lordship took the remonstrance in good part, defended himself, and shortly after sent him to the North-West. Calcutta "gup" said that he was sent there to escape the alternative of giving him a seat in Council, where his anti-Oudh annexation views, and his independence, might have proved troublesome. Mr. Colvin was appointed Lieutenant-Governor of the North-West Provinces (or Agra), on the death of the celebrated "big collector," Mr. Thomason (1853). "When thus appointed," writes "Indophilus," with the highest appreciation of his friend, "there was certainly no man in the service whose name stood higher for activity, ability, and force of character, and he had been already marked out as a fit man for Council." The magnitude of such a government as that of the North-West Provinces cannot be easily understood by Englishmen, who would seem to prefer any study to that of the geography and history of India. It may give some idea of the extent of territory to remark that the provinces which, with very few exceptions, have come under the far-famed "settlement" are about equal to England and Scotland, without Wales. In point of population (already given) they nearly equal Italy, including Sicily and Sardinia; while the gross revenue realized from them exceeds by one-half that of the Kingdom of Belgium.* From an able Bengal civilian, who knew Mr.

* *Calcutta Review*, No. 24, December, 1849, p. |416.—"The Settlement of the North-West Provinces."

Colvin well, we learn that as Lieutenant-Governor he laboured under the great disadvantage of being a stranger to the Province. This prevented him from being one with his officers from the first. But he became popular with most, and always had the reputation of singular fairness. His outsider position, however, led him to consult others as well; and he was thought to lean too much on advice, and to act too little from his own motives. Still, with these disadvantages, in his high position, John Colvin exhibited an astonishing industry and mastery of detail. Perhaps, after all, the grand difficulty in official life is to do little things well. He was perpetually "asking questions, gathering opinions, collating facts, and he carried this to an extent rarely equalled."

Such a mode of conduct was necessary to a governor who had not the practical professional knowledge of Mr. Thomason, who had been a magistrate and collector, and had made settlements; or of Sir John Lawrence, who had "served in every department from top to bottom." It is particularly mentioned that the earnest adoption of everything that was good in Thomason's plans, shows how thoroughly Colvin had the public interest at heart, furnishing "an honourable contrast to the usual disposition of public men to depreciate their predecessors, and to connect their own names with new measures, of which they alone would have the credit." His laudable desire to test the qualifications of his officers by inviting conferences, and making each state his opinion, reminds us of a story of Holt Mackenzie given in the article before quoted,* when the brighter days for the North-West had just arrived, and it was acknowledged that the Revenue Officers alone were able to correct the abuses of an age passed away. Holt Mackenzie was the man who made this discovery. We read that he saw the only way to obtain "an accurate knowlege of a practical, but complicated subject, hitherto little understood, was to go familiarly among the people whom it concerned; to "talk to them in office and out of office." His advice to the collectors was, "*Take your gun in your hand, and go among the people;*" to the commissioners, "*Get your collectors together over a good*

* Page 429.

bottle of claret, and then talk to them about the settlement." The reviewer fears that one part of his counsel was often followed without the other. So, like Holt Mackenzie, John Colvin was a great advocate for relaxing the stiffness of official intercourse where information was to be gained; but he flourished at a time when drinking was less in fashion, and there was little danger of meeting a Shearman Bird of Dacca, who was said, during his life, to have consumed enough claret to float a seventy-four!

Ever anxious to place merit above seniority, he strove to get the right man into the right place, and the judiciousness of some of his appointments was of course questioned. He was the steady friend of improvement in every phase, and in the all important matter of detecting and suppressing crime, a supervision which kept the whole machinery of the police on the alert, he showed remarkable energy. The capture of a dacoit or murderer was, with Mr. Colvin, not only a fact to note, but one to receive deep consideration. In the Revenue Department, he did much for the settlement of the Saugor and Nerbudda territories then recently attached to his Government; and he was arranging for the renewal and revision of the settlement in the North-Western Provinces, which was about to expire. [The custom was to strike an average; the revenue which each village could bear was estimated, and a settlement was made for the whole community, to last for thirty years.]* He was "strongly impressed with the importance of moderate and fixed assessments of the land revenue as the foundation of all improvement." On all matters relating to public works and education, Mr. Colvin brought his usual energy and minuteness to bear. It might almost be said that with him it was not enough to see the bricks in position, but he must also satisfy himself (often so necessary with dishonest native contractors), of the quality of the cement by which they are to remain as a work. Under him, in the Public Works Department, the new system arising from the abolition of the Calcutta Military Board, and the placing of all works, civil and military, under the local governments, came into operation.

* This famous settlement was completed by the great authority on Indian Revenue matters, Robert Mertins Bird, in 1841.

He prosecuted to completion the Ganges Canal, which immortalises the names of Thomason and Cautley, and opened the canal himself. Road making, under his really useful administration was advanced everywhere. He extended the machinery for popular vernacular education to all the districts, which had previously, as an experiment, only existed in a few. The writer of his memoir says most forcibly what, having gone thus far, the dullest reader can easily believe, that, "in all miscellaneous improvements, Mr. Colvin was most zealous and public spirited, as was to be expected from his turn of mind, which readily grappled with anything and everything that presented itself." Not the least of his merits was his conduct towards the press, which was always "liberal and successful." " Indophilus " particularly mentions that Lord Auckland had the cordial support of the Calcutta press during the alarm and depression caused by the Afghan war, which support, of course, was wisely encouraged by Mr. Colvin; or we may say that the good will of the press, cheered a Governor-General while his career was fast closing "in difficulties and darkness." The Lieutenant-Governor's continual desire like Mr. Thomason, to propagate useful information through the press was manifest throughout his administration. It was a common saying that Mr. Colvin "overgoverned." Business greatly increased; the secretaries could not nearly keep pace with the *mens æqua in arduis* of their energetic chief. But now a cloud appears on the horizon, and the labourer is to be taken from his works of peace and improvement. Just one hundred years after Clive "seized the keys of Hindustan" for the East India Company, the mutiny of the Bengal native army broke out—a mutiny English readers who have not been in India should ever keep in mind, not of the Indian army, but of the army of Bengal. It was the sudden revolt of an army, so far as friendship with the British was concerned, insincere and hollow, with sepoys "full of treacherous hypocrisy." Feeding and glutting themselves on their liberal masters, they quietly and cleverly bided their time for rebellion and murder, the flame of which they were to fan with their ill-gotten gains. For a very long time, it has been well and truly said, avarice was "the sheet anchor" which kept the vessel of the Bengal army in tolerable safety; and to show the saving propensities of the sepoys we read that one regiment in Pegu saved three lacs of rupees (£30,000).* But now the minds (if such treasures they really possess), of the sepoy dominating majority, became fairly unsettled, and the time appeared to have come when the Indian statesman's prophecy was to be fulfilled, and a large portion of our countrymen were to get up in the morning with their throats cut! Englishmen began seriously to muse on the probable overthrow of a splendid empire, and to wonder if such a state of things could really be produced by the revolt of a Sepoy army! Having thus touched on the native troops of the mutiny, we trust that, even in the sketch of a distinguished Anglo-Indian, a slight digression may be pardoned if, thinking it will add to the interest of our little volume, a reminiscence of days gone by (nearly thirty years ago) is given, from which it may be deduced by those about to pass a competitive examination, that the French were the original authors of the Sepoy mutiny. This time we give the great nation the credit of the invention, for they used to be rather prone to invent "everything which the cunning rogues, the English, unmercifully appropriate as their own." They invented fluxions, not Newton; and logarithms, not Napier; the vaccine was discovered by a French physician at Montpelier, long before Jenner was heard of; the Lancaster system of education was discovered by the Chevalier Paylett, before the revolution; Lerebours invented achromatic telescopes, not Dollond; and the French even contest the invention of Sir H. Davy's safety lamps; so now they had better take the entire credit of the Indian mutiny. But there is one thing clear : if there had been no Bengal native army, there would have been no sepoy mutiny; and, consequently, no such terrible massacres as those of Delhi, Cawnpore, and Futtehghur. What would Dupleix and Labourdonnais— the grand promoters of French power in the East—have thought of such an insurrection, could their apotheoses have visited India in fatal 1857 ?

* The Indian Crisis, 1857.—*Calcutta Review*,, No. 58, December, 1857, p. 435.

It is interesting to read how in 1644, just nine years before, Fort St. George (Madras) was raised to the rank of a presidency, "Thirty recruits and a considerable amount of ordnance and military stores" were landed from England, for it was not till nearly a century later that the idea occurred to Clive of partly conquering and keeping the country by its own inhabitants. This famous notion of the Peon, or native foot-soldier, was taken by our great countryman from the shrewd Frenchman, Dupleix, which fact was, on one occasion, strongly remarked on to the present writer, while on a visit to the Governor of Pondicherry. The conversation turned on the political exploits of Lord Ellenborough, and our wonderfully constituted Bengal native army, for no one ever dreamt then that in another twelve or fourteen years, such a large, mutinous crew would nearly ruin our power in Hindustan. "Look there, sir," said the sailor governor, pointing to a marble bust of Dupleix at the end of the room, "there is the man who taught you how to conquer India with its own inhabitants. You are of course aware that Clive took his idea of the native soldier entirely from this clever Frenchman?"—The Bengal army in particular, went on increasing till 1857, when the grand explosion took place, so what (with a few European troops) served the purposes of Clive, Dupleix and others in the East, during early European conquests, was no longer to be relied on. And it is curious to note how, after the mutiny (as if out of compliment to Clive, who won his first glories in Madras), the order of faithfulness to British rule in the native armies was clearly seen to run—Madras, Bombay, Bengal.*

We left John Colvin about to be taken from his peaceful labours to face "the stern realities of the military insurrection." The chief importance of Agra lay in its proximity to the great native independent states, to the dominions of Holkar and Scindiah, and to Rajpootana. Being also the seat of Government in the North-West, and with its fort and strategical position affording the nucleus of a strong military centre, it is difficult to imagine any

* See article in *Broad Arrow*, "Our Hold of India."—February 24th, 1872.

position at the time involving higher responsibility or requiring more commanding powers of action than that in which the Lieutenant-Governor was placed. As it turned out, "the worst massacres took place at Futtehghur and Cawnpore. There was the undying malice of the Nana, the almost entire absence of European soldiers, the contiguity of the newly settled kingdom of Oudh, and the excitable nature of a martial population, not yet tamed into forgetfulness of their old predatory habits." In a very different position was the great ruler of the Punjab. "Indophilus" tells us that "John Colvin's government was itself the focus of the insurrection. Lawrence may be said to have been his own commander-in-chief, and after an European force had been detached to Delhi, immediately on the outbreak, he still had at his disposal seven European regiments (including one sent from Bombay to Moultan), besides European artillery, and a local Sikh force of about 20,000 first-rate irregulars of all arms." The civil governor of the North-West, as the posts were stopped, could not even communicate with the commander-in-chief. The Punjab ruler had three days' knowledge by telegraph (by which he is said to have saved India) of the insurrection at Meerut and Delhi, and had time for arranging for disarming the Sepoy regiments under him. Mr. Colvin had no warning, and the military revolt had "actually taken place within his goverment, and the mutineers were in possession of Delhi before he could begin to act." He had only time to look about him, and perhaps hear people invoking Lord Dalhousie, who had recently left India,* in the forcible language of a lady poet of the rebellion:—

> " Come back to us : the tiger, which we deemed
> So tame, has broken loose, missing thy hand,
> Most firm, yet gentle ; and this glorious land
> Is full of his foul slaughters."

But when he did act, he acted with promptitude and vigour. About a week after the Mutiny began, or on the 17th May, Lord Canning telegraphed to Mr. Colvin, thanking him most cordially for what had been "so admirably done," and for keeping that most valuable of

* In March, 1856.

treasures at such a crisis—"a stout heart." At Agra he held a parade of the troops, clearly explaining to them that the Government had no intention whatever to interfere with their religion and caste; he strengthened the fort, and threw into it a large amount of supplies; he raised a body of volunteers (horse), who afterwards did good service; and called upon Scindiah and the neighbouring native states to use their contingents in keeping open the roads and preserving the peace of the country. In a spirit which Vauban or Cormontaigne would have admired, he strongly deprecated any "premature abandonment of our position." He wrote to the Governor-General on the 22nd of May:—"It is a vitally useful lesson to be learnt from the experience of present events that not one step should be yielded in retreat on an outbreak in India which can be avoided with any safety." Surely the strictest and most able and impartial civil or military critic will confess that John Colvin had nobly done his duty up to this mark. But now was about to come the unfortunate proclamation—the "mild proclamation," as it was jeeringly called—which, rightly or wrongly, has been seized upon by historians and other writers to detract from his fame. The "quality of mercy" in a ruler had never been so severely called in question before. Even a faint shadow of mercy was quite out of the question until the fearful crisis was over. The unfortunate proclamation came about in this fashion:— As early as the 15th of May, Mr. Colvin urgently recommended the issue of a proclamation by the Governor-General, to disabuse the Sepoys of the delusions under which they laboured, and to give a bridge for the faithful to walk over and separate themselves from the mutineers. On the 24th of May he reiterated the advice. He was strongly opposed to a general severity towards all, thinking that such action would "estrange the remainder of the army." "Hope," he wrote, "I am firmly convinced should be held out to all those who were not ringleaders, or actively concerned in murder or violence." He wished the Commander-in-Chief to be authorised to act upon such a line of policy, adding, "When means of escape are thus open to those who can be admitted to mercy, the remainder will be considered obstinate traitors, even by their own countrymen, who will have no hesitation in siding against them." The subject being of "vital and pressing importance," Mr. Colvin requested "the earliest answer to this message." The pressure to act in some manner regarding a proclamation must have been very strong indeed. The idea of a successful issue of his own model had evidently taken firm hold on his mind; and certainly, at such an awful time, to many it seemed to depend, like a man's fortune, on the toss up of a halfpenny whether success would follow, or otherwise. Without waiting for an answer from the Viceroy, on the following day (May 25th) he reported that he had taken *the decisive step*. " Supported," he wrote, " by the unanimous opinion of all officers of experience here, that this mutiny is not one to be put down by high-handed authority, and thinking it essential at present to give a favourable turn to the feelings of the Sepoys who have not yet entered against us, I have taken the grave responsibility of issuing on my own authority the following proclamation." Order and control in many of his districts had vanished. His latest letter from Meerut was now seven days old, and not a single letter had reached him from the Commander-in-Chief.* Surely India was never in such a mess, nor Local Governor placed in such a disagreeable plight before. We seriously cannot help thinking that, had Lord Dalhousie been in power, Mr. Colvin would not under any circumstances have issued his proclamation; but would have contented himself with other means at his disposal for keeping order and preventing the spread of disaffection—at least, until he heard from the Governor-General. The Lieutenant-Governor seemed to have some intuitive knowledge of the *slowness*, where grave political matters required speedy decision, of Lord Canning's mind! Action was indeed necessary at Agra; but the very commencement of the Lieutenant-Governor's proclamation was unfortunate :—" Soldiers engaged in the late disturbances,

---

* Who was preparing for the siege of Delhi. On his march thither General Anson died of cholera, brought on by overwork, at Karnaul, 27th May.

who are desirous of going to their own homes, and who give up their arms at the nearest Government civil or military post, and retire quietly, shall be permitted to do so unmolested." While all Anglo-India was, with the deepest execration, thirsting for revenge on the merciless rebels; while Siva wore his most destructive attire, and his wife, Kali, her most ghastly necklace of skulls; while even their fat, elephant-headed son, Ganesa, seemed to have abjured his protective qualities for ruthless slaughter, and (in Shaksperian language) if ever hell was empty and all the devils present in a tempest, it was now, it certainly did seem hardly the time for any show of mercy. Action of some sort, however, was necessary. But without a large European force to back Mr. Colvin's efforts, what was to be done? The concluding paragraph of the proclamation is decisive enough as to punishment:— " Every evil-minded Instigator in the disturbance, and those guilty of heinous crimes against private persons, shall be punished. All those who appear in arms against the Government after this notification is known, shall be treated as open enemies." It was almost beyond human judgment, in such an unprecedented crisis, " to know what were good to do;" so the author of the proclamation, from a strong sense of duty, risked his reputation by an act which was sure to become more public than any other. "Indophilus" cites two cases from history which justify Mr. Colvin, so far as precedent is concerned. These are— the Mutiny at the Nore, and the Irish Rebellion; and any one carefully reading the Royal Proclamation on the former, and the preamble of the Irish Act of Parliament of George III. on the latter insurrection, will see that the course adopted by John Colvin was the usual one on such occasions. In an ordinary state of public feeling, it is remarked "that unsparing military execution would not have been considered justifiable until the attempt had been made to distinguish between the leaders and followers, between those who struck the blow and added outrage to insubordination, and those who passively or willingly yielded to the movement of the body to which they belonged." To this it was replied that there should have been no parleying with rebels, and that the armed opposition should have been put down before discriminating between different degrees of guilt. On this point "Indophilus" remarks, that if Mr. Colvin had waited till then, it would have been too late. "The object was, to apply a solvent to reduce the compact mass of rebellion to its elements, and to give to the well-disposed an opportunity of returning to their allegiance, leaving the guilty remainder to their well-deserved fate." Less reflective men might have acted better, seeing that it was during an *extraordinary* "state of public feeling," and on the principle of violent diseases requiring violent remedies. But such a mode of action was not to be expected from the high, judicial mind of John Colvin. The proclamation was universally approved at Agra. It seemed to his advisers that it was the right thing to do at that time, and under those circumstances. And this forces a remark somewhat similar to what Johnson applied to the writing of the poet Savage under difficulties:—" How many other able and distinguished civilians in India, had they been at Agra, would have acted better than Colvin?" But the difficulty of obtaining evidence as to guilt on giving up arms was severely commented on by the head of the Indian Government. A new proclamation, directed by the Governor-General, fell flat just as much as his Lieutenant-Governor's did; and, taken as a whole, it was identical in substance with a telegraphic message from Lord Canning, "bearing the same date as the proclamation, but received subsequently to its being issued." Colvin wrote to his family, that they might understand the grounds of his conduct:—"That those who had taken a leading or a deliberately malignant part in the revolt would ever seek to take advantage of the notification, we knew to be quite out of the question. The chance that seemed open, through the proclamation, of escape to such persons, was what called forth the heavy censure at many distant points: but we who were nearer the scene, and knew the real spirit of the revolt, could not entertain such a supposition." If Mr. Colvin had lived to complete his defence, he might have added, "that the Governor-General afterwards himself issued a circular letter, in which the principle was fully admitted that a distinction ought to be made between the innocent and guilty even in Sepoy regiments which have murdered their officers, and that punishment ought to be founded upon some proof of individual guilt; and the Governor-General's circular was issued on the 31st of July, when all hope of securing an immediate political result by inducing the comparatively innocent to separate themselves from their more guilty associates had passed away—which was not the case in May, when the character of the insurrection had not been fully developed." "Indophilus" concludes this masterly part of his memoir by remarking, with the clear judgment and impartiality of a true friend and critic:—"The difficulty of obtaining evidence must have been encountered at some time or other, unless it had been determined to make no distinction between the Sepoys belonging to the offending regiments, whatever their individual conduct might have been." On the question of Lord Canning being blamed for his clemency, an able writer, the year after the mutiny, was of opinion that nobody ever blamed the Governor-General for being clement. He was *not* clement in the commencement of 1857, and had no chance of being so; the sepoys had it all their own way. "What we all objected to, was Lord Canning's *discourse* about clemency at a time when Europeans were prostrate at the mercy of a bloodthirsty enemy." When Delhi was taken, India saved, and Lucknow had fallen, it was the time for "mercy and pacification;" for then "the crisis was overpast." Another able writer—one very far from being prejudiced either in favour of Lord Canning or Mr. Colvin—shrewdly remarks: "If many guiltless must have fallen at first under the blind rage of the English or the grosser greed of the Sikh soldiery, it seems clear that some needless waste of lives and property, sowing in its turn rich crops of fear and hatred in the minds of people otherwise loyally, at any rate peacefully, disposed, must be laid to the rash zeal of those civil officers for whose guidance Lord Canning framed the resolution of the 31st of July."* Doubtless, Mr. Colvin had similar

---

* Trotter's "History of the British Empire in India," vol. ii. p. 285.

motives when, in the early development of the mutiny, he issued his proclamation.

Lord Canning's proclamation of May 16th has been compared to pouring a bottle of oil upon a stormy sea "to quell the wild tumult of its waves;" but, notwithstanding, to the Governor-General's credit, he, at the same time, awoke to unmistakable energy, which showed that he did not put his trust in papers or other state craft. He immediately summoned European troops from all quarters, despatched ships to intercept the Chinese expedition under Lord Elgin, and called for speedy and large reinforcements from home. He also proclaimed martial law in the disturbed districts. It should also be kept in mind that Mr. Colvin was the first in the latter particular by asking leave to proclaim martial law around Meerut; that, while the cantonment fires—those "red forerunners of evil"—were raging "in the very seat of his rule," he showed remarkable energy; and that, at the end of May, two companies of native troops having mutinied at Muttra (twenty miles from Agra), he disarmed the remainder of the two regiments to which they belonged (the bulk of them slipping off to Oudh or Delhi); in their default, the English band of volunteers which Mr. Colvin had raised, taking their place, and doing admirable service. * It was Mr. Colvin, also, who first urged on Lord Canning that the returning Persian force be at once ordered round to Bengal. Judged by such activity of mind for the public welfare, the subject of our sketch appears in a fair way to be more admired by posterity than by some highly-intelligent Anglo-Indians of the present time; like many writers, too prone to judge a man's career by one action. only. John Colvin said truly, in the letter to his family, already quoted —that his "proclamation remained a mere trifling incident in the great series of events." From this sketch, perhaps, the useful lesson may be gained, that all proclamations in India, at a time of extraordinary revolt, when every calculation, on ordinary grounds, for its suppression, has a very great chance of being in error, are utterly useless. There

* Towards the end of May, in connection with the progress of rebellion near Agra, may particularly be mentioned the brave stand at Mainpoorie, to the eastward, by Lieutenant De Kantzow, "a noble example," as Lord Canning well said, "of courage, patience, good judgment, and temper."

is no help for it at present, but to be constantly prepared, at all the important posts in the country, with a strong European force, and such aids for a general plan of fortification as our best engineers may deem advisable. A force of 65,000 or 70,000 men is certainly the minimum of European troops we should have in India, including a very strong force of artillery, of which the Oriental mind has a wholesome dread (the Burmese used to style even our 12-pounder rockets "devil-sticks"); and then, with such a speedy mode of transport of fully equipped batteries by rail to any scene of outbreak or disaster, as that recently carried out* by Sir Charles Reid—under whom a fully equipped battery of artillery was moved from Umritsur to Meean Meer by railway at a few minutes' notice, by a telegram—and with the hope of 30,000 more men from home and the colonies, ready for service in India at a day's notice, with various important changes in the constitution of our native armies, which need not be mentioned here, India would become tolerably safe; and it will remain so, till, the people having, through its being made known to them by every available avenue, learned the force and excellence of Christian truth, the transition state of the Native mind, prophesied by Sir Charles Trevelyan, shall have arrived, and we behold a nation " born in a day!"

Mr. Colvin's life was now fast drawing to a close. So much responsibility had rarely been laid on one man's shoulders, and no wonder his health was shattered. That terrible energy, which kills more public men than is generally supposed, was now in full play. A hostile force, composed chiefly of the Neemuch Brigade, arrived within a short march of Agra. Quarters had been prepared for the entire Christian population in the old Royal Residence, which had little of the character of a fort; and into this place of refuge they went, while the main body of our much smaller force marched out to meet the rebels. On the 25th of August, the fort had 4,289 inmates, including the European Regiment and the Artillery. There were 2,514 women and non-adults. But everything had been foreseen and arranged, and the bad effects of compressing such a multitude into a small space, prevented. That watch-

* November, 1874.

ful care of others, which so distinguished his life, now became more and more apparent. But the Lieutenant-Governor had received his death stroke. The guns of the fort commanded all that was left of the vast Government he had striven so hard to improve. Even the remnant was threatened by a war-cloud from the direction of Gwalior. Mr. Colvin's first attack of illness immediately preceded his removal into the fort; but, in spite of the advice of kind friends, he would not cease from work. Eventually he was transferred to "the freer air of cantonments," which gave him but temporary benefit. His son, Elliott, who was out in the district, was just recalled in time "to see and be recognised by his father." Mrs. Colvin was in Switzerland, on her way home to England. "On Wednesday afternoon, the 9th of September," writes "Indophilus," "he sank quietly, without pain, to his last blessed sleep," and was buried inside the fort on the following morning. In the notification of his death by the Government of India (September 19th), a fine passage occurs:—"Worn by the unceasing anxieties and labours of his charge, which placed him in the very front of the dangers by which of late India has been threatened, health and strength gave way, and the Governor-General-in-Council has to deplore, with sincere grief, the loss of one of the most distinguished among the servants of the East India Company."

He could discuss literary and political subjects with the ablest men of the day; but "the warm and genial qualities of his heart were his crowning excellence." Colvin is described as one of the last of our Indian statesmen who derived their inspiration by immediate tradition from Malcolm, Munro, Metcalfe, and Bentinck. "These wise masterbuilders completed the edifice of our Indian Empire on the solid foundation of good faith, justice, and personal respect. Many of their disciples devoted themselves to the interests of the natives with a self-denying zeal which has been seldom equalled."

Had he lived a short time longer, we can imagine with what delight he would have read of the brilliant siege of Delhi (20th September), when the tide of disaster turned, and India passed out of its "dark phase of mourning;" of the deeds of the "glorious Nicholson," and of Hodson, "the

Cavalier of Cavaliers;" all turning him to think of the people, justice, and the settlement in his loved North-West Provinces, where "the labours of Robert Bird, Thomason, and Colvin will not be in vain." Reviewing the life of Mr. Colvin, we cannot help being of opinion that, during his Indian career, he did his vast amount of work ever under the strong impulse of duty. For such a crisis as the great Sepoy rebellion, he may be said to have been, like Lord Canning (who won high honours at Oxford), over-cultivated. More rough and ready material, with half the brains, perhaps, would have done better at such a crisis. Military men are not, as a rule, so highly educated as civilians who rise to distinction. But their profession particularly fits them for action in troublous times; and this tends to impress us with the idea that men like Sir John Malcolm, Sir Henry Lawrence, Sir James Outram, and Sir Herbert Edwardes, can go anywhere and do anything. The frequent over-cultivation in the civilian tends to make him halt between two opinions, to seek a reason for all he does, which will not do in a crisis requiring speedy action. The military political, without any judicial or legal training, has only his common sense to lead him straight to the point. This is apt to remind one of the well-known story of the great Lord Mansfield, who, being asked by a distinguished general officer, with judicial as well as military duties to perform, what he should do, as his inexperience and ignorance of technical jurisprudence would prove a serious impediment to his efficient administration of justice. "Make your mind perfectly easy," said the great judge; "trust to your native good sense in forming your own opinions, but beware of attempting to state the grounds of your judgments. The judgment will probably be right—the argument infallibly wrong." Mr. Colvin left seven sons, three of whom are in the Bengal Civil Service, Bazett, Elliott, and Auckland Colvin, the latter holding the important post of Secretary to Government, North-West Provinces. The fourth son, Clement, is in the India Office, was recently Private Secretary to the Duke of Argyll, and is now in that capacity to Sir Louis Mallet, Under Secretary of State for India.

While concluding this imperfect sketch of a distinguished Anglo-Indian, the clock announced that 1874 had passed away; the writer, therefore, cannot help remarking how admirably the severe trial of the old year—the Bengal famine—has come to a close. Wonderful energy has been shown by Englishmen in the year that has gone, which must prove to the natives of India that, in works of real necessity and charity, Great Britain is ever to the fore. India must now be fully aware that, under Providence, we can arrest the disastrous famine as well as put down the deadly rebellion. In the fatal year 1857, at the very outbreak of the mutiny, the writer occupied an important post near Hyderabad, the huge and wicked city of the Dekhan, where, although we had one rather serious disturbance, peace was well preserved through the tact of the Nizam's most able Minister, the illustrious Salar Jung, the prudent action of Colonel Davidson, the Resident at Hyderabad, and the precautionary measures taken by the officer commanding the Subsidiary Force.* This slight reminiscence compels a thought of how glad we, in India, were to part with a year which had been so fatal to so many of our brave countrymen; and, although we have still to be with the " avenging angel " during that period, while the, in many respects, glorious old year of 1874 (to many like an old friend) has just departed, perhaps it will not be out of place to give the following admirable sonnet, from the " Poetry of the Rebellion," which would have done no discredit to Wordsworth, on

1857.

" Depart; depart ! We ever bid farewell
To our old years with a quick, sudden pain
Around our hearts, as if we would again
Recall the past by working of a spell ;
But thou art different, and we would compel
Thee from our homes, if power were to constrain
Thy speedy parting. Wane, O quickly wane,
Sad moon, and let us hear the signal bell.
Old year, wrap thy blood-stained robes around,
And take thy staff within thy trembling palm,
And leave us ; wait thou not for blessing-sound,
For lingering clasp of hand, soothing as balm :
We standing in a silentness profound,
Shall watch thy going, still, relieved, and calm." †

MARY LESLIE.

* Brigadier (afterwards Major-General Sir Isaac Campbell) Coffin.

† *Calcutta Review*, No. 62, December, 1868, p. 360.

BRIGADIER-GENERAL NEILL.

(A BRIEF REVIEW OF HIS MILITARY CAREER.)*

THE "Second Burmese War," like, perhaps, most other recent military narratives, has been entirely cast into the shade by the more stirring and novel matter of the Bengal Sepoy Revolution. Such a cloud, so awful in result, being as every one hopes, about, to give way to a prospect "bright and advancing," the minds of some may once more turn to Pegu, the province but a few years conquered, where, during the times of bloodshed and rebellion, during a chaos of darkness, disorder and ruin, throughout a large portion of India, the sunshine of a tranquil and increasing prosperity has steadily appeared; and where now, it may safely said, Justice really breathes, and Civilisation, after a hard struggle, is really born.

On the present occasion, however, let us allow Pegu to claim our sympathy for another reason. It is the land where Havelock and Neill first displayed those peculiar qualities which eventually led them on, in Bengal and Oudh, to success and victory.

True enough, neither of them were leading men,—the *fulmina belli*, as they have since been styled,—neither of them held the rank of General in Pegu; but Havelock, with his Company of Europeans, in the first, and Neill, with his Adjutaut-General's duties, in the second Burmese War, did quite enough to shew, that, if opportunity offered, they would one day make a mighty progress on the path to fame.

To both this opportunity came rather late in life; but not too late to exhibit judgment combined with "dash" and

* [Written at Nagpore, December, 1858.]

vast powers of enduring fatigue, reminding us of Clive at Arcot or Plassey, and of the ablest soldiers that have been reared in this our "nursery of Captains." Literature, also, is indebted to the departed heroes. Both were military writers of no ordinary capacity; and we naturally grieve to think, that the pen of Havelock which wrote the "Campaigns in Ava," more than thirty years ago, and that of Neill, which recorded the "services of the First Madras European regiment,"—the immortal Fusiliers,—will never tell us more than has already been told of that glorious career of triumphs at the crowning goal of which Neill fell and Havelock died,—the former dying, in the strictest sense, "as heroes wish to die," and the latter departing while nobly reviewing the conduct of a well-spent life.

Havelock, who had chronicled the privations and sufferings of the troops at Rangoon in 1824, had throughout his career seen death in all its varieties; and his remark to Sir J. Outram, in the last victory, "I have so ruled my life that, when death came, I might face it without fear," perhaps owes some of its power and beauty to scenes of suffering he had witnessed in the land of the Golden Foot.* The exit of this hero points to a remark of old Montaigne— "Where death waits for us is uncertain; but let us everywhere look for him. The premeditation of death is the premeditation of liberty; he who has learnt to die has forgot what it is to be a slave."

That noble-minded Frenchman, Montalembert, has done full justice to Havelock, and to that admirable spirit of the Puritans which still exists in our Army.

To the memory of both heroes their countrymen have done great honour: and, as belonging to Madras, we read with pride what has been done to raise a monument to Neill,* as well as to assist the widow and the fatherless of the Madras Fusiliers, which regiment has played so distinguised a part in putting down the rebellion.

It was during the march of the Martaban Column, in

* It was at Rangoon that Sir A. Campbell, the General Commanding, when informed of the enemy approaching one of our posts, said, "Call out Havelock's saints; they are never drunk, and he is always ready."— *Biographical Sketch*, p. 39.

† [The statue at the Presidency, since raised in honour of Neill, is a most interesting work of art.]

1853, that our attention was first drawn to Major Neill, Assistant-Adjutant-General. Every one remembers Napier's account of the British Infantry soldier in the "Peninsular War;" and on seeing Neill, with his powerful frame, and lofty port, forming a noble specimen of military bearing, one might well have supposed he was proud to have risen in a corps which possessed, rather than these features, the quality of sustaining fatigue with incredible vigour, undeniable firmness in battle, and "the fount of honour full and fresh within;" but which attributes, as was afterwards apparent, he also shared in common with the Madras Fusiliers, as hardy and daring a body of infantry as the world ever saw.

As Captain of the Grenadier company of his corps, he was an especial favorite with the men. Of this we have been well assured by those who have served under him in the ranks.

His services in Turkey, during the recent war with Russia, belong more to the pen than to the sword. Instruction in military duties, and attention to discipline, for which some years of service in the Adjutant-General's department* should well qualify a zealous and efficient officer, had probably something to do with laying the foundation of Neill's after fame in India.

His services in Burma had procured him the army rank of Lieutenant-Colonel; and he served as Brigadier-General with the Turkish Contingent. On the eve of his return to India, General Vivian† wrote to the Court of Directors, with a view of bringing under their notice the estimation he felt for Neill's merits and services, particularizing the zeal and efficiency with which he commanded a division of infantry, from the period when the Turkish Contingent was organized "until its re-transfer to the Sultan's goverment." This was duly communicated to the Government he had the honour to serve; and by the time he arrived in India, about the end of March, 1857, but a very few months had to elapse, before he would do full honour to that Government.

* Havelock had been Quarter-master-General of Queen's Troops, and afterwards Adjutant-General.
† [Sir R. J. H. Vivian, K.C.B. Now G.C.B., and late Member of the Indian Council.]

Before viewing his career, in the last stirring scenes of his life, a slight retrospect may not be uninteresting.

When Neill arrived in Burma, in 1852, it may be said he had seen no field service, although the date of his commission as Ensign was as far back as January, 1827.

Spectamur Agendo, the motto of his regiment, with its long list of triumphs, commencing at Arcot and Plassey, was to be fulfilled by Neill and his gallant corps, a century after Clive had won India for us, in Bengal and Oudh, rather than in Burma, the country which the Fusiliers now visited, to support the glory of our arms, for the second time.

The fame of this distinguished corps is well known to the reader of Indian military history. It was in the year 1755, that the Madras Artillery and the First Madras European regiment were first regularly incorporated. In 1756, the English and French forces on the Coromandel Coast were nearly equal, each consisting of some 2,000 Europeans and 10,000 natives. The British force included H.M.'s 39th regiment, *Primus in Indis*. The Madras Artillery and Fusiliers may be said to have born the brunt of the early (which is, in one sense, the principal) portion of the conquest of our Indian Empire. In those days of Lawrence and Clive it was difficult indeed to make way against French intrigue and native treachery; and, when, notwithstanding, vast progress had been made, and numerous deeds of valour had been accomplished, we at length find the two corps present in Bengal, retrieving the fallen fortunes of that Presidency; and now, about a century after Clive's defence of Arcot, they were serving, each for the second time, in Burma, while fortune had favoured Bengal. and allowed it to pride itself on nearly all the recent military glory of the East!" *

The doings, on the 4th of June, at Benares will be touched upon in due time; but in connection with the foregoing historical remarks, it may not be out of place here to note that, on the said 4th of June, Lieutenant Crump, of the Madras Artillery, rendered important services at Benares, and fell in the gallant discharge of his duties at Lucknow.

* Pegu, a Narrative, &c., p. 65.

At the time of meeting the Assistant-Adjutant-General while on service with the Martaban Column, to procure notes on the subject of the then very recent relief of Pegu, in which he had shared with his commander, General Steel,* was of more importance to us than to photograph the future hero. One day, after a long march, he acceded to our request to furnish some, and the result was a donation of six or seven pages of closely-written manuscript, when the column reached Tonghoo.

From those materials the chief portion of the ninth chapter in "Pegu, a Narrative of the Second Burmese War," was composed, with an endeavour to preserve as much as possible Neill's own views on the relief of Pegu, and the subsequent operations, about which, having been present, and possessing the experience of a military writer, he would, doubtless, give the world a valuable opinion.†

Nothing could be better than Neill's reasons for fully expecting that General Godwin would, after relieving Pegu, and in order to free the garrison from the near position of the Burmese Army, wait for the land column, which was, on its way from Rangoon, proving that he quite understood the value of combining Artillery, Cavalry and Infantry, especially where a small body is to attack a large one. And yet it seems simple enough, though even Generals not unknown to fame have occasionally disregarded the solution of the problem, that well-equipped artillery, especially when furnished with plenty of canister, (say Brigadier Miller's allotment), compensate for small numbers of infantry; and after success by either infantry or artillery, against a comparatively numerous force, without cavalry how is it possible to follow up and cut off the enemy? Military judgment was the grand requisite wanting in the present instance; and there can be no doubt that General Godwin, with an enemy before him without any disposition to retire, should have either himself waited, or deputed his next in command, General Steel,

---

* Sir S. W. Steel, K.C.B., a distinguished (Madras) Indian Officer.

† For those who have not perused the Author's "Narrative," the chapter is given entire at the end of this sketch; and it may aid the better understanding of the few critical remarks on the operations which here follow. The letter which accompanied the MS. is also given.

to wait for the column, so as, in the gallant Neill's own words, to "disperse the enemy with effect."

When the time for action came, even under unfavourable circumstances, decision of character, as shown in the following remarks, gleams forth in the character of Neill. During the operations, dispositions were made for attacking in two columns, of which the left was placed under General Steel; but, the attack of the left column having been countermanded, the "rapid dash" Neill wished with all his heart was not made; and so the enemy walked leisurely off. And again, during the same operations, while a good opportunity offered, he deplores the want of "a steady active advance to bring our troops into action." In alluding to these two occasions, Neill's own words are almost entirely used in the "Narrative." "These plans of attack were admirably conducted until it came to the moment for acting, when it appeared as if the veteran chief lacked decision, and seemed to be unconcious of the enemy passing away before him."

But, with that generosity which might be expected from a noble-minded soldier, he highly praises the relief of Pegu, General Godwin's great "coolness under fire," and the "entire disregard of self" evinced by the gallant chief, which few who had seen him on service could have failed to observe.

And again, it is from Neill's manuscript the sentiment comes, that, during "the three days' work," none displayed "greater endurance than General Godwin himself, and several of the oldest officers who accompanied him."

Alas! how many of the devoted band have since died or fallen in battle, including Neill and Renaud, the Fusilier Officers; both, it may be said, "in the blaze of their fame."

Neill, like the knight of old,* whose chivalrous death he seemed to emulate, doubtless looked into his heart and wrote; so judging from the above strictures on the operations in Burma, he would have acted strictly in the way he recommended; and, judging from the attributes he so warmly praises in others, it is pleasing to think, and his short but brilliant career in Oudh eminently supports

* Sir Philip Sidney.

the assertion, that these attributes shone with a peculiar lustre in his own character. Qualities such as he possessed are rarely to be found combined in one man; and now he comes before us as the Officer of the Madras Presidency, the right man in the very nick of time, to do what Clive did a century before with a handful of the very same Regiment, and even to do more than retrieve the fallen fortunes of Bengal,— to strike deeply at the root of a deadly mutiny which threatened an Empire, show a bold front to Rebellion, and save Benares, the stronghold of Siva, the destroyer, the city of the sacred bulls and sacred waters, with temples second only in mythological and religious importance among the Hindus to Jagannáth, the "Lord of the world." *

Benares, the "Lotus of the world," has been graphically described by Heber and Macaulay. The picture of Siva, as drawn in the Puránas, seems strongly prophetic of the vile arch-fiend of Bithoor, whose bloody work was so soon about to commence. Siva in Benares, in the pride of Satanic majesty, appearing here and there, at one time sitting in his chief temple "covered with the ashes of a funeral pile, ornamented with human skulls and bones;" at another, wandering about, with dishevelled hair, "sometimes laughing and sometimes crying."

At this stronghold of Hinduism, Colonel Neill, with only a detachment of his Fusiliers, arrived on the eve of 4th June, the night of which had been appointed for a general rising in the "holy city." Here, in the strictest

* [The story of Neill at the Çalcutta (Howrah) railway station has been told in various ways. The most striking picture which rests on the mind is as follows:—Neill's sudden arrival at the station with a portion of his gallant Fusiliers—the determination of the Colonel to wait for the rest of a detachment—the carriages filled with passengers for "up-country," Europeans, natives, and East Indians—the surprise of the station-master and railway officials at being told to wait, and, on the arrival of the missing men, unload, and make way for the troops—the natural hesitation on their part—the determined look of Neill, and glance at a Corporal's guard who would execute if the order were not immediately obeyed— Neill assuming *pro tem*, the position of station-master—a few rather strong oaths decidedly audible—the bewilderment of the various passengers— the eventual "clearing" of the train, and its occupation by the Fusiliers—the sullen looks of the guard and engineer, as the train moved off under such extraordinary compulsion with a whistle and a scream to Benares!]

sense, thought was action. This was the first arrival of an additional European regiment in Bengal, and hopes of relief from Europe were yet distant. Down went the spirit of mutiny before the judicious arrangements and untiring energy of Neill! With only 200 men of his own Regiment, and about half a battery of guns,—at first, through causes afterwards explained, hindered rather than assisted by the Sikhs he had so much admired in Pegu,— he dispersed the mutineers with great slaughter, restored order and confidence, and saved Benares. The vast importance of this service, we are afraid, has not yet been quite understood. It was the first stroke in earnest made by British power at the root of the Indian rebellion. Neill had anticipated the movement of the mutineers as one who knew how much reliance to place on Native character; and his triumph was complete.

Clive declared, if he had known the Native language he never would have conquered India; for he might have believed all the lies that he heard, and have been cheated accordingly. Neill seems to have had the great General in his eye when commencing his labours; so, whether it be at the Howrah terminus, or at Benares, we have few words, but a good deal of action, and abundance of decision of character. A mind such as his, which acknowledged only one path, the path of duty, was the right sort of mind for this most formidable crisis. Jomini, in his "Art of War," in enumerating the qualities most essential for a Commander, declares they will ever be a "great character, or moral courage, which leads to great resolutions; then *sang-froid*, or physical courage, which predominates over dangers."* Neill was the man to make and to carry out great resolutions. The slightest pusillanimity or want of decision at Benares might have lost us Calcutta; and who can say what would have been the end of such a disaster?

When comparative order had been restored, Neill passed on to Allahabad. Celebrated as to position for a great city, situated at the junction of the two mighty streams, the Ganges and Jumna, from which, so far as the cleansing away from sin is concerned, the city has, perhaps, as great

* "Art of War."—Article, Military Policy.

a religious importance as Benares, the destroyer was very likely to be equally busy at work.

What Bishop Heber thought, that it might revive to greater prosperity than it possessed when he beheld it, seems now, from the improvements being carried on, to be in course of realisation; and, not the least honour to Allahabad, at the present time, it was from this city came forth the State paper which so nobly defended the policy pursued in Oudh during the rebellion, putting many literary rebels to confusion, and proving the writer to be a statesman worthy of the great name he bears, and, in some respects, deserving to be styled, as Canning said of William Pitt, " the pilot who weathered the storm!"

Had Burke lived in our time, he might have exclaimed, " What a deadly and cruel rebellion!" and pronounced the crisis to be one more difficult to steer through than had perplexed an English statesman since the Conquest.

The progress of Neill up the valley of the Ganges—a mission of relief, as it has been styled, "bringing retribution in his van and leaving order in his rear"—adds an extraordinary lustre to the stern excellence of his military character.

On his arrival at Allahabad, with a small detachment of the Fusiliers, although too late to save the Europeans from the mutineers, he was yet in time to restore order, to defeat and put the rebels to flight; and, on this occasion, the Sikhs, who were in the fort, again elicited his admiration, fighting as they now did with extraordinary vigour.

The remainder of the Fusiliers having arrived were dispatched by Neill, under Major Renaud, in advance, towards Cawnpore. A force of some 800 or 900 men was placed under this admirable officer; and on the same day, the last of June, General Havelock arrived at Allahabad; and the chief command of the small but gallant army was accordingly transfer to him. Up to this time, our Brigadier-General had been the foremost man in the valley of the Ganges.

The magnanimity of Neill on this occasion—the most galling that can be to a true soldier in command—was quite as conspicuous as his gallantry and devotion to the public service after he had left Calcutta. Instead of his energy diminishing, it steadily increased. As in most revolutions and political convulsions, there is room enough for many great men, so it was in this deadly Indian rebellion. Envy or jealousy formed no portion of Neill's failings. Cawnpore had now to be re-taken, Lucknow to be rescued, and the most bloody massacre of the innocents in history had yet to be avenged. Havelock's victorious progress to Cawnpore is well known; and, distinguished among the brave who fell in it is the name of Major Renaud, of the Fusiliers. General Havelock had left Neill at Allahabad, who now, it may be said, having saved that station, was ordered by his superior to push on with every available man and join him at Cawnpore. He arrived on the 20th of July. The relieving General was assisted by Neill across the Ganges on the 21st; and then began his celebrated march to relieve Lucknow. Left at Cawnpore, in supreme command, the energy of Neill's character seemed to burn brighter than ever. At Benares, Allahabad, and Cawnpore (where he organised a local police) he showed administrative ability—that kind which was adapted to such a crisis—only second to his power of military command. Some may think him severe in punishment. On our first seeing a private letter from one of the Madras Fusiliers to a friend, describing how the captured Brahman Sepoy murderers, before suffering a well-merited death on the gallows, were ordered to be flogged into the slaughter-house at Cawnpore, and there compelled to clean up the blood of the poor victims they had so mercilessly shed, it became a question which to admire most, the originality of the mode of punishment or its tremendous severity. Neill did this! But, after all, was it a severe enough retribution? Could it bring back the loved and lost? Havelock's force, from 1,200, had increased at Cawnpore to 1,500. Neill had also sent on numbers of soldiers he could not spare to answer the call of the daring General in advance for reinforcements. In one of Havelock's letters at this time, alluding to some traitors in his force, "traitors in heart to their fostering government," whom he had ordered back and placed under the care of Neill for work in the intrenchments, he significantly says—" He will look after them." This reminds us of what Wellington might have said of Picton, in an emergency, being quite sure he would do his duty.

The period was a terrible time of suspense to the British in India. All eyes were turned to the progress of Havelock towards Lucknow. But his force was inadequate; and cholera, that "angel of death," which so frequently appears in our Indian armies,* had been lessening it as well as the enemy. Having done all that man could do, the General abandoned the attempt, to use his own words, "with great grief and reluctance," re-crossed the Ganges, and on the 13th of August he was again with the indefatigable Neill at Cawnpore.

Immediately after Havelock's arrival, we find our Brigadier-General marching out of the entrenchments, which, with his usual foresight, he had made, and with his accustomed daring and ability completely defeating a rebel force which was endeavouring to prevent our communication with Allahabad. The return of Havelock's force to Cawnpore, it is supposed, saved that city from the troops of the Nana, which were gathering like a thunder-cloud around it. In this case, as throughout the rebellion, the mysterious workings of a kind Providence became strongly apparent. Passing over the well-known advance against Bithoor, after which victory Havelock's most memorable despatch was penned—and where the Madras Fusiliers were, as usual, second to none—we now behold the trio of heroes, Havelock, Outram, and Neill, setting out on one of the grandest missions in the world's history, the second effort for the relief of Lucknow.

General Outram, with that high-souled knowledge of what is noble and right, although the senior, left Havelock in command.

A month had elapsed since the return of the first relieving army to Cawnpore. Even now, with the reinforcements brought by Outram from Allahabad, the force was deemed hardly adequate to the mighty attempt about to be made in Oudh. Two brigades of infantry, one of

* Cholera first began its devastations among our troops in the great Mahratta War, in 1817, under the Marquis of Hastings.

artillery, and a few cavalry, made the whole amount of the relieving army. Neill's brigade, the first, was composed of three Royal regiments and his own First Madras Fusiliers. This column of men—or rather, in the old Guard phraseology, this column of granite, was composed of rare fighting material, and commanded by generals not "rocked and dandled" into command, but who had in war, if not in politics, in the spirit of the great Burke, *Nitor in adversum*, fought their way to distinction.

The relief of Lucknow was an enterprise of the most extraordinary character. When Napoleon found all Europe arrayed against him, neither he nor his brave followers put forth more human effort than that which, during a time when those we had taught the art of war had turned against us, appeared in the commanders and men who now pushed forward to effect this grand object. There is nothing in history to compare with it. The relief of Lucknow, in the face of such overwhelming numbers of the enemy, stands forth unique in its peculiar intenseness from every other military effort. The Residency might fall into the enemy's hands before it could be reached—the Cawnpore massacre, on a more awful scale, might be repeated; so on went the band of heroes, in the face of every danger, to the relief of suffering humanity. The fortified outpost of the Alumbagh reached, the battle won there made hope beat high for a moment in every heart. The relieving army was at the entrance of the city. The determined resistance, however, at the Kaiser Bagh, proved the determination and force of the insurgents to be even greater than was supposed. To go on appeared the only chance of success. Night would soon overtake the weary British troops; and had night come on, without the object gained, annihilation would have been certain. But forward they rushed in the face of death—through a miracle the Residency was gained, and the evening of the 25th of September saw Lucknow relieved! But the gallant Neill, who had reached the entrenchments, was no more! In the heat of the conflict, actuated by a noble vengeance, he had rushed forward to rescue some guns, and was struck on the head by a bullet from one of the innumerable loop-holes; and so, like

Brunswick's Duke at Waterloo, "foremost fighting fell!"

He fell, it is said, while passing through a gateway at the head of his own loved Regiment (there was also H.M.'s 78th Highlanders, whose brave men knew well the worth of Neill), and had paused only to assist from his flask a poor soldier who was wounded by his side—which pause, it may be remarked, cost him his life!"*

And thus his career ended with a glorious act of charity, which has caused his end to be eloquently compared to that of Sir Philip Sidney on the field of Zutphen.†

In the land of his birth—the land of Wallace and Burns, where there are now some alive who remember the bright-eyed reckless school boy—there is a tombstone to the martyrs of the Covenant, with the inscription commencing, "*Halt! passenger!*" thus arresting the attention of the inquiring traveller. Beside Neill's grave might be raised a stone with the words inscribed on the monument of a French General, so much admired by a melancholy poet (Kirke White)—"*Siste viator, heroam calcas!*" ‡

It is difficult to recollect a more striking or brilliant close to a military career than that which has been now so briefly and imperfectly recorded. There hardly seems to be a single flaw in the picture. The energy of the man, his heroic devotion to the State; the resolute execution of his plans in the face of every difficulty, which is always considered a grand test of strength of character; his magnanimity in supporting Havelock to the utmost of his power; his nerve, firm and unquailing like that of a Napier; his consummate tact and talent for resource under circumstances, the like of which the world never saw before; the kindness he ever evinced for his men; his noble death,—all afford a splendid example of one who

---

* Lieut. Crump was killed while in the actual performance of extricating a gun from a position exposed to the heavy musketry fire of the enemy.

† "'Give it to that poor man, his necessity is greater than mine.' And when after we are gone, our children's children shall be taught the last words of the gentle warrior poet at Zutphen, shall they not also read with glowing hearts and moistened eyes of the last deed of the undaunted Neill dying at Lucknow?"—Speech of Mr. Ritchie, in Calcutta, Feb. 4th, 1858.

‡ Stop, traveller—thou treadest on a hero!

had adopted the science of war as his profession, and, by striving to become a master in it, did full honour to that science.

Not the least pleasing remembrance, while thus remarking on the character of Neill, is the manner in which he has been treated by public meetings and the public press.

There is, generally speaking, no sickening adulation—little distortion of facts—the truth comes boldly forward—the man is understood, and justice is done. It has been so, likewise, with regard to Havelock and Nicholson; and, perhaps more than with any of these, in the case of Sir Henry Lawrence, who, approaching if not equalling the military qualities possessed by the others, has the honour of having devoted a large portion of his fortune and time to the organisation and foundation of the noble military asylums which bear his name. High dignitaries of the Church, Members of Parliament, men of nearly every shade of opinion, have joined to do honour to the memory of the fallen heroes of this sad Rebellion. But, why call it sad ? True enough, it is sad to the bereaved; but to the world, and to humanity, the darkness, even now passing away, is only the forerunner of a lasting marvellous light !

It must have been strange to hear a Member of the British Senate talking of Neill, Nicholson, and Havelock as "not only three of the greatest soldiers, but three of the wisest statesmen that were ever entrusted with authority in India or any other part of the world." We are pretty sure, had they been alive, they would have disowned the latter portion of the compliment and transferred it to Sir Henry Lawrence. Clever administrative ability, which really good soldiers sometimes possess, and wise statesmanship, are two very different things; in the world of mind bearing about the same relation to each other as the Principia of Newton to the Elements of Arithmetic. But excess in panegyric in such cases is pardonable.

Each of the illustrious four died the death of a soldier; and, in the mighty enterprise in which they were engaged, it was such a composition of glorious natures which put life into the business of putting down the rebellion.*

* See Lord Bacon's Essay on "Vain Glory."

G

In the case of Lawrence it is consoling to know that the brother, who has rendered such eminent services to the State, is yet alive to put us in mind of him.

The best thing that has been said of our hero by the British Press is that, "from Benares to Cawnpore, the march of Neill was as the track of England's avenging angel!" *.

It would be useless to attempt a comparison between Neill and other Generals. He reminds us more of Clive than of any other, the "merchant's clerk" who suddenly "raised himself to celebrity," and who, as "the heaven-born General," retrieved the fallen fortunes of our late most noble and most munificent masters, the East India Company. Neill never had the opportunity of devising or conducting war on a grand scale. To this the nearest approach is his share in the organisation of the glorious advance upon Cawnpore and Lucknow.

The historian of the Peninsular War condemns the injudicious juxtaposition made by some, in military talents, of Crawfurd and Picton beside their master, the illustrious Wellington.

Great opportunities and great power have, it is true, a wonderful deal to do with bringing out the lasting effect of a really good General's picture. Had Neill lived, and these requisites been eventually his fortune, it may be reasonably supposed he would have risen to be considered as occupying a place in the first rank of our Generals; and his name now certainly stands very high among the best and bravest Commanders who ever led on British troops to victory. The mention of Picton and Crawfurd forces a comparison between Havelock and Neill, with regard to the assistance rendered by one to the other while on service.

During the fight on the Coas, Crawfurd asked Picton for the support of his division, which was angrily refused, while, as the eloquent historian asserts, it should have been "eagerly proffered."† Neill sent every available soldier to assist Havelock. Take him for all in all, he surely did enough worthy of imitation. And when, in an after age,

* *Westminster Review.*
† "History of the Peninsular War," Book XI., chap. iv., p. 415.

the account* of this Rebellion shall be read in the page of some future Orme or Malcolm, as one of the blots on the page of history, the star of Neill's glory will even give a lustre to the page; and then, as now, young military readers will not cease to admire his chivalrous courage, his power of enduring fatigue, his untiring energy, and his noble end. Paradoxical as it may seem, it is the appearance of such qualities in military commanders, during great emergencies, that will do much to usher in the blessings of peace—when the power of Christianity and the advantages of education shall be acknowledged by Hindu and Mussulman alike—when no arsenals shall resound with the busy clang of machinery in working out scientific inventions for the destruction of our foes—when the world-renowned British bayonet shall cease to be required in the charge to extirpate tyranny and support the cause of freedom—when the thunder of our batteries of Artillery and the crack of the long-range rifle shall no longer be heard in the land—when the trumpet shall hang in the hall, and men shall "study war no more!"

NEILL IN BURMA.

LETTER FROM THE LATE GENERAL NEILL, WHILE SERVING IN BURMA, TO THE AUTHOR.

" My dear ——,

"I am quite ashamed to send you such a scrawl, and so stupidly put together; but I was so interrupted I had not time to set my mind to the work. If it, such as it is, will be of any use to you, I shall be very glad. You will do well to compose something more worthy of your book, of your own, from the information I give, which I believe to be correct; and the opinions I have given are my real sentiments: they need not be yours. I return your Prospectus. D—— subscribes to your work; the

* [This has been done by Sir John Kaye.]

only staff man who has not seen the paper is B——. I wish you every success, and only regret the assistance, if any, I have given is so paltry.

"Yours very sincerely,
"J. G. S. NEILL.

"*Tonghoo, 5th March,* 1853."

THE RELIEF OF PEGU,

and other Operations: written chiefly from Notes furnished by the late General Neill. (From "Pegu, a Narrative, &c.," p. 120.)

THE most energetic measures were now taken at Rangoon by General Godwin to answer, with all possible speed, the needy call for relief which came from the Pegu garrison. Rangoon had not been in such a state of excitement since its capture by the British in April. Had the tide of fortune at length turned against us? Had the mine of Burmese vengeance at length been sprung, to tell us that the dynasty of Alompra was not yet in danger, and rouse us into action?* In any way, a great event had taken place. The wonted energy of our chief, when anything like danger was to be encountered, proved him to be the man for the emergency. But General Godwin, unfortunately, had much difficulty in providing transports for the troops for the relief of Pegu.

[Here commences the use, by the Author, of General Neill's notes on the relief of Pegu, &c.]

Two hundred and fifty Madras Fusiliers, under Captain Renaud, had been obliged to return to Rangoon in consequence of the disabled state of the river steamer *Nerbudda*, in which they had embarked. These troops were transhipped to the *Mahanuddy*, a vessel whose boilers had seen rather too much service. It was not, therefore, until both these steamers had been repaired, that the Head Quarters, in the *Nerbudda*, and the Madras Fusiliers, in the *Mahanuddy* were enabled to leave Rangoon. At noon of the 12th of December (1852) both vessels steamed on until sunset, the *Nerbudda* leading. At daylight next morning, which was very foggy, all the boats con-

---

* While these pages are going to press (1858), a most wonderful event has taken place to point a moral for the future historian. H.M. steamer *Megæra* has landed the ex-King of Delhi at Rangoon, to be imprisoned in Burma, we presume, for the remainder of his days.

veying the other troops, under convoy of Captain Tarleton, R. N.,* proceeded with the *Nerbudda* up the river; the other steamer was supposed to be following not far astern. They approached the village of Lomen Seedee as the mist was rising, which was found, as expected, occupied by the enemy, and the river staked abreast of it. We were quite prepared for the foe; guns loaded, and a party of 25 men on each paddle-box—the starboard furnished by the Madras, the larboard by the Bengal, Fusiliers. We had evidently taken the Burmese by surprise; some of them were seen about the village, also a large party with some horsemen moving about on the plain. The left bank, near where the steamer was anchored, was an open plain; higher up, and out of shot, stood the village. The troops were soon landed; and it was speedily determined to occupy the villlage as affording shelter, it having been taken for granted that the enemy had retreated. The Bengal Fusiliers were therefore moved up to some of the nearest houses, when about twenty shots were fired on them from the high grass and jungle adjoining. One man was slightly wounded; the Burmese escaped without either being seen or fired upon. The village was then occupied, the Madras Fusiliers being on picquet in advance. The *Mahanuddy* not having yet arrived with the remainder of the Fusiliers, the other steamer was therefore sent down to bring the men up. The day wore on, and there being no appearance of the steamer, arrangements were made to pass the night in the village, and picquets were thrown out; but no attempt was made to drive the enemy further away, or out of the village of Upper Seedee, about a mile distant. This village had on several occasions—particularly the last, when the boats were obliged to retire—annoyed the Navy considerably; and the occupation of it might have been attended with little or no loss had its entrenchments been turned by a small party, and the enemy there, about 300 or 400 men, driven off, and perhaps intercepted.

About midnight a volley was fired into some of the houses, by which one Bengal Fusilier was killed and another was mortally wounded; a sailor was also mortally wounded. Irregular firing now commenced, and the sentries at other points of the line also giving the alarm, some firing—which was fortunately put a stop to in time—had nearly caused considerable confusion, to which the increasing consternation of the servants and few camp-followers would have materially added.

* [Now Admiral Sir J. W. Tarleton, K.C.B., and Lord of the Admiralty.]
† [See Narrative, note at page 118.]

Two hours after this disturbance, the bamboo flooring of one of the houses occupied by the followers fell in, and caused great alarm; the troops, of course, without inquiring into the cause, stood to their arms and behaved steadily. The steamer returned during the night with Captain Renaud's party, their detention having been caused by the *Mahanuddy* unfortunately grounding. The troops were landed early in the morning, and by 7 a.m., the whole force advanced in the following order:— Two ship's guns, dragged by sailors of the Royal Navy, under Captain Shadwell, R.N.; 250 Madras Fusiliers, under Captain Renaud; 150 Bengal Fusiliers, under Major Gerrard; and 300 Sikhs, under Major Armstrong, formed the advance of 700 men—General Godwin commanding, with Brigadier Dickenson. Two hundred of the 10th B.N.I., under Captain Monro; 450 Bengal Fusiliers, under Colonel Tudor,—650 men,—formed the reserve, under Brigadier-General Steel, C.B. The force moved off, marching away from the river, so as to avoid Seedee; and on nearing a small village came upon the high road leading to the S.W. gateway of the mound or old wall round the ancient city of Pegu. In the out-skirts of the village about 300 of the enemy were posted, and on the plain about 100 Cassay horse.* On the approach of our advanced troops, the enemy cheered and came on towards us, their Infantry flanked by their Cavalry. Our skirmishers pushed on, answering their cheers; firing commenced, and the Burmese retired, the Infantry into the jungle in our front, the Cavalry keeping to the plain on our flank. As the head of the column was entering the jungle near the S.W. angle of the mound, a short halt took place; the guides had evidently been leading the column in the wrong direction for that point. Counsel was now taken of an excellent guide in Captain Renaud's service, who, having urgently represented that the defences at the west point were particularly strong,— as was subsequently seen,—and that the proper way, which he offered to show, was by the east side, he was at once directed to lead the column. The force continued its march, and after a very fatiguing morning's work reached the gateway in the eastern bund. † Here the head of the column first came in contact with the enemy. Captain Renaud's party quickly pushed over the bund. The Burmese came down through the jungle on the flanks of the column, and opened fire on the reserve; their fire was speedily answered, and they were compelled to retire. All then pushed forward and got within the bund. Firing had, up

* See note at the end of this chapter.
† An artificial mound of earth.

to the time of the column entering the bund, been heard near the pagoda. Telescopes were now in requisition, but nothing could be seen of the garrison. A man was at last discovered on the pagoda; he was made out to be a Burmese soldier; he was immediately afterwards declared to be a Madras Lascar. General Godwin, who had been in a state of intense anxiety, was at once relieved. The force now pushed on to the east gateway of the pagoda; and it was not until a very short distance from it that we observed the garrison, and then learned that the line of bund and old pagodas from which it was commanded had been occupied by the Burmese until within a few minutes of our entering the fortress, that we had taken them in reverse, and that, had we been aware of it, by detaching a party to our right on entering the first bund we might have cut many, if not all off. The troops were now "dead-beat;" and, quietly rising with terrific glow, shone forth the fierce Burmese sun—than which the heat is nowhere more intense, except perhaps occasionally in China. Few out of the whole force were equal to more exertion during the heat of that day. It had been a long and fatiguing march, but not yet was there to be a rest of any duration. All the troops crowded into the pagoda, and completely covered its area. Then commenced cordial greetings of welcome; tales of adventure experienced within the last few days; and the frequent remark of the soldier to his comrade on the care-worn and fagged appearance of some of the relieved. The men were lying about, taking their rest, when, about 4 p.m., a fire was opened upon them from the old commanding ground, which the enemy had again occupied. In a few minutes several men were hit, and it became necessary to dislodge and drive them out of the defences along the river bank, and south and west faces of the bund. These services were performed in a very brilliant manner by the troops employed; and this being the first time we had an opportunity of beholding the Sikhs acting by themselves, their progress was attentively observed. Nothing could have exceeded their enthusiasm, and their forward propensities are beyond a doubt.* They advanced steadily and coolly across a piece of open ground fully exposed to the fire of the Burmese, who, posted on the mound, were completely covered by the jungle; they pushed on, however, without answering the fire, and when sufficiently near ran in on the enemy and gallantly drove them from their position. The

* On several occasions in Burma, the truth of this valuable opinion was confirmed. These remarks on them are the gallant Neill's own words. The concluding paragraph is the Author's.

same men whose bravery had given Lords Hardinge and Gough their peerages, who had proved themselves to be one of the most formidable foes the British ever had to encounter in India, were now nobly acting on our side in defence of order and a just government, 2,000 miles from the land of their birth, from the land where the pride of the Khalsa army, but yesterday, became mutinous, disorganised, and fallen !—The Bengal Fusiliers had been directed to clear the works to the south and west, which they soon did in an effective style, destroying the stockades and defences, out of which they expelled the enemy. All the troops returned after dusk to the pagoda, well tired out: they slept under what cover they could get; many being without great-coats suffered much during the night from the cold damp and dew, which, no doubt, laid the foundation of much of the subsequent sickness and mortality. From what we saw of the Cassay horse, and the activity of the enemy in evading us on the plain, we all looked forward to the arrival of Colonel Sturt's land column, * with a portion of Burgoyne's Troop of Madras Horse Artiliery, Sappers, Ramghur Cavalry, and 67th Bengal Native Infantry; feeling assured the mounted men would give a good account of the cunning Burmese soldiery on the plains over which they had to pass to reach Shoé-Ghyne or Sitang; and more particularly on the following morning, when the whole Burmese army of about 9,000 or 10,000 men were observed from the pagoda taking up a position and entrenching themselves on the plains about the village of Kully, between four and five miles distant, on the Shoé-Ghyne road.

It was now but natural to believe, that General Godwin would not venture an attack upon the enemy in such force without aid from the expected land column in the shape of Cavalry and Artillery. In the first place, he could have no guns with him, for he had "no means of drawing them;" and in the second, without Cavalry, in any fortunate movement made by our Infantry, he had not the means of following up and cutting off the enemy. But no doubt the General's presence was urgently required at Prome. To him time was everything. He would not be content with the glorious achievement of having relieved Pegu, but he was determined also to free that garrison from the near possition of the Burmese Army ! It is difficult to say whether others similarly situated would not have been inclined to act otherwise; but we think that the majority,

* Of some 700 men, which General Godwin had dispatched to co-operate with his other force.

under the circumstances, would have waited for the land column, As to time, there was Brigadier-General Steel, a distinguished Company's Officer, who could have waited to disperse the enemy with effect, while the senior General was steaming to Rangoon or to Prome, ready to gain any amount of glory that might be in store for him. But it was ordained otherwise. On the 15th, orders were issued for the force to march on the following morning. During the day this was countermanded, in consequence of the Commissariat supplies not being brought up. The Burmese were still observed entrenching themselves about the village of Kully, and showed no intention of retiring.

On the 16th, nothing was heard from Colonel Sturt's column. According to orders issued on that day, the force—composed of 570 Bengal Fusiliers, 182 10th B.N.I., 330 Sikhs, 150 Madras Fusiliers, and 30 Sappers; total, 1,260 men—was warned to be prepared to move on the following morning. The men were directed to carry their great-coats, and one day's cooked provisions in their haversacks. A memorandum was also required from Commandants of Corps of the positive requirements of their men in the way of shirts and trousers, with a view to their being procured from Rangoon; men and officers having left Rangoon for this service with the least possible quantity of clothing. None of the officers had horses, Generals Godwin and Steel excepted; and the rations for the force were carried on in carts drawn by buffalos.

The force moved out of the pagoda, following Captain Latter's guides. We wound slowly through the jungle to the north of Pegu, and emerged on the plain about half-past 9 a.m. So little were the enemy expecting us that the garrison of Pegu saw from the pagoda their elephants feeding in the jungle near us, and had we been aware of it we might have captured them all. On our column reaching the plain, signal guns were fired from the enemy's lines, evidently to collect their people. On reconnoitring their position, it appeared to be three lines of entrenchments, the right on the river, and extending across the Shoé-Gyne road, far into the plain; on the left of the road, which was the centre of their position, ran a jungly nullah, which we subsequently found had been so spiked and entrenched that had we advanced by that route, our loss would have been very considerable from a foe *who out-marched us and fought under cover.* * General Godwin determined to turn

* This is a grand difficulty we have to contend with in Burmese warfare. Should unfortunately any rupture hereafter take place in that quarter, light guns and plenty of Irregular Cavalry will be invaluable; also howitzers for boat service.

the left of their position, and moved to the right. The Cassay Horse approached and kept pace with our column, moving on our right flank. After the force had turned the left of the first line of entrenchments it was halted, and dispositions made for attacking in two columns; one—the left—under General Steel—the other under General Godwin. The left column was soon in its place, impatiently waiting the signal to advance: it was not given; the enemy were seen moving in huge masses from their left; and it is the opinion of some that had the left column been permitted, it could have cut them off. An Aide-de-Camp was sent off to General Godwin to inform him of what was going on in front, and returned with an order that the attack of the left column was not to take place, but was to stand firm and cover his flank when he attacked. At this order considerable disappointment was felt by the left column. General Steel rode back to join our chief on the right; and Major Seaton, of the 1st Bengal Fusiliers, and his men had to remain inactive, seeing an enemy they could by a rapid dash get in among and severely punish, walk leisurely off. When the advance by General Godwin at last took place, the enemy were in full retreat; a few only remained on our front; and although the attacking party, European and Native, more particularly the Sikhs, were exceedingly forward and energetic, our men were never able to approach sufficiently near to do the execution they would have done, had they been permitted to attack at the proper time. While the column was halted, the Cassay Horse on our right were emboldened to make a charge. They rode down with some spirit, but none of our Infantry field officers being mounted, they had not sufficient command over their men, some of whom in the hurry and excitement fired too soon, and were followed by the rest of the line; a few saddles only were emptied, and the Cassay Horse got out of shot at the quickest possible pace. The Burmese retreated by the Shoé-Ghyne road, and the column was halted in a tope of trees which had formed their head-quarters. After more than an hour's halt, the men stood to their arms, and formed upon a road leading nearly west. Hopes were now entertained of again speedily beholding the enemy, Although not a vestige or trace of any number of men was observed along the road, yet on the repeated assurance of the guides, the march in that direction unfortunately was persisted in, which ended on our reaching the village of Lephandoon before sunset. With the exception of a broken down buffalo cart and an old woman—there are no patriots in Burma so staunch as the old women, come friend or foe—the post was found abandoned. The old woman stated in a lively manner that the enemy had not been there that day. General Godwin, it is said, expressed his extreme displeasure at the conduct of the guides. Many now thought that instead of halting in the tope, the enemy should have been at once followed up along the Shoé-Ghyne road; as the men had not marched far, and their blood was up, they could have kept up a hot pursuit for many miles, and, perhaps, although unaided by Cavalry, they would have captured some guns and baggage, also carts and other carriage, which we much required. The guides, on this occasion, seemed to have taken us off the proper line of pursuit, which was the more provoking, when it was considered that they were under the charge of one who possessed a vast knowledge of the Burmese language and character.

For the night the force occupied the houses on the left bank of the river at Lephandoon, and after sunrise on the 18th moved off in a north-easterly direction. After proceeding some distance, we came upon the Shoé-Ghyne road, about two miles north of the tope where we had unfortunately halted the day before, and proceeded along it. Every yard showed the traces of a multitude having crowded along it in great confusion. The road was narrow, through thick grass and paddy, and in some places tall elephant grass, all sufficiently thick to impede the march of Infantry except on the road. Approaching the village of Montsanganoo there was a thick belt of jungle, but it was found unoccupied. The force passed through it and found shelter in huts and sheds. A vast plain extended to the front and on our right. The guides declared that the enemy had pushed on, and were at least twenty miles off. Under such belief, all ranks got under such cover as the place afforded, and it was determined to return on the following day to Pegu Lomen. About one o'clock p.m. it was reported that two of the Cassay Horse had appeared in front of the position occupied by the detachment of the Madras Fusiliers. A staff and two other officers, accompanied by two men, went out along the northern road to reconnoitre, and the Burmese being within long rifle range, two shots from a Minié were fired at them; the first, at about 460 yards,* went sufficiently close to one to make him bow his head; another, at about double the distance, also fell close. The horsemen making off at their utmost speed, the party moved on to a wooden bridge, from which they had retired, and where a better view of the country in our front

---

* Since then, the Enfield Rifle, with a range of 900 yards, has been introduced into the Indian Service.

was expected. From this nothing could at the time be seen, except a village and some large houses to our left; some Poonghi houses on the road, about a mile in advance of the bridge, and a large village some distance to the right; in many places it was thought a line of newly turned up earth could be distinguished, as if extending from the houses on the road, on both sides, towards the villages on the right and left. Not a sowar was to be seen except the two horsemen above noticed, who, observing the party stationary at the bridge, began to approach slowly. It was at this time that Captain Travers, General Steel's Aide-de-Camp, rode up on his brave little Arab, *Selim*, and galloping past the party, the Cassay Horse wheeled about. The gallant Aide-de-Camp dashed on after them, and had gained within 100 yards of the last, when many more men suddenly rode out to meet him, and numbers of the enemy showing themselves about the houses, the energetic Captain was compelled to pull up.

As he walked quietly back, the Burmese horsemen following at a respectful distance, the whole extent, from village to village, became alive with men. A long line rose up from their entrenchments, where they had been lying concealed, and the houses and villages were soon filled. A peremptory order at this time arrived for the party to return to their lines, upon which our opponents fell back on theirs. The presence of the whole enemy within two miles of his head-quarters thus by chance became known to General Godwin from the unauthorised act of two or three officers and men going out beyond the outposts to reconnoitre. The position occupied by the British was better adapted for affording shelter to the troops than for defence; a few huts on the right, a shady tope, and some sheds on the left, the rear close on a jungle, and a nullah which turned up round our left flank and extended nearly to the right centre of the enemy's position, would have enabled him at any time, day or night, to have brought his whole force unperceived into our rear and left flanks and to have occupied the thick jungle within half musket shot of us. There was certainly something wrong in the present state of affairs. The guides asserted that it was all a mistake; there was no enemy near. However, an old ruined pagoda in the jungle, in rear of our head-quarters, and which had been used by the Burmese as a look-out, enabled others to see them as they had been reported; and a body of their Infantry moving down into the belt of jungle in front of their centre, an officer with a small party again went towards the bridge to reconnoitre, when the enemy attempted to cut off their retreat. More of their troops pushed forward; but our party was brought slowly back, keeping clear of the jungle, which was now occupied by our adversaries, and bringing down, following them at a respectable distance, considerable numbers of their Infantry, with a few horse. The bugles in camp now sounded, the men stood to their arms in a few minutes, and the force moved on to meet the foe, who on seeing our troops advance fell gradually back on his entrenchments, our skirmishers dislodging those who had entered the belt of jungle on our left. After crossing the bridge, two columns of attack were formed; the right intended for General Godwin, the left given to General Steel. The right had some little distance farther to march; General Godwin did not accompany it, and the next senior officer lost no time in getting into motion. The left column was halted and held back by General Godwin's personal order. Thus, in the opinion of some, was a chance of fairly and successfully closing with the enemy lost, who, as on the previous day, retreated slowly and surely. There can be little doubt that a steady, active advance would have brought our troops into action; but apparently General Godwin was not desirous of risking such a contact. The skirmishers of the left column only were engaged; the right carried the village on the enemy's left. Night closed in, and the force marched back to their former ground, where they found that the sheds they had protected themselves in during the day had been set fire to. The following morning we left Montsanganoo after sunrise, and reached Pegu about one o'clock p.m.

REMARKS.*

The operations on the 17th and 18th showed that had Colonel Sturt's column been waited for, the army of the enemy would in all probability have been entirely destroyed. No country could have been more favourable for Cavalry, and the few patches of jungle their Infantry might have found refuge in could have been cleared by our own. But between Kully and Montsanganoo there was a sufficient space of open ground for the destruction of the force. A blow might have been struck at Kully on the 18th or 19th, which would have paralysed them with terror, and compelled them to submit to our power, and from the carriage the enemy's camp would have supplied, a rapid movement on Shoé-Ghyne would have obtained us possession of that town, and the almost certain annihilation

* These, almost entirely by General Neill, are valuable.

of that boasting Burmese army. It is a humane wish to be lenient with the actions of men. We must narrate, however, that this grand opportunity was lost by not waiting for a more efficient column, which marched from and back to Rangoon without once coming into action. The exposure and fatigue the troops underwent on the 17th and 18th caused much sickness from cholera; the Bengal Fusiliers in a few days lost upwards of twenty men. The Natives also suffered considerably. General Godwin, as is ever the case, showed the greatest coolness under fire, and an entire disregard of self; and nothing could have been better than the relief of Pegu, and the plans of attack on the 17th and 18th. These were admirably conducted until it came to the moment for acting, when it appeared as if the veteran chief lacked decision, and seemed to be unconscious of the enemy passing away before him. Whatever may have been General Godwin's motives for not attacking his enemy with vigour on the 17th and 18th—and he had shown himself quite capable of vigorous and successful attacks even during the second Burmese war—whatever may have been his motives for not waiting for Colonel Sturt's column, or leaving General Steel to follow up the enemy when the Horse Artillery and Cavalry arrived—he relieved Pegu and turned the enemy's position on the 17th with little or no loss to his own troops.

The three days' work on the 14th, 17th, and 18th of December tried the stoutest and hardiest of the force. Some old campaigners declared the "Punjab" was a joke to it as far as fatigue went. None displayed greater endurance than General Godwin himself and several of the oldest officers who accompanied him.

The Cassay Horse.

The Muniporeans, or people of Cassay in particular, abound in great numbers, and they are much prized as clever workmen. Owing to their superior skill in the management of the horse, the Burmese Cavalry is almost exclusively composed of them; and they are distinguished by the national appellation of "the Cassay Horse."—Major Snodgrass's "Narrative of the First Burmese War."

MAJOR-GENERAL W. F. BEATSON.*

"At the grand ball at the Hotel de Ville on Saturday last, the lion of the evening was Brigadier Beatson in the uniform of the Nizam's cavalry. The French ladies declared they had never seen anything so splendid. 'Quel bel uniforme, mais quel bel homme aussi,' was whispered everywhere. 'Qui est il?' 'Je crois qu'il est le Sultan ou le Grand Mogul.' In fact, they were quite puzzled who he could be—'perhaps a new candidate for the Presidency of the Republic!' If it had depended on the ladies at the Hotel de Ville he certainly would have been elected!"—"Bravo! Brigadier Beatson outshining Louis Napoleon in his own capital! Think of that, officers of the Nizam's army, and plume yourselves." †

A letter from Paris, dated 5th January, 1852, contained the above item of interest, which, among those who knew the Brigadier well, probably excited but little surprise either in Bombay or the Nizam's dominions, where, on account of a local revolution in dress—which Brummell might have envied, but which had brought dismay to those officers not overburdened with rupees—it had really seemed as if the apparel proclaimed the man. ‡ And yet the subject of our sketch was no fop, but one of the most able, zealous, and hard-working soldiers who ever entered the Indian army. Throughout life, honourable distinction was his steady aim. Wherever he went he seemed marked out to be "the observed of all observers;" yet, strange to say, after long and faithful service, he died without a single mark of distinction from his country to add to his name. That he was indeed a distinguished Anglo-Indian

* Written in January, 1875. † See *Bombay Times*, February 7th, 1852.
‡ "For the apparel oft proclaims the man."—*Shakspeare.*

will be seen from the following record of military services. But first it may interest those who were his friends to learn that he was born at Rossend Castle, Fifeshire, N.B., about the year 1805. General Alexander Beatson, Governor of St. Helena, was his uncle—the distinguished Madras officer who had planned the attack of Seringapatam, and wrote the history of the war in Mysore. Sir Charles Oakeley (Governor of Madras) married Miss Beatson, General Alexander Beatson's only sister. The father of our hero was Captain Robert Beatson (Beatson of Kilrie), of the Royal Engineers, who had three sons appointed to the Bengal Native Infantry. William Ferguson entered the Bengal army in 1820. Being on furlough, he (with the sanction of the British Government) served with the British Legion in Spain, in 1835-1836, first as Major, afterwards as Lieutenant-Colonel commanding the 10th, or Munster Light Infantry, at the head of which regiment, he was severely wounded. For his services in Spain he received the Cross of San Fernando from Queen Isabella, and Her Britannic Majesty's permission to wear it in September, 1837. Beatson was not the only Indian officer who, under Sir De Lacey Evans, won distinction in Spain, but he was certainly one of the foremost in what was considered a good cause. Nearly forty years have not entirely changed the drama in that unfortunate country—so difficult to govern—for we have just seen Don Carlos again fighting for the crown, yet, in spite of his energy and pluck, defeated and discomfited; while Queen Isabella is in Paris, and her son, with the romantic name of Alphonso, ascending her throne! It may truly be said, that if Hindu sovereignties fall to pieces, so do European.

Beatson returned to India in 1837, and having been appointed to the important command of the Bundelkund Legion, received the thanks of Government for the capture of Jignee, in Bundelkund, in 1840; and of Chirgong, in 1841.

In February, 1844, he received the thanks of the Governor-General's agent, Scindiah's dominions, for recovering for the Gwalior Government forts and strongholds in Kachwahagar.

In March, 1844, he played one of his best cards by volunteering with his Bundelkund Legion for Sind. For this he received the thanks of Government; which volunteering, the Governor-General declared, placed the Government of India under great obligation.

In March, 1845, he was mentioned in Sir Charles Napier's despatch, regarding the campaign in the Boogtee Hills; which service called forth the approbation of Government.

In July, 1846, the conduct of his Legion while in Sind, was, much to the satisfaction of the Commandant, praised in General Orders by the Governor-General, Viscount Hardinge.*

Having been appointed to the command of the Nizam's Cavalry, we find Brigadier Beatson, in July, 1848, receiving approbation from the Government of India for taking the Jagheer and fort of Rymou from that troublesome, ever-warlike, and energetic race, the Rohillas; and in November, 1850, he recaptured Rymou from the Arabs.

In February, 1851, he captured the fort of Dharoor, one of the strongest in the Dekhan.

In March, 1851, the Resident at Hyderabad paid Beatson a high compliment, by issuing the following General Order:—

"Brigadier Beatson having tendered his resignation of the command of the Nizam's Cavalry, from date of his embarkation for England, the Resident begs to express his entire approval of this officer's conduct during the time he has exercised the important command of the Cavalry Division.

"Brigadier Beatson has not only maintained, but improved, the interior economy and arrangement of the Cavalry Division; and the value of his active military services in the field has been amply attested and rendered subject of record, in the several instances of Kangoan, Rymou, Arnee, and Dharoor."

The Brigadier appears to have tendered his resignation rather hastily, for we find him, shortly after, asking Lord Dalhousie's permission to withdraw his application; but

* Lord Dalhousie arrived in India on the 12th January, 1848, and on the 18th Lord Hardinge left Calcutta on his way home.

his Lordship, with characteristic decision, did not approve of the "wavering spirit" of even so distinguished an officer. So Beatson proceeded to England.

We next find him in Turkey, on special service (1st May, 1854), with rank as Colonel on the staff in the British Army. He received the rank of Lieutenant-General in the Turkish Army on his arrival at Constantinople. For his services on the Danube he obtained the gold medal from the Sultan, the "Nishan i Iftihar." In 1854 he was with the Heavy Brigade at Balaklava and Inkerman, and was mentioned in General Scarlett's despatch regarding the famous charge which has made Balaklava immortal. "During the time he was with me" (writes General Sir J. Scarlett, when recommending him to Head-quarters in October, 1856) "as Lieutenant-Colonel Beatson, he proved himself a most active and useful officer, as willing to work as the youngest Aide-de-Camp, with the experience of active service before the enemy. He was with me under fire the early part of the 25th October, 1854, near the Turkish forts. He was by my side at the charge of the Heavy Brigade—and rode by my side down the valley in support of the Light Brigade—under as severe a fire as troops were ever exposed to, and had his horse struck by a spent shot in the side. During the whole of this day he behaved with the greatest gallantry and coolness, and entirely supplied the place of my Aide-de-Camp (Captain Elliott), after the charge of the Heavy Brigade, in which Captain Elliott was severely wounded." He received the British and Turkish silver medals for the Crimea, the former with three clasps.

On the 1st November, 1854, Beatson was given the local rank of Major-General in Her Majesty's Army in Turkey; and he organised 4,000 Bashi-Bazouks. This corps was composed of confessedly the most difficult troops in the world for European officers to deal with; but for which the commandant's "long experience among the Arabs and Rohillas of the Nizam's cavalry peculiarly fitted him."

It was "during the transfer of the command from Colonel Beatson to Colonel Smith" that the events were said to have occurred which were set forth in the well-known trial in the case of Beatson v. Skene. The consul at Aleppo (Mr. Skene), who was with the commandant of the Bashi-Bazouks at the Dardanelles, was reported to have brought against him the extraordinary charge of attempting " to incite to mutiny the troops he had been appointed to command, so as to prevent others succeeding him therein." The value of such a charge was at once apparent when he was specially employed to aid in suppressing the great mutiny in India, after being charged with attempting to create one in Turkey.

Resting assured that he would be able to clear his fair fame,* he returned to India on the breaking out of the mutiny in 1857, when he was immediately employed on the highly responsible duty of raising and organising two regiments of cavalry, which, under the name of "Beatson's Horse," he took into the field. For services with one of the regiments of this brigade, the 18th Royal Irish, and Bombay Artillery, he received the thanks of Sir Hugh Rose in February, 1859. Sir Hugh Rose (now Lord Strathnairn) had made known to the Bombay Commander-in-Chief the satisfaction he derived from the manner in which Colonel Beatson discharged his duties while under his command, and praised him for zeal and energy in carrying out his instructions. Sir Hugh was perfectly aware of his "readiness to encounter any hardship or fatigue for the good of the service." He returned to England towards the close of 1859.

We have before us a "Supplement" of Beatson's services under four successive Governors-General, Lords Auckland, Ellenborough, Hardinge, and Dalhousie. Lord Canning made the fifth; and, though engaged under the lamented Viceroy in a peaceful but brilliant service, Lord Mayo, the sixth. Under Lord Canning's successor, Sir John (now Lord) Lawrence, whose reign appears to have been one of consolidating the Empire after the mutiny, Beatson's name does

---

* On the grounds of the communication being "privileged," the verdict of the Jury was "for the defendant." "The Jury wish to express their strong opinion of regret that, on discovering how unfounded the reports were, the defendant had not thought proper to withdraw his statements." The trial took place on Beatson's return from India, after the mutiny, and it cost him £3,000. The case was fully noticed in the London and provincial journals of January, 1860.

not come much before the public. Shortly after his return to India, or about the years 1864-65, there was almost nothing for him to do; so he could only wait patiently for what he was generally confessed to have very strong claims —the command of a division. This he at length obtained from the Commander-in-Chief, Sir William Mansfield (now Lord Sandhurst); but he and his friends felt that the high and lucrative appointment, worth over £4,000 a year, came rather too late in life. * Still the old soldier was very thankful for the great honour paid him, through which the wonted energy might again burst forth; and he had hope of retrieving his pecuniary losses.

In the Allahabad Division, "up in the morning early" (as was ever his custom), and action everywhere among the troops, soon became the order of the day. A sham fight was taking place at Allahabad, while the troops in some other cantonments were only just arriving on the ground! Lord Chatham's famous maxim, "If you do not rise early, you can make progress in nothing" (advice doubly valuable in India, where the sun, if you would be cool, compels you to rise early), was never absent from Beatson's mind; and we cannot help thinking it not improbable that, had he been in command at Meerut during the 10th and 11th May, 1857, at the first outbreak of the mutiny, he would have headed a party of horse, galloped off, and not left the saddle till he had done his utmost to secure the mutineers on their way to Delhi, and bring them back, under a strong guard, to their proper station!

Early in 1869, we find him in command of the Sirhind (Umballah) Division, where the grand Durbar, in honour of Shere Ali, the Ameer of Afghanistan, was held, under Lord Mayo, with unusual splendour.

Beatson was now in his glory, and put forth all his energies to deserve the thanks which he so generously received for his admirable arrangements regarding the troops; and our friend, the Ameer, doubtless, went back to his own country, having formed a very high opinion of our Army, under the Chief, Sir William Mansfield, and his

---

* Beatson was a full Colonel in the Army, November, 1854; a Regimental Colonel in May, 1864; Major-General, 8th January, 1865; and was appointed to command the Allahabad Division, 3rd October, 1866.

soldier-like Lieutenant, General Beatson. This was the brilliant service before alluded to; and Lord Mayo's Durbar, we may hope, Shere Ali considered, in every sense, a victory of Peace! If such friendships last, the designs of Russia (if such there be), or any other great power, against our splendid dominion, will vanish like mist before the morning sun.

Our distinguished Anglo-Indian's career is now drawing to a close. The "last of earth" is not far distant. Originally of a strong constitution, his health, from over-work and anxiety, now gave visible signs of being somewhat shattered; and, while commanding at Allahabad, he lost his wife, on which occasion he sent a letter to the present writer detailing the sympathy shown in his bereavement by all the officers at the funeral. More than a year of his divisional command still remained to be served; but he determined to visit England early in 1870, leaving the year in reserve for his return. Shortly after reaching home he lost a favourite daughter, which affliction he bore with truly Christian resignation; and before his health was fairly established—although much improved—he, soon after the sad event, left for India to accomplish the "one year more," which has killed, and will yet kill, so many Anglo-Indians! His condition in the loved land of his best achievements gradually became precarious, and he was recommended to Malta for change of climate. Thence, at the end of January, 1872, he returned to England to join his only surviving daughter, Mrs. M'Mullen, who had recently lost her husband, Major M'Mullen, "while on active service in India." On arrival, he was so weak that he had to be carried from the ship. Early in February, the London journals contained the following announcement:— "GENERAL BEATSON.—This distinguished officer died on Sunday (the 4th) at the Vicarage, New Swindon, the residence of the Rev. G. Campbell, aged sixty-seven."[*] Gazing on him in his last sleep, he reminded you of an effigy in a cathedral of one of the knights of old, with a visage conscious of having, during an eventful life, done much hard and chivalrous work. Or he might have given some the idea of a dead warrior on the hard-won field,

* Then followed a record of his services.

with, as Aytoun describes the "dead Dundee," a slight smile on his visage, as if, in the splendid lines of Campbell—conscious of leaving "no blot on his name," he dared to

" Look proudly to Heaven from the death-bed of fame."*

Having now endeavoured to do some justice to Beatson's military career, it behoves us to make a few remarks on his character, which may afford a key to the strange fact of his dying without a mark of distinction after his name. He was impetuous in most of his dealings with mankind, to a remarkable degree; and he seemed to consider that every one should be subservient to his rule. He was safe enough if you did not differ from him; but if you once disagreed it seemed as if you would never again recover his friendship. Although a first-rate officer, and strict disciplinarian, and, from the nature of his profession, obliged to succumb in weighty matters to the higher powers, still this unfortunate spirit of dislike of correction, or advice, sometimes followed him into quarters where, had he acted otherwise, marks of high favour and distinction were certain. He knew nothing of that important thing, " to listen discreetly;" and he totally disagreed with shrewd Mirabeau, "that to succeed in the world, it is necessary to be taught many things which you understand, by persons who know nothing about them." Too often discarding the science of etiquette, he thought little of patience as a social engine; and, with Beatson, " to listen, to wait, and to be wearied," the certain elements of good fortune, were quite out of the question. Eccentricity has been well defined as "disdaining to walk in the vulgar orbit." But the subject of this sketch would sometimes walk in no orbit whatever, excepting that described by himself in his periodical revolutions. There can be no doubt that he had numerous very fine qualities; but disappointed ambition seemed occasionally to freeze "the genial current" of his soul, and in a few of his deeds there was an evident want of discipline of the mind. After all, how many well-known men, in and out of the Services, are deserving of the same remark, and have shown, more or less, qualities which stood in the way of Beatson's advancement and distinction.

* "Lochiel's Warning."

One good anecdote of him may be told, showing his impetuosity, even at the quiet *chota haziree* (small breakfast) after parade. It was in Central India, when the fame of "Beatson's Horse" was beginning to attract attention, that, as the commandant and his officers were seated round the small table, preparatory to the larger and later repast, Beatson suddenly drew his sword, and made a smart cut at the helmet of one of the officers, who naturally looked up from his tea, inquiring the reason for such an assault. "I only wanted to find out whether or not your helmet is sword-proof," coolly replied Beatson. That he was a favourite among many of his officers is undeniable; and the following extracts will show how he was appreciated in the Bundelkund Legion, and the Nizam's Cavalry. Take him in what light we will, Beatson will long be remembered as one of the bravest and best soldiers of the old India Army.

PAPERS RELATING TO GENERAL BEATSON'S INDIAN CAREER.

No. I.

Extract of a Letter to Government from GENERAL FRASER, *Resident at Hyderabad, dated 6th March,* 1848.

" I have always been anxious to diminish, as far as possible, the debts of the Cavalry Division, and it is a source of gratification to me to find that the Brigadier has taken such steps as may tend to effect this desirable object.

" I am happy that I am enabled to speak in terms of high approval of Brigadier Beatson. He was not appointed at my recommendation, and there was another Officer who I thought had superior claims to the Cavalry Division, from having served in it for many years with credit and reputation; but there is no man with whom I could be better satisfied than with Brigadier Beatson, nor any one, in my opinion, who would be better suited to command the Cavalry branch of the Nizam's Service."

[General Fraser was a distinguished Anglo-Indian, a capital Persian scholar, and well-read on nearly every subject. He held several important political appointments during his long career. The writer recollects him at Hyderabad, in 1846, remarking, as we entered with our swords on (according to custom) before breakfast, " Take off your swords, gentlemen ; this is a time of peace ! "]

No. 2.

Extract of a Letter from Col. Wood, *Military Secretary to* Lord Hardinge, *dated* 18*th October*, 1848.

" It now appears that Col. Tomkyns has applied for an extension of leave, only to the 29th February next, and that on his re-assuming his command, Major Beatson, who is officiating for him, will be deprived of his appointment.

" The G. G. considers the claims of this Officer on the Government are very strong, having, whilst in command of the Bundelkund Legion, consisting of Cavalry, Infantry and Artillery, done good service to the State, at a most important crisis, when our troops refused to march to Scinde, which his troops volunteered to do, the command of which he has been deprived of by the men of the Legion having been drafted into the regular Regiments of the Bengal Army.

" Under these circumstances the G. G., although he acknowledges that Major Ingles, having commanded a Regiment of the Nizam's Cavalry for 17 years, would be a very proper Officer to command the Cavalry Division, does not feel justified in passing over Major Beatson in favour of that Officer."

No. 3.

The following is the Inscription on a Sword presented after the Bundelkund Legion was broken up :—

To Major W. F. Beatson, *late Commandant-in-Chief of the Bundelkund Legion.*

From his friends of the Legion, in token of their admiration of him as a Soldier, and their esteem for him as an individual—1850.

No. 4.

The following accompanied the presentation of a handsome piece of Plate, from the Officers of the Nizam's Cavalry, after BRIGADIER BEATSON gave up command:—

"We have availed ourselves of this method of testifying our regard for you personally, and our admiration of your talents and abilities as a Soldier, under whose command we have all served, and some of us have had opportunities of witnessing your gallant conduct in action with the enemy, and your sound judgment, upon all occasions, when Brigadier in command of the Nizam's Cavalry, both in Quarters and in the Field."

No. 5.

Extract of a Despatch from the COMMANDER-IN-CHIEF *to the* GOVERNOR GENERAL, *dated Head Quarters, Simla,* 19th *October,* 1853.

Recommending "The introduction, under an Inspector, or other properly qualified Officer, of a well-considered and uniform system in the Cavalry, so as to ensure effectually, for the future, the most perfect efficiency attainable.

"In the event of these suggestions meeting with the approval of the Most Noble the Governor-General-in-Council, I am to observe that Major W. F. Beatson, late Brigadier in the Army of his Highness the Nizam, whose return from furlough is shortly expected, appears to His Excellency, from his long experience, a fit Officer to investigate into the state of the Irregular Cavalry, and to prepare such rules and regulations as may conduce to its perfect organisation."

COLONEL W. H. SYKES, M.P., F.R.S.

THE death of Colonel Sykes, M.P., at the ripe age of eighty-two, has removed from us a man of no ordinary mental calibre, and whose like we may not soon see again. He was emphatically, as a contemporary has styled him, "the M.P. for Hindustan." India was the darling of his heart through two generations of men, and when he could not get India to talk about, he was off to China to discourse about the Taepings, or some other political subject of the Flowery Land. India, past and present, was alike known to the gallant and philanthropic Colonel; and from his extensive reading and vast experience he had the power of doing much good; but he knew not the secret of being concise, or of seizing on various occasions the main points of an argument, which injured his value in the eyes of the world. Great in statistics, great in a knowledge of the origin and progress of Eastern commerce, great in a knowledge of ancient India—his "Notes" concerning which form one of the most interesting works on the mysteries of Buddhism in the world—great in his devotion to the officers of the Indian army, and always kind and considerate to officers and others requiring his assistance and advice, the departed Colonel was in many respects a remarkable man. As Director and Chairman of the East India Company, a large amount of patronage was in his gift, and for nearly forty years we fully believe that he never lost an opportunity for exercising his power of doing good. The subaltern of the fine old Indian army, wanting his book patronised by the Court, was sure to go to Sykes. If it could be done—*he* was the man. The widow and the orphan, too, how often have they had to bless his name! Some who read this will remember the Colonel's famous remark—"I never ask favours from the Government"—which has damped the spirit of many an aspirant to fame. That tall figure with the benign countenance has now passed away; but none who have heard his speeches, read his works, or had an interview with him, will easily forget such a friend as William Henry Sykes.*

The Liberal Member of Parliament for Aberdeen, of whom the above brief sketch is given, died in London on the 16th June, 1872. He was the son of Mr. Samuel Sykes, a representative of a branch of the Sykeses of Yorkshire, and was born in the year 1790. He joined the Bombay army in 1804, and in 1805 served under Lord Lake at Bhurtpore. At the battles of Kirkee and Poonah he commanded a regiment of native troops.

He was actively employed in the Deccan in 1817 and 1818; and in 1824 he was engaged by the Bombay Government as Statistical Reporter—a position which he held till he finally quitted India in 1831. In 1840 he was elected a Director of the East India Company. He gave his services to the public gratuitously as a Royal Commissioner in Lunacy. In March, 1854, he was elected Lord Rector of Aberdeen University; and, to crown the zeal he displayed for India, he was subsequently chosen Deputy-Chairman of the East India Company, and served as Chairman of that great Corporation in the eventful years of 1857-58. He had represented Aberdeen since 1857, at every general election the gallant and learned Colonel having the preference. He belonged to many learned societies at home and abroad, and had held the presidential chairs of the Royal Asiatic Society, of the Statistical Society, and of the Society of Arts. In 1856 he received from the citizens of Bombay a medal, for his strong advocacy of a system of native education; and only a year or two before his death he was presented with a handsome silver candelabrum, subscribed for and presented by the officers of the Indian army "in grateful appreciation of his persevering and disinterested advocacy in the House of Commons of the rights and privileges" of that body. Turning from the learned "Notes on the Religious, Moral, and Political State of Ancient India"—which

* Written in June, 1872.

alone occupy some 250 pages, or nearly the entire volume, of the Journal of the Royal Asiatic Society, for May, 1841 —we find among his scientific and literary works one on the "Organisation and Cost of the English and French Armies and Navies," and upwards of sixty papers published in the transactions of various learned societies, "mainly on the ancient history, antiquities, statistics, geology, natural history, and meteorology of India."*

The general complaint, remarked on by the wise Seneca, of the shortness of life, and his answer—*Vita, si scias uti, longa est*—" Life is long, if you know how to use it "—were known to few men better than Colonel Sykes. Not long before his death, the writer had occasion to pay him a visit in Albion Street, Hyde Park. The conversation turning on work for the Anglo-Indian at home, on its being remarked to him what a vast deal of work *he* had got through since he left India (more than forty years ago), he replied—" But there is little use in living now; the *vis vitæ* has gone !"

Some twenty years before, the conversation with him, when he served as a Director in Leadenhall Street, had been on Buddhism and Monsieur Manupied's wonderful work, bringing out a comparison between some of the Buddhistical writings and those in Isaiah ; now it was on the great question of the day—Education !

Perhaps no Anglo-Indian ever moved in a higher circle of society than Colonel Sykes. He was the friend of several distinguished men, among others, Lord Rosse, the inventor of the mighty telescope, with whom the writer found him busy on one occasion; and, during the first conversation above alluded to, he remarked on being obliged, from ill health, to decline all invitations, even from those related to the Royal Family. This is mentioned to show that, in spite of a few short-comings as a public man, there was some attractive metal about him, even in a social point of view. Early in June, on leaving the House of Commons, we believe that he said to a brother Member with whom he had been associated for years, while supporting him on leaving the House, " I'm going home—I don't think I shall ever return !" The remark was too true ; he went

* See *Broad Arrow*, June 22nd, 1872.

home but to die. Sykes comes under the head of useful and hard-working rather than of brilliant Anglo-Indians. Those who knew him well declared that he thought he knew every thing better than anybody else; and surely, when we consider that he was a soldier a year before Nelson won the battle of Trafalgar, and then an ardent student, such pride of knowledge may be excused. A duplicate of the man can never possibly appear: he belongs to a school fast passing away; but younger men will do well if they evince the same amount of energy and industry in the public service, which so long distinguished Colonel Sykes.

THE GENIUS OF ANCIENT BUDDHISM.

[Under the above head, the conclusion of Colonel Sykes' famous paper, "Notes on Ancient India," may be given as an example of his style. When we consider that the religion of Buddha numbers some 400,000,000 members, the subject should be one of no common interest.]

WITH a few words on the genius of *ancient* Buddhism, and the possible cause of its fall in India, I shall close these notes. The Buddhists, like many other Eastern nations, believed in the transmigration of the soul. To terminate the probationary state, and to obtain final liberation or rest, *nirvana* or *nirbutti*, that is to say, the stoppage of the further transition of the soul, was the sole worthy object of man's existence! The only path to this object was through the grades of the clergy. The conditions were, the "*most perfect faith, the most perfect virtue, and the most perfect knowledge.*" It was insufficient for the laity that they believed in *Buddha*, Dharma, *Sanga*, *i.e.* Buddha, the law, and the clergy or church; of which there is elsewhere an analogue in " God, the law, and the prophets :" it was only by receiving the tonsure, and enlisting in the ranks of the church that they even made the first step towards salvation. It was then, that, abandoning the world and its concerns, pledged to absolute poverty, to support life by eleemosynary means, to chastity, to abstinence, to penance, to prayer, and, above all, to continued contemplation of divine truths, they rose in the grades of the church, until some one amongst them having obtained the most perfect knowledge, the most perfect virtue, and the most perfect faith, became Buddha, or infinite wisdom; that is to say, the soul ceased to wander,—its final rest was attained, and it was absorbed into the First Cause. It has been attempted to brand this doctrine with atheism; but if it be so, then are the Brahmans atheists, for it is part of their esoteric system.* Those of the Buddhist clergy who could not attain nirvana, in their renewed births were supposed to attain a form amongst the grades of beings either celestial or terrestrial, approaching to perfect happiness in the *proximate ratio* of their attainment of *perfect knowledge*, and in these states they might rise or fall, until *final liberation* was attained. The souls of the laity went on transmigrating through animal or vegetable life, without even passing the threshold to salvation. It was a strong motive with every man, therefore, to join the clergy, and even the painful lives the latter led, did not prevent the proper relation between producers and non-producers in the social system being subverted. The accumulation of the clergy was pregnant with evil. Their standard of excellence was infinitely too high for humanity; their tests for its attainment too severe; schisms occurred, disorders broke out, relaxations in discipline followed, and these circumstances, in the progress of ages, combined with the severe pressure upon the laity for the support of the enormously disproportioned numbers of the clergy [*vide* Mahawanso], loosened their hold upon the veneration and affection of the people: they silently fell off from a system which was so onerous, and merged into the Vaisya or Sudra ranks of the Brahmanical faith, precisely as is described by Hiuan thsang to have been the case at Patna in the seventh century, when " the Buddhists were living amongst the heretics, and no better than them." In this corrupted stage of Buddhism, the fiery Saivas mustered in sufficient force to effect its overthrow; the clergy, and such of the laity as espoused their interests, were either slaughtered, or driven out of India to a man, and the rest of the laity had little difficulty in transferring their allegiance from one idol to another, (for from works of Buddhist art, and from what we now see of its practices in other countries, it must then have lapsed into little better than rank idolatry,) and Buddhism thus finally disappeared from India, leaving, however, indestructible vestiges of its former

* Wilson, Second Oxford Lecture, p. 64.

glory, and many of its practices amongst the Hindus, as noticed by Dr. Stevenson; the Saivas leaving also, as I elsewhere have had occasion to notice, monuments of their triumphs!*

In case I am asked for the specific object and *cui bono* of my labours, my reply is brief and simple. The startling accounts of India by the Chinese travellers in the fifth, sixth, and seventh centuries of our era, prompted me to subject details so novel and unexpected to the test of such contemporary or previous evidence, as might be obtainable. The Chinese travellers have come from the ordeal unscathed, and the accumulated facts in the preceding pages satisfy me that the narratives of what they saw, in their chief features, are as worthy of credit as those of the travellers of any other time or nation whatever, at least those of Fa hian. With respect to the *cui bono*, if it be proved that Brahmanism is neither unfathomable in its antiquity, nor unchaugeable in its character, we may safely infer that, by proper means, applied in a cautious, kindly, and forbearing spirit, such *further changes* may be effected, as will raise the intellectual standard of the Hindus, improve their moral and social condition, and assist to promote their eternal welfare.

* Journal of the Royal Asiatic Society, No. iv., page 205.

MAJOR-GENERAL W. H. MILLER, C.B.*

WILLIAM HENRY MILLER appears in the "Madras Quarterly Army List," in June, 1860, as Regimental Lieutenant-Colonel, a Colonel in the Army, and Aide-de-Camp to the Queen; his season of appointment to the Madras Artillery dating as far back as 1823. The same interesting work—more interesting to many than either romance or history—records that Colonel Miller served with the force of Colonel Evans, C.B., employed against the insurgents in the Nuggur Province of Mysore, in April, May, and June, 1831; with the Saugor Field Divison in the Bundelkund campaign, of 1858, in command of the Artillery Brigade; present at the actions of Jheenjuñ, April 10th, and of Kubraee, April 17th, 1858; the Battle of Banda, 19th April, 1858. Received three wounds, one on the hand, one on the face, and lost his right arm.

From the fourth of the seven ages of man (according to Shakspeare), we make a retrograde movement to "the infant," and find that, as the son of Major Miller, Royal Horse Guards (Blues), William first saw the light in May, 1805, at or near the town of Windsor. To his father, one of the best informed officers of the day, the son owed much of his education; and that love of argument in conversation, which so distinguished him in after life, was due to paternal tuition. The Millers seem to have caught some infection from the vastness of the Scotch intellect during the eighteenth century, of which we read in Buckle's remarkable book on " Civilisation." Of the two fundamental divisions of human inquiry—the deductive and the inductive—during that renowned period of invention, all the

* Written June, 1873, partly from a sketch printed at Ootacamund, Neilgherries, 1866.

great thinkers of Scotland chiefly cherished the deductive philosophy which, in comparison with the other, was deemed " remarkable for boldness, dexterity, and often rashness." From Patrick Miller, of Dalswinton, over his carronades and paddle-wheels, down to his grandson, the lieutenant fire-worker in the Coast Artillery, the spirit of investigation was apparent. Such a state of mind, preferring facts to theories, was not less valuable to the soldier, Miller, (especially in the scientific branch of the Army) than to the eventual vindication of his grandfather's right to be considered the sole originator of Practical Steam Navigation.

After some thirty-five years of uninterrupted Indian service, in the different capacities of surveyor, commissary of ordnance, and regimental officer—all blended with that love of *shikar*, which the Iron Duke rightly deemed a grand qualification in the British soldier—William Miller was appointed by Sir Patrick Grant, the Commander-in-Chief of the Madras Army, to the command of the Artillery Brigade of the Saugor Field Division, which division, under General Sir G. C. Whitlock, the great question of the Banda and Kirwee prize-money afterwards rendered even more famous in the eyes of the world than its glorious deeds in the field.

To one who was fond of, and knew so much about, horses and cattle, this well-equipped division (including a more than usually effective siege-train) must have presented a cheerful picture—one that would have received ample justice from the genius of Landseer. All the animals were in splendid condition, and well adapted to aid the work of giving the *coup-de-grace* to the Sepoy rebellion. The Brigadier was a thoroughly practical man. Not a few of the stores for the large train were weighed out and packed under his personal inspection. While Commissary of Ordnance his plan was to keep various books, in which the materials for making up stores were carefully jotted down, as well as a vast quantity of practical information, invaluable to the Ordnance officer. " Give me facts, I am sick of theory; give me actual facts!" said James Watt to Boulton; and, doubtless, so thought, while about to set forth on his warlike mission, the grandson of Patrick Miller,

I

of Dalswinton. Bundelkund was to be the grand theatre of action. It was in the height of the hot weather of 1858 that the Column encountered the Nawab of Banda. During the action which ensued, Brigadier Miller's gallantry, while in command of the Artillery, was conspicuous. Attempting to silence or carry away one of the enemy's field guns, which was playing hard upon the Division, he had his right arm shattered, and received a sword cut on his head, and other wounds. Through medical skill, and a strong constitution, a valuable life was spared; but the arm had, at Banda, to be eventually amptutated near the shoulder.

"After the battle," wrote a most intelligent officer in the force, "the fearful weather under which we marched to Kirwee—when strong men dropped motionless, and too soon lifeless, day by day—will never be forgotten by those who shared it." [The General was proud to the end of his days of the Artillery he commanded at Banda, on the 19th April, and of how they did their duty in the famed relief of Kirwee, 25th December, 1858, under the personal command of General (afterwards Sir George) Whitlock, on which occasion the Cavalry and Horse Artillery marched eighty-seven miles in thirty-seven hours.] *Honor fidelitatis premium* was the motto chosen for an interesting pamphlet on the Division, recording the exploits of the Madras troops, who "from the hour when the gallant Neill led his little band of Fusiliers across the surf down to the Battle of Banda and march to Kirwee, had proved themselves to be soldiers of whom Charles the Twelfth, or the Great Condé, would have been justly proud." Among the recipients of honours distributed after the war, was the Artilliery Brigadier, who had fought so fearlessly and well; he was appointed Aide-de-Camp to Her Majesty, with the rank of Brevet-Colonel, and eventually a C.B., on obtaining the honorary rank of Major-General. In 1866 General Miller was among the first recipients of the good service pension allotted by Her Majesty to distinguished or worthy Indian officers. He retired from the service, and left India in 1860-61.

Shortly after his retirement General Miller set his powerful mind to work on the scientific subject of the origin of Practical Steam Navigation; and the result, after unwearied investigation, was a published letter (1862), "vindicating the right of Patrick Miller, Esq., of Dalswinton, to be regarded as the first inventor." For many years, in a foreign land, the grandson had been displeased to hear that others were pursuing the triumph which belonged to his illustrious relative, whose experiments in artillery and navigation, including those in the latter with steam, are well known to have cost Mr. Miller above 30,000*l*. The "Letter," published in the form of a neat *brochure*, is addressed to Bennett Woodcroft, Esq., F.R.S., author of "A Sketch of the origin and progress of Steam Navigation."

In his "Vindication" the General exhibited a forbearance, a generosity, and an impartiality, not common in a matter of scientific controversy, and did much to fix old Dalswinton in a conspicuous niche in the temple of fame. The question of Army prize, in connection with the well-known Banda and Kirwee case, occupied unceasingly the last seven or eight years of General Miller's life; and, as President of Committee appointed with reference to the money and jewels taken in the campaign in which he had played so distinguished a part, the *hoc age*, or do it with all thy might, principle of work, was ever apparent in one of the most unselfish of men. The worry and vexation which his generous labours frequently entailed, doubtless tended to hasten the General's end; and, after a brief illness, the fine old Anglo-Indian soldier died peacefully at his residence in Kildare Gardens, Bayswater, on the 15th May, 1873. His remains were interred in Kensal Green Cemetery, May 21, in the presence of numerous mourning and sincere friends and companions-in-arms.

In his manner General Miller was genial and attactive in an extraordinary degree. Tall and erect, with a rather powerful frame, *le général sans bras* (as the French used to style him), with his amiable visage set off by a venerable beard, seemed to make friends everywhere. In the omnibus or railway carriage he had always a little troop of patient listeners to his occasional droll remarks and brief anecdotes, and in the former vehicle on one occasion he kept two old ladies chained to their seats, to their dismay, long after the appointed place of exit. He was generally at first averse to novelties of any kind. He preferred the old stage coach to the railway carriage, and shot with the flint gun (and killed right well, tóo) long after percussion caps had come into use. The old soldier in London, now turned into a *commissionaire*, who could display medals, and especially if he had lost an arm, was sure to meet with his sympathy or assistance. At home, the fund of anecdote he would pour out was sometimes surprising. He knew everything about Anglo-India in the old time, and would bring "old familiar faces" back before you in rapid succession. In Indian sporting matters he was a first-rate authority, and the well-known heroes of the turf of a past age in our "Nursery of Captains" were most of them known to him.* Himself a fearless rider, he would discourse on the merits of once renowned jockeys. He would tell you of the mighty hunters, whether with hound or spear, such as John Elliott and Backhouse, and of some of the chief turf men in Bengal—Stevenson, Bacon, Grant, and John White. He would bring before you the feats of Stevenson, the father of the turf in the Bengal Presidency, and the eccentricities of Mac Dowell ("Arab Mac") who claimed that honour in Madras. He had stories of Apthorp, Humffreys, and Shirriff—all renowned tiger-killers—and Duncan Mackenzie ("Mr. North"), Edward Gullifer Showers (Artillery), and the two Macleans, were cited as "among the glorious old 'Mulls,'" who in their day shed glory o'er the turf, as Cunningham (Cavalry) did in Bombay. He had even stories of the famous Arabs of the time, such as Pyramid, Feramorz, and Hurry Skurry—those "equine sons of the desert," as he styled them. He would then strike off to affairs at home, and talk of history, politics, and the drama. Of the latter he was especially fond, and he would tell you about the old actors—of whom he had seen many—dwelling on Liston's wonderful face, for instance—with a genial humour worthy of *Elia*. In politics the General was a strict Conservative : and, with a Tory journal in his hand, he seemed to bid defiance to all the world, which frequently led him into severe wordy conflicts with his political opponents. Well-read, and possessing a most retentive memory, his weak point now came forth—

* See "Sketch of Sporting Literature in India," in which the General is the "choice spirit of a world gone by," therein alluded to.

impatience of contradiction. And yet with his opposing style of argument he was one of the kindest and most charitable of men. A genial laugh or smile soon succeeded the motion of the empty sleeve. Charity with him was not a mere name. With but limited means he was ever ready to do a good action, when in his power; and he did it with much delicacy and good feeling. To give the last touch, he was eminently just and liberal, and loved for his justice and magnanimity.

NOTES.

I.

THE SAUGOR FIELD DIVISION.

The Saugor Field Division consisted of a wing of the 12th Royal Lancers, under Colonel Oakes; the 43rd Regiment, under Colonel Primrose; the 3rd Madras European Regiment, under Colonel Apthorp ("Tiger Apthorp," so called from being such a good shot); a troop of European M. H. A., under Major Mein; F Troop of Native H. A., under Major Brice; a Horse Battery, under Captain Gosling and Lieutenant Pope; the 50th M. N. I., under Colonel Reece; and the 1st M. N. I., under Colonel Gottreux. Captain Palmer's Company, R. A., with Lieutenant Morgan; and last, though far from least, the 2nd Ressalah of the Hyderabad Contingent, under Captain Macintire, completed Whitlock's Field Division, in which were some of the best officers in the Madras Army.

The Staff consisted of Colonel Hamilton, Adjutant-General; Major Barrow, Commissary of Ordnance; Major Ludlow, Field or Chief Engineer; Head of the Commissariat, Captain Barrow; Major Lawder, Q. M. G.; and Dr. Davidson, Surgeon-in-Chief, with whom the writer had served in the second Burmese War. All the men were eager for service—"the boys" in particular; for so the men of the recently raised Madras 3rd European Regiment had been styled by their former Colonel (General Whitlock), who was now about to lead them on to victory!— *Bondela Khond*, the land of the Bondelas, was to be the grand theatre of action.

II.

COLONEL WALTER CONINGSBY ERSKINE, C.B.
(EARL OF KELLIE).

The Honourable Colonel Walter Coningsby Erskine, C.B., also retired in 1861, after distinguished political service in Central India during the mutiny. We mention this, as the subject of the foregoing brief sketch was cousin to the very recently deceased Earl of Mar, now (1866) succeeded in the estates by Colonel Erskine (cousin to the late Earl), under the title of the Earl of Kellie. So much for the rise of the cadet who went out to the Bengal Presidency in 1827. To future historians, among the various fortunes of the famed Erskines of Mar, not the least remarkable will be that of the soldier (and after political) who found his way to India! We may here state that John Thomas Erskine, 13th Earl of Mar, son of John Francis, 12th Earl, married Miss Janet Miller, daughter of Patrick Miller, Esq., of Dalswinton, in Dumfriesshire, and had issue one son, the Honourable John Francis Miller Erskine, and two daughters. The now deceased nobleman, John Francis Miller Erskine, 14th Earl of Mar and Kellie, was born at Dalswinton about the year 1794-5.* He must have been born in the old mansion; for the present was not erected till some years after. However, the grounds, and lake (on which the first steamboat experiment took place) remain the same; and while we think of the place as hallowed by scientific achievement, history reminds us that here was born the descendant of an Earl, who had the "custody of his infant Sovereign, Queen Mary," till 1548; and from whom was descended the next Earl, his son, who had charge of James VI., afterwards King of England, when an infant. This Earl, the sixth of a great line "whose origin is lost in its antiquity," was highly distinguished by his Sovereign, and, as we read, bringing the immortal inventor of abridging calculation by Logarithms to memory, "was the friend and fellow labourer of Baron Napier of Merchiston!"

[Lieut.-Colonel the Earl of Kellie died at Cannes, 15th January, 1872. He held several military and civil appointments in India; received the thanks of both Houses of Parliament, and was created a C.B. (Civil Division) for his conduct in the Indian mutiny; he also had medals for the "Sutlej" and "India."]

* In his early days he served in the Army, and was present at Quatre Bras and Waterloo. He died at Alloa House on the 19th June, 1866, in his 71st year.

MAJOR-GENERAL ALBERT FYTCHE, C.S.I.*

GENERAL FYTCHE, late Chief Commissioner of British Burma, was born in 1823, and educated at Rugby and Addiscombe. At the age of sixteen he obtained his commission in the Bengal army, and (like many distinguished men) commenced work in earnest at an early age. Before he was twenty, while serving as a lieutenant in the Arakan Local Battalion, he did credit to Rugby and Addiscombe while gaining his first laurels (1841) by routing out and punishing a wild hill-tribe, known as the Wallengs, who had committed several raids on the British frontier. It was a difficult service. The position to be attacked was on a precipitous mountain, 4,000 feet high, with sides so steep that the inhabitants of the place could only ascend it by ladders. In the face of strong opposition Lieutenant Fytche dislodged the enemy, and for this gallant attack received the thanks of the British Government. In 1845 he joined the Commission of Arakan; but in 1848 he left civil employ to take part in the second Sikh war, and distinguished himself at Chilianwallah and Guzerat. During the latter famous and decisive action, he was selected by General Sir Walter Raleigh Gilbert to storm the key of the Sikh position, and in performing this important service Lieutenant Fytche was severely wounded. He also joined in the pursuit in which the Ameer Dost Mahomed Khan was so nearly taken prisoner. After the Sikh war Lieutenant Fytche returned to the Commission of Arakan, but in 1853 was appointed Deputy-Commissioner of Bassein, in the new British province of Pegu, where he performed services which must at once recommend themselves to every

* Written in March, 1873; forming portion of a sketch of the General's "Administration of British Burma." The growing importance of Burma must form an excuse for the administrative details here given.

saving War Minister or economical Chancellor of the Exchequer. They are recorded in a "Narrative of the Second Burmese War." On one occasion Captain Fytche penetrated to the haunts of bands of armed robbers, who were ravaging the country, accompanied by a band of irregular followers whom he had raised and drilled himself, and by this daring act succeeded in routing and dispersing the enemy, and restoring tranquillity in that quarter of his district, with a wonderfully small bill of costs for an army. On another occasion, which even more strongly recommends itself, the Captain attacked a strong entrenchment of the banditti, and shot their chief with his own hand. But his most daring and economical exploit was against the ex-Governor of Bassein, who had collected an army of 3,000 men, with a gathering of camp followers which raised the aggregate to about 10,000; Captain Fytche attacked them, after a forced march, with his detachment of irregulars, accompanied by four field-pieces; the engagement was most successful. Captain Fytche, with an energy worthy of a Malcolm or an Outram, not only dispersed the enemy and killed their leader, but captured nine guns and upwards of 3,000 stand of arms, and so much plunder, that with the proceeds he was enabled to pay all the expenses of his carriage and other charges without the cost of a rupee to the State.* On this occasion we were led to remark:— "With such a force, the blue-jackets and four field-pieces, we think that a successful march might have been made even on Amrapoora, 'the city of the immortals,' itself!"

As we cannot here detail the Captain's numerous other exploits for the next few years, all performed in the most gallant manner, let us pass on to 1857, when Major Fytche was appointed Commissioner of Tenasserim and Martaban, a most important post, which he held with great credit for a period of ten years. Tempered by the Commissioner's judgment and discretion, which greatly adorned his administration, under his mild rule the territory enjoyed an order and tranquillity which formed a significant contrast to the more demonstrative proceedings

* See "Second Burmese War."—Pegu.—pp. 385-389.

which were carried on in other provinces of the British Empire in the East. In March, 1867, Colonel Fytche was appointed to the still more important post, in succession to Sir Arthur Phayre, of Chief Commissioner of British Burma and Agent to His Excellency the Viceroy of India. His four years' administration date from March, 1867, to March, 1871; and before taking his departure from the Province on furlough to Europe, the Chief Commissioner put upon record some interesting particulars respecting the past history of this administration, and its progress during the time it had been entrusted to his care. His distinguished predecessor, Sir Arthur Phayre, previous to his departure from Burma, had submitted to the Government of India statistical tables of the progress of the province prior to 1867; and so the wholesome practice has been established in Chin-India (as the French geographer, Malte-Brun, aptly styles India beyond the Ganges), of an administrator finishing his chequered course by displaying his talents as author or reviewer. General* Fytche had just reason for entering on a comprehensive review when we consider that the main portion of his life had been spent in the country, and that for more than thirty years he had been serving in one or other of the three divisions of Arakan, Pegu, and Tenasserim.

Passing over some valuable particulars, especially concerning the rapid improvement of Arakan and Tenasserim (which provinces came into our possession in 1826) under British administration; at the present time, when, probably in a true spirit of wisdom suited to the age, annexation is *not* the policy of our Indian Government, it is interesting to read General Fytche's remarks on Lord Dalhousie's not taking a mode of action which, in our opinion, might have led to making northern Burma British, and the omission of which, for political reasons, appears to the General to have been open to question. He alludes to the "premature withdrawal" of the expedition, in 1852:—" Had that force been allowed to remain a few weeks longer, our political relations with the Court

* Appointed Major-General in the Army, November, 1868, and Companion of the Exalted Order of the Star of India.

of Ava might have been established on a lasting basis, which would have proved beneficial to both states. Fortunately the result has been in a great measure achieved in later years, partly by diplomatic action, and partly by a spontaneous display of friendship and confidence on the part of his Majesty the King of Ava, which was previously unknown."

It is curious to remark that when General Fytche came to India (1841), while the Government was rashly contemplating the occupation of Afghanistan, Burma was so little cared for that a withdrawal from the country was more than once seriously contemplated. The revenue was insufficient to meet the expenditure, and the public opinion of civilised nations had not yet reached the fertile valley of the Irrawaddy, from the sea-coast upward to the wild tribes which intervene between Burma and China, which region "was in the hands of a cruel and barbarous despot utterly ignorant of the great world around him."

General Fytche, in a "Memorandum," reviews his administration during four years under the several heads of Foreign Policy, Internal Administration, and Public Works. Under the head of Foreign Policy his review of the progress of our relations with the Court of Ava—especially at a time when the Burmese Embassy, after receiving the utmost consideration and attention, has so recently left London—is highly interesting.

The other countries upon our frontier also come well under notice.

When entrusted with the administration of Burma, early in 1867, one of the Chief Commissioner's first objects was to open up a friendly intercourse with the King, and to endeavour, through Major Sladen (who was at that time his assistant at the Court of Mandalay), to remove all suspicions from the mind of His Majesty, and to convince the Burmese Government that the only object of the British was to promote, by mutual concessions, the material interests of the two States. At that time so little had been accomplished in the way of developing the trade with Upper Burma under the treaty of 1862 (which proved to be of little or no advantage to British interests and trade), that during the whole interval that had elapsed between that year and the date of Colonel Fytche's taking charge of the administration, in 1867, only four merchant steamers had made their way to Mandalay. One of his earliest measures was to provide for a more rapid and regular communication, not only between Rangoon and the frontier town of Thayetmyo, but between Thayetmyo and Mandalay, the capital of Ava, and with the stations in the Ava territory still further inland, as far as the remote and decaying commercial city of Bhamo.

While Commissioner of Tenasserim and Martaban, in 1864, Colonel Fytche had carried on some important negotiations with the Siamese Commissioners especially appointed by the King of Siam, respecting the line of boundary between British territory and that country. Matters, unsettled for forty years, were brought to a successful issue. Proceeding to the boundaries in person, in less than two years, through the Commissioner's negotiations, the line of frontier was surveyed and demarcated,* and duly ratified by a treaty between the Government of India and the King of Siam.† This business appears to have been so well managed that it was natural to expect great results from the visit of the new Chief Commissioner to Mandalay, in 1867. Colonel Fytche succeeded in negotiating a very important treaty with the King of Burma—forming the basis of our present political relations with the Court of Mandalay—under which the oppressive monopolies of the King were abandoned, and a fixed rate of frontier duties was finally settled; whilst the country was fairly opened up to European enterprise, and with such advantageous results to British merchants that during the following year the trade with Upper Burma was nearly doubled. At the same time Colonel Fytche won the confidence of the King, and thus obtained His Majesty's permission to the despatch of an expedition, under Major Sladen, towards Western China, *via* Bhamo, with the view of re-opening an ancient and important trade between Burma and Western China, which had been closed only ten years

* An excellent and much-lamented officer, Lieutenant Bagge, R.E., was employed in this work.
† See Appendix, No. V.

previously in consequence of wars between some Mussulman tribes known as Panthays, and the Chinese local governors. Opening up the old trade route, among other grand objects, had the important one of encouraging the influx of population into British territory.

By this expedition in 1868, the energetic and fearless Sladen did for this part of Asia what Sir Alexander Burnes had effected by his travels into Bokhara; he cast a line of light—*une ligne lumineuse*, as the great Humboldt said of Sir Alexander—around a hitherto unknown region. The Major succeeded, not only in visiting Bhamo, but in penetrating the Kachyen hills as far as Momein, and opening up communications with the Panthay chiefs of Talifoo, the capital of Yunan; so the Chief Commissioner has good reasons for thinking there can be no question that with a rapidly-increasing steam communication with Bhamo,* the old trade will speedily revive, and the river Irrawaddy become the Ganges of Burma.

The value of Pegu as a British possession in the East is particularly noticed by General Fytche.

Indeed, it may be safely asserted that without Pegu our possessions in Burma are of comparatively small value; but that with Pegu our territory in Burma has become "one of the most prosperous provinces of our Eastern Empire." Beyond all question, the General's four years' administration of Burma has been eminently successful, externally as well as internally; and at its close, it is highly pleasing to note the following results:—

" A British officer has been appointed to reside permanently at Bhamo. A mixed court has been established at Mandalay for the trial of cases in which British subjects are concerned. Every year Upper Burma is brought more and more into communication with the western world; whilst the prosperity of British Burma is such, that within the last ten years her population and revenue have both doubled; and whilst she has to maintain herself against a frontier more considerable and difficult than that of the Punjab, she contributes one-sixth of her revenue to the Imperial treasury, after meeting all charges, military and civil."

* In 1869, Captain Strover was appointed to reside at Bhamo as assistant political agent.

As regards roads, railways, and other public works, very much was effected under General Fytche's administration. A complete system of Imperial roads was prepared, and a line of railway was surveyed between Rangoon and Prome.* Embankments were constructed, whereby large tracts of culturable territory, which had been abandoned to swamp, have been rescued. New lighthouses were constructed at Krishna Shoal, China Buckeer, and Eastern Grove. Plans were submitted to the Government of India for connecting Burma with India by a submarine cable. Gaols and civil courts were constructed at every important station in Burma, in the place of the wretched huts which had previously done duty. Education was promoted, and strong efforts were made to utilise the hundreds of monastic schools (under the yellow-garbed *Poonghis*, or priests) throughout the province, and to render them available for the better instruction of the masses.

The employment of Burmese officials had been largely promoted; a more regular system had been introduced into the revenue and judicial courts, throughout the province; a vaccination department had been organised, and local gazettes established in English and Burmese, bearing favourable comparison with those published in the Presidencies of India.

So much, then, for British Burma under General Fytche; a province which has improved in a greater ratio than, perhaps, any other in British India, and which the Chief Commissioner thinks it will be always well to administer in accordance with the national institutions.

Education in India is a great question, and has been so since the days of Lord William Bentinck. The present Viceroy, Lord Northbrook, was not out of order when he declared that the Indian education question was a greater one than that which has "temporarily checked Mr. Gladstone." † In Burma, or India beyond the Ganges, there are some peculiar features about the question not to be met with elsewhere. Allusion has been made to the monastic schools under the Poonghis, reminding us, so far as zeal in the teachers is concerned, somewhat of schools

* See p. 29.
† Speech at opening of the University Hall, Calcutta, March 13th, 1873.

under the parish priesthood of Ireland. About 1865, the Chief Commissioner (Sir A. P. Phayre) had drawn up a famous Memorandum on Vernacular Education for British Burma, and the plan was at length to be given a trial. This drew forth a strong protest from an opponent of the scheme, who thought that it was so thoroughly antagonistic to the principles on which the Buddhist priests live and have their being, that it could not be otherwise than a failure. The champion of the masses in Burma argued thus:—What is a Poonghi? A Poonghi is a man who has given up all intercourse with the outer world, as far as worldly affairs go. His great object in this world is to practice virtue, and to become proficient in the various qualifications as ordained by his religion. The subjects which we would all like to see more largely diffused in the Burman mind are purely worldly—land measuring, arithmetic, history, and geography, &c. That the Burman priests hold school, is true, but to convey to the English mind the nature of the instruction given, we should call them Sunday schools. The boys go to the Kyoungs daily, to be taught their religion only. To get the priests to be secular, you must strike at the root of their religion, which is to renounce everything pertaining to this world. General Fytche, throughout his administration, studied the nature and character of Buddhist schools; but, although he thought very highly of Sir Arthur Phayre's suggestion, that the monastic schools might be made the basis of a national system of education, increased knowledge of them opened the Chief Commissioner's eyes to difficulties which had not appeared to his predecessor—still, difficulties not insurmountable. As we do not wish to weary our readers, we shall give no further details on this matter, but merely remark that there is not a village in Burma which has not a school, and there is, consequently, scarcely a Burman to be found who cannot read, write, and cypher in the vernacular.* In 1866, Mr. Hough had been appointed Director of Public Instruction; there were also four circuit teachers—the whole forming the educational department.

* Compare with Bengal, where, says Mr. Wodrow, Inspector of Schools, only two and a half to three per cent. of the people can read and write their mother tongue.

Previous to this, the present writer had the honour of being appointed by Sir Arthur Phayre, the first Inspector of Civil Schools in Burma. In 1870, upwards of 12,000 youths were being instructed under British superintendence. While Commissioner of Tenasserim, General Fytche believes that he founded the first school in British Burma for the exclusive education of girls; and after taking charge of the province, both the General and Mrs. Fytche endeavoured to promote female education by every means in their power. This was, indeed, a move in the right direction; for, after all, female education is the grand lever for mental progress in Eastern lands.

Progress is the word we should more frequently apply to India and Burma. India is, or at least should be, of no politics. It only acknowledges one law—the law of progress; and, like the science of geology, what in the history of that progress is its "goal to-day," may be its "starting point to-morrow." In looking at Burma, therefore, let us observe this "princess among the provinces" in such a fair light. In British Burma the progress of education is encouraging.

It must have been pleasing to General Fytche, at the close of his administration, to know that the bonds of relation between the British Government and the Court of Ava were drawing the two countries into closer communication than could have been anticipated at any previous period. The King had sent several young Burmese to Europe to be educated, whilst he welcomed any European merchant or official who paid a visit to his capital. Siam —a country whose frontier is conterminous with that of British territory—was also in a satisfactory condition; and we all know that the promising young King, of many names, last year* paid an interesting visit to India. Doubtless it is, in some measure, on account of the tact and wisdom of our "politicals" that the Kings of the East are becoming less shy of us than formerly. We have had embassies from proud Burma and exclusive Japan in London; and this year the Shah of Persia, after saluting the Czar, is to honour us with a visit. For the first time in the world's history the Shah will leave his dominions

* January, 1872.

for Western Europe; and his arrival in the modern Babylon will of course set young people a-reading "Lalla Rookh" (tulip-cheek); fashionable novels will for the time give way to the "Veiled Prophet of Khorassan :"

"That delightful province of the sun,
The first of Persian lands he shines upon;"

and young students, with a "coached" knowledge of Hafiz, will be ready for examination in Persian. The advent of the Persian monarch we should look upon as a most important political, as well as social, event, since, through the Shah's dominions, in case of Russian attack, the approach to India *must* lie.* Next year, perhaps, to crown our foreign policy, we may expect the Golden Foot himself, and then there will only be the Emperor of China† left who has not honoured us, but who, with his young bride, when (with the permission of the Board of Astronomers) he does come, will be heartily welcome! Britannia is extending her hand to all the world.

Returning to Burma. The tribes on the Arakan frontier and region beyond—wild, savage people, of a very primitive type—occupied General Fytche's attention. He found that they practised the system of kidnapping and slavery amongst themselves, which his administration did his best to suppress. Early last year (1872) the Loshai country, lying on the south-western frontier of Bengal, and extending thence to Burma, became the scene of a campaign. The hardy mountain tribes, who for years had made raids on the neighbouring British territory, were punished, surveys were made, and more knowledge of the country gained. At that time the General had for several months left his post of Chief Commissioner; still he must have been deeply interested in the operations, as they tended to solve the questions connected with the administration and political control of these remote regions.

The internal administration of British Burma, from 1867 to 1871, seems to have been a complete success; and it was most gratifying to the administrator to observe

* And *not* by way of the "disputed frontier."—Sir Henry Rawlinson.

† [His Celestial Majesty died at Pekin in January, 1875, at the early age of 19.]

the large increase in the trade of the province, especially in the year 1868-69. This commercial progress was no doubt due in great measure to the new markets which were opened up in Upper Burma, in consequence of the treaty which General Fytche had concluded in 1867.

The defences of the Province were in a most unsatisfactory condition. The great pagoda of Rangoon (stormed by the British in April, 1852), with the arsenal lying to its westward, were neither entrenched nor rendered secure. "Practically, it may be said that, at the commencement of 1867 the province was—setting aside the presence of the troops—in a defenceless state by sea and land;" and on his departure, with the exception of the near completion of the Rangoon pagoda and arsenal defences, General Fytche could not record that the province was in a more advanced state in the matter of defence than it was four years before. But so far as the local administration was concerned, the needful steps had been taken for materially improving the military position of the province, which should never be left without a considerable European force, and, in our humble opinion, which should have its frontiers strengthened by a fortress system similar to that now being adopted in Germany.* With reference to the well-timed despatch of Colonel Jervois, R.E., by the Home Government of India, to look after the defences of Calcutta, Bombay, and Aden Harbours, and the approaching visit of the estimable, but now lamented, Earl of Mayo to Rangoon, when it was thought that the merchants would urge on the Viceroy the importance of our founding an extensive traffic with South-Western China, we wrote :† " The defences and battery at Monkey Point, which commands the Rangoon River, will require the attention of Colonel Jervois. Monkey Point must be put in the strongest state of defence; and to do this an intelligent artillery officer suggests that two more forts should be built, one on the Poozendoung Spit to the left, and another on the Dalla side of the Rangoon River. These with the

* Their system of classifying forts, and the adoption of strategical railways, demand our attention in India as well as in Burma.
† 25th January, 1872.

Monkey Point Fort, would render the passage impracticable, and this is absolutely necessary in case a Russian, American, or even German squadron should one day visit the future Liverpool or Glasgow of Chin-India. At Lord Mayo's request, the Secretary of State for India allowed Colonel Jervois to visit Burma with the Viceroy, from which no doubt good results have been obtained.

General Fytche alludes to the interest felt in British Burma by his Excellency Lord Mayo; and it was a matter of sincere regret to the Chief Commission that His Lordship's visit to Rangoon, which was seriously contemplated in 1870, should have been indefinitely postponed. The General thus missed a grand opportunity; and we much regret that neither of the two administrators of British Burma (Phayre and Fytche) could welcome to its shores the high-souled and chivalrous Viceroy.

It may here be remarked that the Chief Commissioner had an interview with Lord Mayo in Calcutta, early in 1870, and took back with him to Burma his Lordship's reply to a Rangoon address. His Excellency declared the growing prosperity of British Burma to be specially interesting to him, and promised a visit to the province as soon as public duty would permit. Such a visit we ventured to think would greatly tend to facilitate the discussions on the necessities of Burma in the Executive Council of Calcutta. Since Lord Dalhousie's time no Governor-General had visited Pegu. The remarkable words uttered by the Viceroy to the Burmese community at Rangoon, in January, 1872, will not be forgotten so long as Arakan, Pegu, and Tenasserim remain British; for they contain the grand desire of our Indian Government at home and abroad :—" We govern (said Lord Mayo) in order that you should live in peace, prosperity, and happiness; that you should be free to come and go; that whatever you possess should be secure; that all your rights should be preserved, and your national customs and habits respected."

In closing our remarks on a very useful four years' administration we must not omit a name regarding public works particularly alluded to by General Fytche: the name of Fraser will ever be linked with Rangoon and British Burma. After the capture of the citadel, a Colonel

Fraser (Bengal Engineers) became the architect of new Rangoon, which seemed to rise as if by magic from the old; and of late years another Colonel (Alexander) Fraser, of the same corps (now Royal), in addition to other important duties, has completed many lighthouses around the Burmese coast. "The name of Colonel Fraser," writes General Fytche, "must ever be associated with the ease and safety with which a hitherto dangerous coast may now be navigated." British Burma, through the triumphs of science, can now fairly say regarding her coast—

"Steadfast, serene, immovable, the same,
Year after year, through all the silent night
Burns on for evermore that quenchless flame,
Shines on that inextinguishable light." *

Having now given so much of work well done, let us think for a moment how few persons in this country understand the vast trouble and responsibility attending the Chief Commissionership of such a province as British Burma. True, he is monarch of all he surveys; but everyone expects a berth from him, and all sorts of adventurers besiege him for appointments. Even the loafer from Australia, with some got-up story about coming over with horses to Calcutta, prowls about as if he had a right to be employed. On one occasion an adventurer, with an extraordinary quantity of what is vulgarly called "brass," solicited employment on the ground that he could do it "cheap,"† as if he were talking of mending a coat or taking a contract, when, for the important duties required, the man would have been dear at any price! To steer well clear of such annoyances requires some tact; and in all cases, to put the right man into the right place has been an object steadily kept in view in the administration of British Burma.

IN a record of General Fytche's services, drawn up in March, 1873, after alluding to the prospects of the ancient and important trade between Burma and Western China being

* "The Lighthouse," by Longfellow.
† We heard this from Sir Arthur Phayre himself.

re-opened—" for which Great Britain should largely pay when such a consummation would be fraught with so much benefit to British trade at home "—it was remarked (notwithstanding a difference of opinion as to some of the political actions of the late Chief Commissioner) that his labours had "smoothed the way for a new and mighty field of enterprise." The noble Irrawaddy would sooner or later become the Ganges of Burma. And, in conclusion, it was stated :—"Mounted on the pedestal of purpose, wherever good could be effected, it was, often in the face of difficulties, readily accomplished ; and now we look with pride on British Burma, as a province which has improved in a far greater ratio than perhaps any in British India,—the result of such able administrators as Phayre and Fytche."—

General Fytche's seat is Pyrgo Park, Havering-atte-Bower, Essex, and he represents one of the oldest Essex County families—the Fytches of Danbury Place and Woodham Walter, and of Eltham and Mount Maskall, in Kent. He is a Magistrate and Deputy-Lieutenant for Essex, and is also a Magistrate for County Tipperary, where he has also an Estate.* So our esteemed Anglo-Indian has opportunities of doing good accorded to few.

THE ANGLO-INDIAN IN PARLIAMENT.

During the three or four years he has been at home, a steady and most laudable aim of our zealous Anglo-Indian has been to serve in Parliament ; and at the last General Election (early in 1874), General Fytche came forward and contested Rye in the Liberal interest. He was defeated, after a severe struggle, by a small majority. Should he eventually obtain a seat, there is every reason to believe that he will do it full justice. As has been remarked elsewhere, India has no politics, or should cause no political bias in the minds of those acting for the benefit of our splendid dominion. "I do this for the good of India," the useful Anglo-Indian in Parliament must consider his watchwords of action. Taking a broad survey of its people and its customs, and musing over the historic fact that ages before Athens and Rome promoted the arts of civilised life and literature India was the seat of wealth and grandeur, it certainly does seem on such grounds, even to Liberals, that the strictest constitutional principles, or say, the highest state of Conservatism, is the safe mainspring for political action in

* Vide Essex County Hand Book, 1875.

Hindustan—"unchangeable in the midst of change"—so, in the House of Commons, we may yet see gifted Members, Liberals for England and Conservatives for India! Any way, the Anglo-Indian in Parliament should now be a more important personage than ever; and in the coming Session we hope to see him, *in a full House*, debating on the highly-important matters, regarding the country to which he owes his all, which will be sure to come under his consideration! The M.P. for Hindustan has gone! Who is to succeed him? We trust it will be an Anglo-Indian orator, not tedious, but copious, explanatory, and fascinating. There is a grand field in the British Senate now open to Anglo-Indians; and if some clever and experienced men whom among them we could name would only seek a seat in Parliament, an amount of practical good might be accomplished, of which at present we can form no adequate conception.*

A few days after sending the above remarks on the Anglo-Indian in Parliament to press, the writer was much gratified by reading the speech of the Marquis of Salisbury, on the occasion (Saturday, 23rd January) of his being presented with an address by the Manchester Chamber of Commerce. His Lordship's views require no comment; and as they exactly chime in with those of the humble author of these sketches, it may be considered wise to insert some of them at this stage, as affording a noble and liberal guide for Secretaries of State who shall have India confided to their charge in generations yet unborn.

PARTY IN THE GOVERNMENT OF INDIA.

At the commencement of his speech Lord Salisbury remarked :—" You have referred to the recent change of government. Indian politics, I am happy to say, are different from all other politics—in this, that we know no distinction of party. Change of government does not of itself mean a change of policy. Opposition on other matters does not mean opposition on Indian subjects. I was well satisfied with the policy of the Duke of Argyll during the time that I was in opposition. I never expressed any dissatisfaction with, and am glad to be able to follow it now that I have acceded to office (applause). I observe that in some parts of the country it is now a subject of political comment—in fact, most political speeches seem to take that for their basis—that there is no substantial difference between the policy of the present government and the last, and

* Written in January, 1875.

political controversy is very much becoming a controversy not as to the nature but as to the copyright of measures that are proposed (laughter). Well, gentlemen, this is not a political assembly, and therefore I shall not say what I might in another place have to say on the subject of the copyright of measures that are proposed; but what is the taunt with respect to other parts of English policy is our object and aim with respect to Indian policy, and our most earnest desire is that (to borrow a figure from a matter which has been a good deal in controversy in India) there will never be any break of gauge observed in the government of India—(applause)—and, in doing so, I must do justice, in passing, to my predecessor."

SIR ARTHUR PHAYRE, K.C.S.I.,

THE NEW GOVERNOR OF MAURITIUS.*

"A CLASS of public servants which has never been equalled upon earth."—Such was the eulogy bestowed by a high authority on the many illustrious men produced under the system of the old East India Company. And, certainly, when we look at their actions, the difficulties they had to encounter, and the vastness of the splendid dominion in which they laboured, the praise seems not undeserved. On the present occasion we desire to say a few words regarding the services of one whom Lord Carnarvon has just appointed to the Governorship of Mauritius,—" another example," it has been well observed, " of the system under which a new career is opened to those public servants who have attained a high Indian reputation; and we trust that Sir Arthur Phayre will prove as successful in Mauritius as Sir John Peter Grant has been in Jamaica."

Sir Arthur became an ensign in the Bengal army on the 13th August, 1828, a lieutenant in 1835, a captain in 1843, major in 1854, and lieutenant-colonel on the 22nd January, 1859. He was appointed to the Bengal Staff Corps in February, 1861, and five years later held the rank of colonel. In August, 1870, he became a majorgeneral, which military rank he now holds, with the honourable adjuncts of C.B. and K.C.S.I., after an arduous service of forty years in the East.

From the first he was essentially a political officer, for, as in the cases of Malcolm and of Munro, the duties of drill and discipline were second in his mind to the more noble work of settling the affairs of kingdoms. It was during the second Burmese War, 1852-53, after that " brilliant feat of arms," the capture of Rangoon,† and when the important

* Written in September, 1874. † April 14, 1852.

towns of Bassein, Prome, and Pegu had fallen into our hands, while the energy of the great Pro-consul, Lord Dalhousie, on behalf of his favourite annexation, had reached its *acme*, that Captain Phayre was looked upon as the only man fitted to be the future administrator of the conquered kingdom. Pegu, released from the tyranny of the Golden Foot, was, under the Bengal captain, soon to behold Justice beginning to breathe, and civilisation struggling to be born. It was thought that the administrative talents of Captain Phayre—who had been "one of the chief means of turning the swamps of Arakan into the granary of the Bay, and whose forte lies in making a little kingdom a great one"—would soon render Pegu a most important and valuable British possession. About the middle of January, 1853, the new Commissioner arrived at Rangoon with the Governor-General's proclamation annexing Pegu to the British territories in the East. The reading of this document at the stronghold of Gautama we have no doubt Sir Arthur considers not the least important action in his busy life; while hardly less remarkable was another, when, a year or two after, in the marble hall of Government House, Calcutta, Major Phayre, as interpreter, by desire, and in the presence of the Governor-General, announced to the Burmese Envoys—who had come by command of the king of Ava to seek restitution of the whole of the captured provinces—that "AS LONG AS THE SUN SHINES IN THE HEAVENS, THE BRITISH FLAG SHALL WAVE OVER THOSE POSSESSIONS!"—a capital lesson for short-sighted political sentimentalists who talk of giving up any of the conquests of Great Britain."*

When Sir Arthur Phayre had finished his work in Pegu, he was (1862) appointed the first Chief Commissioner of British Burma, *i.e.*, Pegu, Arakan, and Tenasserim. No better representative of his Excellency the Viceroy, could have been appointed; and in March, 1867, when he

* [Nearly the last words uttered by the writer of this sketch to Sir Arthur, in St. James' Square, on the eve of his departure for Mauritius, were on the above subject. The decided speech of Lord Dalhousie will afford to many a melancholy reminiscence of what Lord Mayo (nearly twenty years later) told the Burmese at Rangoon in January, 1872. In his own admirable manner, he said that Arakan, Pegu, and Tenasserim were British, "AND BRITISH THEY WILL REMAIN FOR MANY GENERATIONS OF MEN!"]

gave up his high post to General Albert Fytche, Pegu might have been looked upon as possessing a model administration. Within a period of fifteen years (from 1853), British Burma had attained a prosperity which could be favourably compared with that of any province in India; and in the ten years, from 1855-56 to 1864-65, the revenue was doubled. At the same time, the population—which had been essentially reduced through the devastating wars which for centuries had desolated the entire region from Chittagong to Siam—increased from 1,252,555 to 2,196,180. The Official Report on the administration for 1866-67 does Sir Arthur full justice. The details of his labours are most carefully noticed. At first, writes one of his numerous admirers, "it seemed to announce what we hoped was only a visit to Europe for the recovery of his health. But it was really his retirement from British Burma." In the Report the following remarkable passage occurs—enumerating the qualities so essential for every good ruler or governor: "Whether at the commencement of his career as a district officer, or later when organising a new administration, or lastly as the head of the entire province, Sir Arthur Phayre has always been prominently distinguished by his mastery of details, his exceeding personal devotion to his duties, and his own sympathy with the people of the country which he ruled." His intimate knowledge of the Burmese language, and scholarly acquaintance with the dialects of the races in, and contiguous to, British Burma, and his close study of their history and characteristics, "rendered him an authority on the philology and ethnology of the Indo-Chinese nations" —perhaps, we venture to add, the soundest that England can boast. We have no doubt whatever that the learned and distinguished heads of the Royal Asiatic and Geographical Societies fully appreciate the few Oriental researches Sir Arthur has been enabled to make. Mr. Coryton, in a letter to the Liverpool Chamber of Commerce, takes care not to omit another fine passage of the Report above mentioned, disclosing qualities which will recommend the new Governor to the people of Mauritius :—" His constant accessibility and courteousness to the people of the country, whatever their position, gained for him their confidence and respect to an unusual extent. He was careful of the rights of Government, but zealous and watchful over the interests of the native population. His great administrative capacity has been well shown by the rapid and progressive prosperity of the province, especially in the manner in which it has grown up under his direct guidance and control." Those who know Sir Arthur Phayre and his works well will endorse every word of this praise; and we may add that in the all-important matter of education there could not be a more zealous advocate for the diffusion of its blessings. For this alone he will ever be remembered by the people of Pegu, to whom he strove to give a national system of education founded on the best principles; while, for his works among them in general, Peguers, Burmese, and Karens (Deists, chiefly inhabiting the hills), for many generations to come, will, as in the case of the "Munro Sahib" in Southern, and in that of "Jan Malcolm Sahib" in Central India, make it apparent to the inquisitive traveller in a large portion of Chin-India that whoever mentioned the great Chief Commissioner—as Johnson said when extolling one of the poets—"mentioned him with honour."

In Sir Arthur's opinion, the chief essential for extending the commerce of Chin-India, and that of Great Britain and India with Western China, is *exploration;* and as the British Chambers of Commerce are now much interested in the subject, it may not be out of place to say here, what has been said elsewhere, that, in 1862, orders were communicated by the Government of India to Sir Arthur Phayre, when negociating a treaty with the King of Burma, "to include in it provisions for facilitating the commerce of British merchants with Yun-nan." He still considers that our relations with the Golden Foot threw, and still throw, considerable difficulties in the way; and no one understands the keen trader and monopolising monarch so well as the ruler who is now about to embark on a new scene of action. In a few years, perhaps, the Chinese will have learnt to respect the rights of nations; and it is not improbable that before the expiration of Sir Arthur's new Governorship, through the strong influence of Burma, Siam, and England, "an artificial highway"

will have opened up British trade with the south-western provinces of China. *
The General expected to leave for Mauritius by the last steamer in October. [He left England on the 20th October, 1874, having previously been honoured with a farewell interview by the Marquis of Salisbury at the India Office ; and we have every reason to believe that the great merits of the distinguished Anglo-Indian are fully appreciated by the present Secretary of State.] It is not enough to say that the appointment is an honour to the Indian Army ; many of us see in the laudable action of the Colonial Secretary that the clever and experienced Anglo-Indian " is no longer to be left out in the cold." It is not at all likely that the statesman who ruled so well in Chin-India will make only a second-rate Governor of such an important possession as the Isle so famed in history and romance; and if Mauritius, under Sir Arthur Phayre, does not exactly—as Grattan said of Ireland when boasting of having given her Free Trade—" rise from the sea and get nearer to the sun," we may still venture to predict many great improvements therein. The political school in which Sir Arthur rose to eminence is probably one of the severest in the world. His knowledge of the cunning and duplicity of the Mongol races, kings, and chiefs, with whom he has had every variety of dealing, preventing any chance of imposition on the part of those in whose interests he laboured, will never be without value ; while his rare appreciation of the position and wants of the British merchant abroad, and the desire he ever evinced in Chin-India to be courteous to all, will be sure to gain him troops of friends. [Before the new Governor's departure, he received a deputation from the Aborigines Protection Society. In addition to the state of the coolies, Sir Arthur will, no doubt, bring his practical mind to bear on the sanitary condition of the lower classes of the community and time-expired emigrants, " with a view to the prevalence of epidemic fever and cholera being prevented" from effecting the destruction of life hitherto, at intervals, experienced.]

* [See Appendix v.—" Action in Eastern Asia." A telegram from Rangoon, December 12th, 1874, announced that the Western Chinese Expedition had started under Colonel Browne.]

THE BURMA RACE.*

(A CRITICAL SKETCH.)

"The proper study of mankind is man."—POPE.

[To Oriental students the subjoined sketch, it is presumed, will be of interest. It is founded on one of Sir Arthur Phayre's most learned contributions to Asiatic research; which, apart from the desire of knowledge, evinced the laudable and statesmanlike wish to know all about the people he was called upon to govern.]

THE idea of the Chief Commissioner finding time, amid so much work of a constant attention-requiring, sometimes dry, and frequently unpleasant, nature, to write on the history of the Burma race, is another of the proofs occasionally presented to the world of the Anglo-Saxon's mental energy in lands where the love of deep study among us is not conspicuous;—the chief reason for which, perhaps, being that we are "exotics" or "fish out of water." From time to time, however, in literature and in science, men have appeared in the East who reflect the highest credit on their country; and whose writings and researches will be dear to the memory of the Oriental student till time shall be no more. England may be proud of having had not a few distinguished literary and scientific scholars in India. Colonels Sykes, Young, Boileau, and Davidson; also Captains Macnaghten, Richardson, and Newbold—the first and last in Oriental research and statistics, and the others in general literature—are the chief military names among India's periodical writers. Colonel or General Vans Kennedy, of the Bombay army, in days long gone by, was also one of the greatest of our Oriental scholars and writers.

Burma is now beginning a new life. The *Conquest of Pegu* has been the means of this second birth; and no better manner of showing the world that we do not only conquer a

* "On the History of the Burma Race." By Lieutenant-Colonel A. P. Phayre, C.B., Chief Commissioner of British Burma. (Contributed to the "Journal of the Asiatic Society.") The critical sketch, of which only a portion is here given, was written in 1872, and originally appeared in "Papers on Burma."

country but endeavour to gain a knowledge of its people, could have been adopted, than that which is exhibited by Colonel Phayre in the present pamphlet.

We have before alluded, while writing of Lord Dalhousie,* to what Lord Macaulay says of Warren Hastings, "the Conqueror in a deadly grapple, sitting down, with characteristic self-possession, to inform Dr. Johnson in a letter about Sir W. Jones' Persian Grammar, and the history, traditions, arts, and natural productions of India." And, although Pegu has for some years back been far from a settlement in commotion, still, in like manner, might we suppose the Chief Commissioner of this comparatively new conquest, amid many cares and anxieties, while a peaceful but rather eccentric King was watching the progress of trade among the British in Chin-India, and, as some said, amusing himself by erecting stockades and taking them down again,† and even turning an eye to the improved manufacture of ordnance in England—the Viceroy's Agent, finding a few hours to spare, to gratify his love of study and research, by writing a paper on the history of the Burma Race!

Some years ago, Colonel Phayre was presented by the "King of Burma" (the letter *h* is omitted in what is the most correct spelling of the word) with a complete copy of the carefully preserved "Chronicles of the Kings" of this interesting land, which are styled *Maha Radza Weng*. These chronicles appear to have been compiled under the direction of His Majesty, himself a man of learning and research. Of this "national work," writes the author of the paper under notice,—"All that part of the history which refers to cosmogony and the dynasties of Kings in India, is derived from Pali books, and has no more real connexion with Burmese history than the Hebrew annals have with British history." (Page 1.)

The learned Dr. Mason‡ (who is bringing out a grammar of

---

* "Pegu," p. 400.

† These stockades "in esse" were probably the acts of the "Fighting Prince," and not the King's. [Sending embassies about the world appears to be the new political game on the part of His Majesty. In December, 1874, we read of an embassy from Burma about to visit the Viceroy, the object being unknown.]

‡ [This eminent man has since gone to his rest. He was among the chief of those distinguished Americans who have done so much for the land of the Golden Foot; he was a missionary in the highest sense of the word, and all who take an interest in Chin-India must be acquainted with his famous book on "The Fauna, Flora, and Minerals of Burma."]

the Pali language) writes regarding the Pali, that it is the sacred language of 300,000,000 Buddhists. In it are written the most ancient inscriptions found in India, and the Vernaculars of all Buddhist nations abound in Pali terms and phrases. . . . . "The Burmese books have as many Pali words in them as the English have Latin."

This will at once account for the many discrepancies found by the author of the paper on the history of the Burma Race, whose object is simply to make "an outline of the main facts, yet omitting nothing which is necessary to be known to understand the history of the Burmese race as written by themselves." First, we have the self-development of the world, and the appearance of man therein—the system of cosmogony, with the Buddhist philosophy and religion, being from India. The Burmese Kings, we are told, profess to trace their descent "from the Buddhist Kings of *Kappilawot* of the *Sakya* tribe, to which race *Gautama Budha* belonged."

In the Royal history there is the Buddhist account of the first formation of human society—the election of a King, and the grant to him of a share of the produce of the soil; such legends, according to Colonel Phayre, constituting "to this day the foundation of the authority, temporal and spiritual, of the Burmese Kings."

Those old facts being "for ever present to the minds" of the Burmese, make them interesting in a political, as well as in a historical point of view; for with them, as a matter of course, are wrapped up certain views of the British law of progress at the present day, while Christianity is beginning to assert her triumphal reign on the ruins of old kingdoms fallen to pieces.

The student of Hindu mythology will derive some pleasure from analogy in his study of this paper on the Burma Race. After an inexplicable chaos, the present earth emerged from a deluge.* The subsiding water left a delicious substance, which became spread over the earth. Gautama's throne first appeared above the water. At the same time the occupants of the "heavenly regions," called *Brahma*, had accomplished their destinies. Changing their state, they "became beings with corporeal frames, but without sex." The men arrive at "Paradise Lost," in Chin-India.

"From eating of the ambrosia, the light of the bodies of

---

* For similar curious information, relating to the Karens in particular, see Appendix to "Pegu," a Narrative, &c., p. 500.

these beings gradually declined, and because of the darkness they became sore afraid." LIGHT—what a world of meaning lies in that single word ! And well did Longinus consider the perfection of the sublime reached by the Divine command at the beginning of all things, *Sit Lux, et Lux Fuit!* Yes—" Let there be light : and there was light,"* whether as applied to creation or to fallen humanity, will be found, perhaps, to have sunk more into the minds of the intelligent or thoughtful among heathen nations than any other remark in the literature of any people or race. For, what dreadful ideas do we evolve from darkness! Take light away from the world, and we may as well take life. And it was a full sense of the truth of this remark which caused the mighty but erring genius of Lord Byron to pen that "grand and gloomy sketch† of the supposed consequences of the final extinction of the sun and the heavenly bodies, the very conception of which," says the father of modern criticism (Lord Jeffrey), " is terrible above all conception of known calamity."

From the " beings with corporeal frames," just alluded to, we are informed in a *note* that the people called by Europeans *Burmas*, Burmans, or *Burmese* take their name. In the Burmese language, " the name is written *Mran-má* or Mram-ma, and is generally pronounced by themselves *Ba-má*." Talking of Ava, we find a geographical writer‡ of twenty years back remarking :—" By Europeans the country is generally called Ava, from the common name of the capital ; but, by the natives themselves, it is named Burma, which is a corruption of *Mrumma*, its original appellation."

The truth of this latter remark would appear to be corroborated by the more recent research of Colonel Phayre, by whom we are now referred to the etymology of the word *Myan-ma* or Mran-má. Alluding to a paper by Mr. B. H. Hodgson, published in the Journal of the Asiatic Society, No. 1, of 1853, it is found that the author concludes that the term Burma or Burmese, " which is the Europeanised form of the name by which that people call themselves, can be traced to the native name for man. This, however, is open to some doubt ; but Mr. Hodgson's general conclusion that the languages of the Himálálayan, Indo-Chinese, and Thibetan tribes are of one family is fully justified."

The name, then, by which the Burmans are known to Euro-

* Genesis, c. 1, v. 5.
† " Darkness."—Byron's Works, in one vol., p. 564.   ‡ Symonds.

peans, or as the Burmese call themselves, is written *Mran-ma*, and sometimes *Mram-ma*, and is pronounced Ba-má. The Arakanese call themselves Ma-ra-ma, which is "a variation of the same word."

Turning from the roots *mi* and *ma* in the Burmese language, we at length arrive at a most interesting conclusion by the author of the present paper :—" I cannot say how the Chinese got the word, but it is possible that *Mien* was the original name of the race, and contains the root meaning man." However that may be, the word in this or any similar sense is now entirely lost among the Burmese, excepting as noted in the term for woman (*Miên-ma* or *Mim-ma*), and it may be in *Mru* (race). "It does not appear," the author remarks, "as the name of any of the tribes with which the Burmese might be supposed to be immediately connected." On an assembly of the world's first inhabitants, we get at the origin of kings and high priests :— "An excellent man, full of glory and authority, the embryo of of our *Gautama Phra*, being entreated to save them, was elected king, and was called *Maha-tha-ma-dà*. In verse, it is sung that he was of pure nature, of exalted authority, and of the race of the sun. The Burmese "history" then informs us that, like a second sun, this Manoo dispelled darkness or ignorance. To the name of this early reformer, Colonel Phayre appends some interesting information :—" The word appears to mean generally lawgiver or king. The word is Indian not Burman ;" simply, we presume, the far-famed Menu, the Indian lawgiver. From the following may be deduced an argument greatly in favour of the purity and antiquity of Buddhism. Next to the ruler came men of wisdom ; "they were called *Brahmans*. Others tilled the ground and traded ; they were called wealthy men and merchants. The rest being poor persons in humble employments were called *Soodras*, or poor people. Such were the four classes of men." Among them, it is remarked, will be observed that the ruling power is placed first according to the Buddhist system. The Brahmans appear as "literati and ascetics."

We now turn to when the embryo of *Gautama Phra*, a wealthy *Kap-pi-la Brahman*, having abandoned his house, had become a hermit in the Himalaya jungles or mountains. When we are told that eighty-four thousand kings reigned in *Kap-pi-la*, the native country of Gautama, in "distant after times," it is needless to inquire how princes came, or how time elapsed. But "Princes" did come to the hermit's place of secretion (whether a teak or a saulwood forest it is not known). They came to the place "in search of a site for a city." The hermit foresaw, with admirable sagacity, "that a city built there, would, in after time, be of great fame in *Dzam-bu-dee-pa*, the world of man, and advised them to build their city there and to call it *Kap-pi-la-wot*." This, from a note, we learn, appears to signify "the Kap-pi-la Brahman's place of religious duty." Then the Princes consulted together saying, "There are with us no king's daughters of our own race, nor are there any king's sons for our sisters ; if marriages are made with other races the children become impure ; in order to preserve our race, let us put aside our eldest sister as a mother, and we four marry our four younger sisters?" It was done ; and from that day the race became known as the *Tha-kya-tha-kee* race of *Kap-pi-la-wot*. Regarding the elder sister, Colonel Phayre remarks:—"In Burma to this day the king's eldest daughter is not given in marriage, but remains unmarried, at least during the life of her parents."—(P. 4).

Regarding the word Phrá loung (*i.e.*, the embryo Phrá, a term for Gautama Budha) the Chief Commissioner says, "The *Phrá*, now adapted into the Burmese language is, according to Professor Wilson, a corruption of the Sanscrit *Prabhu*, Lord or Master. This appears to be the most probable origin of the word. It certainly is not a pure Burmese word. The orthography of it in ancient stone inscriptions at Pughân is Bu-rhá and Pú-rhá. The Burmese have used the original much as European nations have the Pali word Da-go-ba. The modern word is written *Phu-rá*."

After a terrific enumeration of sons and daughters of kings, we arrive at *De-wa-dat.* "This was the great opponent of Budha Gautama. They were first cousins by birth, and *Gautama* had married *Dewa-dat's sister.*" As the Kings of Burma claim to be descended from the *Tha-kya* race of *Kap-pi-la-wot* to which Gautama belonged, the inter-marriages of that tribe are carefully detailed in the history.

Having brought down the narrative of events to the death of *Budha Gautama*, the first volume of the work proceeds to give an account of the geography of the world of *Dzam-boo-dee-pa*, where the Buddhist Kings reigned. We now come to confusion worse confounded. And, truly, it may be styled, in the words of Colonel Phayre, a "mythological geography." *Dzam-boo-dee-pa* frequently represents "India prominently, and the world remotely."—(P. 7).

As regards the countries of India—all cited by Colonel Phayre—it is remarked, "There appears to be some confusion, resulting apparently from some states having in the course of time subdued others, and from the historian (of the *Maha Ruza Weng*) not knowing that some small states appear sometimes as members of a confederacy in an exensive country called by one general name; and at other times are lost in the establishment of a monarchy." The first volume of the history concludes with maxims for kings and people.

Into Colonel Phayre's critical analysis of the second volume of the "History" we do not propose to enter at any length. Suffice it to say, that a great variety of interesting information is brought forward, from which much that throws light on the Burmese race may be gleaned. The brochure concludes with some most valuable "observations," from which we learn that the physiognomy and language of the Burmese people, as well as those of the adjoining tribes, proclaim them all to belong to the same family of nations as the tribes of Thibet and the Eastern Himalaya. As to whence they came, and how they arrived in Burma, Colonel Phayre writes:—" The theory of Prichard in his Natural History of Man on this subject is probable, is supported by existing facts, and accords with the physical geography of the regions north of the countries now occupied by the Indo-Chinese races." It is thought reasonable to conclude that tribes leaving the south-eastern margin of the great plateau of Central Asia, early in the existence of the human race, " would naturally follow the downward course of streams and rivers." And, among the earlier emigrants from that part of Asia towards the south, " as far as we can now discover, were the ancestors of the present *Mon* or *Talaing* people, the aborigines, so to speak, of Pegu." The Karens also, it is thought, left their ancient dwelling-place at an early period. Uninfluenced by Buddhism, and their language unwritten till the year 1830 A.D., their traditions of their own origin, or at least of the route by which they arrived at their present seats, "are therefore more trustworthy than those of the Burmese or of the Talaings are, regarding themselves." Regarding the physiognomy of the Karens, the Chief Commissioner observes, " I must uphold that their national physiognomy is essentially Indo-Chinese, and their speech connects them with the same family." Again, he says :—" In every Indo-Chinese tribe occasional exceptions to the general flat physiognomy are met with; these are almost always among the men. The women have more frequently the true type of Mongolian or Bhotiya face."

It is then presumed that such tribes as the " Burmese, the Karens, and the Mon, would readily find their way from Central Asia by the courses of the rivers Salween and Menam towards the south. Some would be led westerly, and so gain the valley of the Irrawaddy, in the upper course of that river." Regarding some Buddhist writings preserved in Ceylon, we arrive at the sonorous name of *Thoo-wan-na-bhoomee*. "By that name, no doubt, is meant the country inhabited by the Mon or Talaing race, and their chief city then was on the site of the present *Tha-Tung* lying between the mouths of the Salween and Sittang rivers. . . . That gold was anciently found in that vicinity is testified from the Burmese name of Shwegyeen (Shoéghyne), literally 'gold washing,' now borne by a town on the Sittang ; and gold is still found there, though probably in diminished quantity to what it was anciently. This, no doubt, was the origin of the name 'Aurea regio,' of Ptolemy." Many circumstances seem to show that the *Mon* or Talaing race received Buddhism before the Burmese did. It is difficult to say when the conjectures about Fo—"the son of a prince of India"—the *Samana Kautama of Pegu*, the *Samana Codium of Siam*, and the Foé or Xaca of China and Japan, *all* being the same person,*—will end ; or if they ever end at all, whether the vast research expended on them will enlighten us much regarding the early history of this or that race. If this Fo were the Hindu Vishnu in one of his pretended incarnations, then, doubtless, much in Burmese history, as well as in that of *Thoo-wan-na-bhoomee*, the country inhabited by the Mon or Talaing race, is accounted for. "Although the conversion," writes Colonel Phayre, "of the people of Suvanna Bhumi was planned by people in Gangetic India, it is not probable that so essential a sea-hating people had their own ships to convey the missionaries across the Bay of Bengal. Then, how did they arrive at their destination ?" Regarding the mission to *Suvanna Bhumi*, the writer also remarks :—" It is probable that the people of the Coromandel Coast already had settlements on the Arakanese and Talaing Coasts as places of trade, and the Buhists of Gangetic India would, in all probability, resort to some of the ports on the east coast of the continent, and not far from the head of the Bay of Bengal. At that time it is probable that the people of Telingana carried on commerce with *Suvanna Bhumi*, and the Budhist missionaries would embark in their ships." There is said to have been a Hindu Colony at Moulmein, the site of which was called Ramupoora. Until late years, the Burmese mixed up English and all Europeans with

* CRAUFORD.—See also the author's work on "The Temple of Jagannáth," p. 12.

the natives of India in the one common appellation of *Kulá*, or western foreigners; and it is only since the war of 1825-26, with the British, "that they have learnt to distinguish between the more prominent of the nations lying west of them. But the fact still remains that the Burmese received religion and letters from India."

It now requires a good knowledge of the Burmese language to follow Colonel Phayre. "It does not appear that the Burmese people received their religion and letters through the medium of their cousins, the Arakanese, for that people refer to the eastward as their own source of both. The passage of Indian Budhist missionaries, therefore, from Gangetic India through Bengal and Munnipore to Burma, is a probable event, but it took place much later than has been represented." The Chief Commissioner concludes his valuable paper with allusion to certain customs which "are tenaciously adhered to by the Royal Family of Burma, who consider themselves as ethnologically and religiously the descendants of the Budhist Kings of Kap-pi-la-wot." We shall now conclude this brief and imperfect sketch by referring the reader to Colonel Phayre's valuable paper itself for further information on the Burma race, and by stating from such good authority :—In the matter of the race of the Burmese, they are undoubtedly what is now called Turanian, or by Cuvier and the old authors, *Mongolian*.* The notion of the descent of the Royal Family from Indian Rajas is regarded as incorrect. But it is now admitted that the Rajpoot tribes of India are *Turanian* also, the Brahmans being Aryan, or, as formerly called, Caucasian.

The Overland Mail, of 26th of February, 1870, from Bombay, announced the important news that Sir Arthur Phayre, who had been making antiquarian researches in the north of India, was expected to produce "an exhaustive work on Budhism." In such an event, we may fully expect a line of light to clear up what is still one of the great Asian mysteries.—[As even a Governor and Commander-in-Chief of Mauritius may require an occasional holiday, it is not improbable that some such work from Sir Arthur's pen may yet afford food for discussion by eminent Orientalists.—Nov. 1874.]

* In the "Lectures on the Science of Language," by Professor Max Müller, the Professor says, regarding the question, Whether or not originally Tatar was a name of the Mongolic races :—"Originally 'Tatar' was a name of the Mongolic races. The Mongolic class, in fact, has the greatest claim to the name of 'Tataric.' The recollection of their non-Tataric— *i.e.* non-Mongolic—origin remains among the so-called Tatars of Kasan and Astrachan."

SIR JOHN KAYE, K.C.S.I.

" Etinim talis est vir, ut nulla res tanta sit ac tam difficilis, quam ille non et consilio regere et integritate tueri et virtute conficere possit."—CICERO: " Oratio pro lege Manilia," cap. xx.*

THE retirement† of Sir John Kaye from the India Office, after a long and distinguished period of service, is an important event, on account of the intrinsic merits and vast experience of the late political chief, in whom Conciliation ever found a steady friend, and Annexation a determined foe. Doubtless, the young Bengal Artilleryman, when he arrived in India, in 1833, little contemplated either the transfer of the glorious old Company's government to the Crown, or that (after being for nearly twenty years Secretary in the Political and Secret Department of the East India House and India Office) he should one day retire with so much honour, gained after various political and literary work well and carefully done. But to say that an active mind like Sir John's could be at rest, would be to utter a preposterous fallacy. There is no rest on earth for such men. He, and some of the others whom we have so imperfectly sketched in these pages, remind one of the old Roman alluded to by Sir Walter Scott as anxious to adjust his mantle ere he fell, but who—as the Scottish Shakspeare makes John Philip Kemble say, on his retirement from the stage—like the

> ——— "worn war-horse at the trumpet's sound,
> Erects his mane, and neighs, and paws the ground,—
> Disdains the ease his generous lord assigns,
> And longs to rush on the embattled lines !"

---

* " In truth he is such a man, that no affair can be so great or so arduous, which he cannot direct by his wisdom, maintain by his integrity, and accomplish by his valour."

† " The retirement of Sir John Kaye from his Secretaryship at the India Office is formally announced."—*The Week's News*, October 24th, 1874.

Yes—we may easily imagine, on a war-note sounding from Afghanistan or Central Asia, or in the event of another Mutiny (which God forbid!) the historian, rising even from a sick bed—the old fire returning to the fading eye—eager to seize his pen again!

"Rest!" says an eloquent divine,* "what have we to do with that?" Earth for work, heaven for wages; and so must it ever be with men of energy and intellect who are desirous of leaving "footprints on the sands of time."

We had written thus far, when a friend put Sir John Kaye's "Essays of an Optimist" (of which we had heard, but had not seen before) into our hands. There we found his views on "Rest," including those concerning "Superannuation," and the "Battle with Time;" which we deemed well worthy of attention. In his essay "Of Life," Lord Clarendon advises us to follow the wise rule laid down by an old philosopher—*pretium tempori ponere, diem æstimare;* to consider that "every hour is worth at least a good thought, a good wish, a good endeavour; that it is the talent we are trusted with to use, employ, and to improve." Sir John has not hidden this talent in the dark, "that the world cannot see any fruit of it;" and it is only a mind conscious of much valuable time well employed that could have produced the pleasing essay on "Rest." He thinks a well-timed retirement a most prudent action. "The time must come," he says, "when younger men will do our work better, and, if we remain still at the grindstone, we shall be little more than cumberers of the earth. Nay, we may be something worse—miserable spectacles of decay, not even stately ruins. . . . . Let us take our pensions thankfully in good time; let us be content to be superannuated; let us go cheerfully into retirement before people say that we ought to be kicked into it." But then, he afterwards says beautifully—"It is only through the gates of death that we can grope our way to the fulness of repose." Sir John's striking lines on the "Battle with Time," probably written "on the eve of a crisis," which fortunately "never came after all," and which might be applied to himself, follow the remark that "it

* Dr. Guthrie.

is not good to be stricken down in the midst of the great battle :"—

> "His life was one grand battle with old Time.
> From morn to noon, from noon to weary night,
> Ever he fought as only strong men fight;
> And so he passed out of his golden prime
> Into grim hoary manhood; and he knew
> No rest from that great conflict till he grew
> Feeble and old, ere years could make him so.
> Then on a bed of pain he laid his head,
> As one sore spent with labour and with woe ;
> 'Rest comes at last; I thank Thee, God,' he said,
> Death came : upon his brow laid chilly hands,
> And whispered ' Vanquished !' But he gasped out ' No,
> I am the victor now ; for unto lands
> Where Time's dark shadow cannot fall, I go.' "

Then, reminding us that "death is a fearful thing," and of the immortal lines which Shakspeare puts into the mouth of Claudio,* commencing—

> "Ay, but to die, and go we know not where,"

the subject of our sketch asks—"Ay, but whither ? " and continues :—" It is ill thus to die with the harness on one's back and the battle-axe in one's hand. Better to lay them down ere the dark shadow falls ; and, resting as best we may upon earth, pass away into the Perfect Rest." †

---

* "Measure for Measure."

† "The Essays of an Optimist." By John William Kaye, F.R.S., Author of " History of the War in Afghanistan," " Life of Lord Metcalfe," " History of the Sepoy War," &c., 1870 (*pp.* 285-6-7). We cannot leave such a pleasant volume of essays—written with a smack of the graceful style and humour of Addison, and of the common sense of pious Jeremy Taylor—without turning to one, "The Wrong Side of the Stuff," in a note to which Sir John mentions one day, on passing to office, having seen a Commissionaire, hard by the great palace of Westminster :—"As I neared him, I saw another old soldier approach him—an older soldier, and of a higher rank, with bronzed cheek, and white moustache, and erect carriage, and a noble presence ; one whom there was no mistaking, though dressed in the common garb of an English gentleman. When he saw the medals on the Commissionaire's breast, his face brightened up, and he stopped before the man in green, and, with a pleasant word or two, took up the medals, one after another, in his one hand, and then I saw that he had an empty sleeve. And when I looked at the Commissionaire, I saw that he also had an empty sleeve. And I wished I had been an artist to paint that touching scene." Compare the " older soldier " with a dear departed Anglo-Indian General Officer sketched in these pages !

Something is said in the sketch of Anglo-Indian Periodical Literature about Sir John Kaye, and a portion of his writings, so that it may now be sufficient to add, that the grand secret of Sir John's success in Anglo-Indian literature—particularly in his histories and biographies—lies in the admirable execution of the work, rather than in the interest attached by the British public to the subject. People who want to know about the War in Afghanistan, or Sir John Malcolm, or Lord Metcalfe, go at once to *the* History and Biographies *par excellence;* or, about the Mutiny, to the History of the Sepoy War. Beyond a doubt, then, during such a lamentable state of indifference to Indian affairs—such an obstinate want of British—and even in some respects Anglo-Indian—interest in an Empire which tends to make England glorious, the treatment of the matter is of the last importance; and on this the success of any book on India that is to live will always greatly depend. You have first to conquer prejudice, and then, if you can, become fascinating. Sir John Kaye, throughout his literary career, has been eminently successful in both these particulars. Such remarks may excuse the introduction here of a reminiscence of that mighty wielder of the English tongue—Lord Macaulay. It was in the month of June, 1850, while Macaulay lived in the Albany, writing his " History of England," that the writer of these pages having, after some labour and historical research, arrived in London with a manuscript work on " The French in India," submitted the question to the great historian and essayist, Whether he thought the public would care about such a work at such a time? The reply was prompt, exhibiting the kindness of Macaulay to young authors. (He had not long before gracefully acknowledged a copy of " Orissa."*) Coming from, perhaps, the most brilliant writer of modern times—one of the chiefs of Modern Criticism—his remarks may be given :—" It seems to me that the fate of such a volume as you describe must depend entirely on the execution. There is not, I apprehend, much curiosity on the subject of the French in India. But eloquence and vivacity will

---

* A volume of local, archæological, and other critical sketches, reprinted chiefly from the *Calcutta Review*. (London, 1850.)

make any subject attractive. My own pursuits do not leave me time to give to manuscripts that attentive perusal, without which advice is a mere mockery." We may fairly claim Lord Macaulay as a very distinguished Anglo-Indian,* one of whom it is well known that, from the date of his first appearance in the *Edinburgh*, as a reviewer of Milton (August, 1825), down to the day of his death (December, 28th, 1859), his literary career was a grand continual success.

Few writers can tell an anecdote so well as Sir John Kaye, and it cannot be denied that this is a most excellent gift in an author who would be entertaining. While lecturing in Central India, on Periodical Literature, we quoted an anecdote which gave great amusement, one of the famous Sir John Malcolm, when a boy, appearing before the mighty Court of Directors in London, to present himself as a cadet, previous to obtaining their consent to proceed to India:—"So mere a child was he (says Mr. Kaye), that on the morning of his departure, when the old nurse was combing his hair, she said to him, 'Now, Jock, my mon, be sure when ye are awa', ye kaim your head and keep ye'er face clean ; if ye dinna, ye'll just be sent haim again.' 'Tut, woman,' was the answer, 'ye'ere aye sae feared, ye'll see if I were awa amang strangers, I'll just do weel aneugh.'" And Jock did "weel aneugh" amang strangers. Towards the end of 1781, " John Malcolm was taken to the India House, and was, as his uncle anticipated, in a fair way to be rejected, when one of the Directors said to him, 'Why, my little man, what would *you* do if you were to meet Hyder Ali?' 'Do, Sir!' said the young aspirant, in prompt reply, 'I would out with my sword and cut off his head.' 'You will do,' was the rejoinder,

---

* Thomas Babington Macaulay was born at Rothley Temple, Leicestershire, in the year 1800. His father, Zachary Macaulay, a retired East India merchant, strengthened the hands and helped forward the philanthropic enterprise of Wilberforce. When eighteen years of age, Thomas entered Trinity College, Cambridge, where his career was a brilliant one. He entered Parliament in 1830, under the auspices of Lord Lansdowne, and became Secretary to the Board of Control. About 1834, he became a Member of the Supreme Council of India. In 1838, Mr. Macaulay returned to England with a practical knowledge of Indian affairs ; but he is best known to Anglo-Indians as the author of the unrivalled essays on Clive and Warren Hastings.

'let him pass.'" The "Boy, Malcolm," had been brushed up at home to some purpose.

In the review* of Sir John Kaye's work, in which the above anecdote is quoted, some interesting information is given regarding an early part of the career of one whose biography is now better known than that of other highly distinguished Anglo-Indians of days long gone by.

"In February, 1798, Lord Hobart resigned the Government of Madras, and General Harris acted during the interregnum. The Town Majorship of Fort St. George was in those days an office of greater honour and emolument than it is now, and it was regarded as a perquisite of some one of the Governor's suite. It was therefore given by General Harris to his secretary, and Malcolm held it till the arrival of Lord Clive in August. In this year also he attained his captaincy. And in this year Lord Mornington landed at Madras on his way to Calcutta; and Captain Malcolm took the liberty to forward to 'the glorious little man' some of those papers that he had submitted to Lord Hobart, and to solicit that 'when opportunity offered, he might be employed in the diplomatic line of his profession.' And opportunity offered soon: on the 10th of September he received a letter from the Governor-General, announcing his appointment to be assistant to the Resident at the Court of Hyderabad, and at the same time requesting to see him as soon as he could possibly present himself at Calcutta."

At this time the Nizam was on friendly terms with the French as well as the English. But the English and French were at war with each other; and, as the reviewer remarks, the Nizam ["Putter in Order"] "had no very special preference for either of the parties." One of the first acts of Lord Mornington (afterwards the Marquis Wellesley) was to order the disbandment of 11,000 troops in the pay of His Highness, under the command of French officers, and of course only devoted to French interests. Captain Kirkpatrick and his able assistant did the business fearlessly and well.

* *Calcutta Review*, No. 57, September, 1857. It is a sad reflection to think that this review of the great Political was originally assigned to Sir Henry Lawrence.

"Had Kirkpatrick," writes the eminent biographer, "wanted resolution—had he hesitated, and faltered, and shown himself to be a man of weak-nerved humanity, slow to resort to extremities—in all probability before the end of October, the French lines would have been running crimson with blood. There is an ill odour about the *word* "dragooning," but there is more real kindness in the *thing* itself than is readily to be believed."* John Malcolm proceeded with the colours of the disbanded French regiments to Calcutta; and the Calcutta reviewer, while alluding to Mr. Kaye's account of his important advent, thus gives Lord Mornington's idea of "the right man in the right place," which we think as applicable to the selection of politicals and other officials at home as in India, and which feeling no doubt prompted the selection of the subject of this sketch to fill the high post of Political Secretary at the India Office, as well as the appointment of Sir John Kaye's successor :—" In point of fact, the Governor-General, the 'glorious little man' [since his time we have had another 'glorious little man,' Lord Dalhousie], was one of those few men to whom, being in office, it was of no consequence whether a man were old or not, whether he were a cadet or a colonel, provided he had eyes that could see, a brain that could think, a soul that could feel what was right and what was noble, and a hand that could hold a sword or a pen."

Having alluded to the disbandment of French officers in India, with reference to the all-important matters of Conciliation and Annexation (touched on at the commencement of this sketch), it is natural for one who has long taken an interest in such political acts in the East, to remark how deficient the French in India, during their early struggles, were in the necessary qualities for either. Dupleix could found a factory, but not an empire; Count Lally could blow Brahmans from guns, but could not gain for his country any firm footing in Hindustan; and even long after the days of the Marquis Wellesley, French adventurers joined the great Sikh ruler (Runjeet Singh), and eventually one (whom we knew), General D'Orgoni,

---

* Also quoted in the review : p. 167.

tried to "manage affairs" at Ava! All—all are now departed, and have left no sign!*

It is the best thing that ever happened for England, that, during the early part of her wonderful career in India, France could neither conciliate nor annex! Great Britain has done both successfully; but the days for annexation are now at an end. The mandate has gone forth—to look well after what we have, to resist aggression, but go no farther; and the more pleasant task of the political secretary in days to come will be to conciliate, chiefly with a view to increase commerce and the general prosperity and happiness of the people. Annexation, in the mind of Sir John Kaye, is not to be tolerated for a moment. Talking to him one day on the subject, and casually bringing forward some excuses, in extreme cases, for the political act, such as the "force of circumstances," the writer incurred his displeasure, and was immediately silenced by "The force of circumstances!" being repeated in a disdainful tone. Regarding the annexation of Pegu—perhaps the best and most righteous annexation effected during the last quarter of a century; and even the strongest enemies of the act must admit, that if the Burmese war was a mistake in its commencement it has not been so in the result—it would have been useless to point out to the Political Secretary how valuable the possession of British Burma was to us during the Mutiny; how "the isolation of Burma kept the Court of Ava out of the influences of the mutinies altogether;" how the Bengal Sepoy regiment stationed there found no sympathy from such a different race as the Burmese in the matter of disaffection; how we could spare British troops from the Province at such a time; or how, as is well known, the King sent a donation of 1,000*l.* to relieve the sufferers

* Pondicherry and the other French settlements in India do not affect this remark. The French have *no* power in India. It would be well, however, if we could buy them out of it, as we have done the Danes, which (in case of European complications extending to the East) might save us much trouble. Goa, the Portuguese settlement, is another thorn in our side, which it might be wise to purchase.

by the Mutiny.* But, in the opinion of Sir John, Pegu should not have been subjugated. There should be no annexation at all; no aggressive policy, under *any* circumstances—only conciliatory. He denounces annexation with the same admirable vigour as Lord Brougham displayed when, in the younger days of his eloquence, advocates of the slave-trade talked to him of " rights " and " property "—" I deny the rights; I acknowledge not the property!" So, on the above occasion, the writer left his room convinced that the Political Secretary held annexation to be another " wild and guilty fantasy." And his views on the subject of *control* in India clearly seemed to be, as already remarked in the sketch of Sir Henry Lawrence—*We may protect and help; but on no account are we to take land not our own*, and put the rents into our own pockets! This is at least a *safe*. plan of action, and is, perhaps, the best suited to the present highly civilised times. Long may we be able to carry out Sir John Kaye's conciliatory policy, which he has taken so much pains to establish! As Political Secretary, his courtesy towards native officials who came in contact with him was ever remarkable. He took the utmost pains to avoid, under any circumstances, giving them the slightest cause of offence.

While the Burmese Ambassadors were in London, he did his utmost to give them a good opinion of the courtesy and kindness of the English nation to strangers. He was anxious that nothing should be said or written that would, if it reached the Golden Foot, cause the slightest annoyance to the King of Burma (Oriental princes are more apt and well-informed than we give credit for); so we may truly say, that during his long tenure of office, conciliation and the promotion of goodwill among men formed the guiding stars of his conduct.

In the *East India Register*, from 1856 to 1858, we find Mr. John Stuart Mill—the philosopher whose views have so lately puzzled the reading world—Examiner of India Correspondence. In this department of the Home

* See article on " Lord Dalhousie " in *Calcutta Review* for December, 1859; and article in *Fraser* for July, 1858, on the " Indian Rebellion ;" in which admirable papers this subject is forcibly touched on.

Establishment there appear also two assistant examiners and three assistants—"Edmund D. Bourdillon, W. T. Thornton, and J. W. Kaye, Esqrs." Colonel William Henry Sykes is at this time Chairman of the Court of Directors. But, in 1859, we find in the *Register* that the junior assistant has succeeded his philosophic and experienced chief under the new and more comprehensive title (India having passed to the Crown) of "Secretary, Political and Secret Department." If, as it has been said, it was no common honour for Sir John to have succeeded Mr. John Stuart Mill, we fearlessly assert that it is a still greater honour for Colonel Burne to have been selected to succeed such an able Political Secretary as Sir John Kaye.

In conclusion, the writer of this brief sketch, along with all his friends, wishes him in his retirement health and happiness. Macaulay once said to the electors, talking of resigning and seeking literary repose (pointing to his head)—"This is my stock in trade, gentlemen!" From Sir John's varied and always valuable stock the public are still eagerly expecting some books they have fully calculated on reading; among others, another volume of the "Sepoy War," and a new work, the "Life of Sir James Outram." It is sincerely to be hoped that such literary treasures will not figure among the "unaccomplished purposes" of our distinguished Anglo-Indian.

SIR JOHN WILLIAM KAYE.

[We have much pleasure in re-producing the just and appreciative sketch of Sir John, which appeared in the leading journal, for the benefit of our readers.]

AFTER a service of nearly nineteen years as Secretary in the Political and Secret Department of the India Office, combined with literary work of an arduous character, failing health has obliged Sir John William Kaye to seek relaxation from work.

Sir John Kaye manifested at an early period of his life a remarkable taste for writing and talent for composition. He was educated at the Rev. Dr. Radcliffe's, at Salisbury, and many of his old school-follows to this day talk of his juvenile contributions in prose and verse to a Magazine, in imitation of the *Etonian*, published at the Wiltshire School. By one of those anomalies or chances which so often govern early careers, he was sent to Addiscombe and transformed into a Bengal Artilleryman. His service as a subaltern in that noble corps, far from changing the bent of his mind, formed him into the historian of Indian wars, and inspired him with that regard for the natives of India, and that insight into Indian life and Indian history which have shown themselves in so many of his subsequent writings. Generous in his disposition, and an able writer, young Kaye soon became a favourite in [Indian society, and the ruling spirit in the foremost publications of the day. His literary pursuits obliged him, however, to leave the Artillery, and ill-health drove him to England; but not before he had established, almost single-handed, the *Calcutta Review*, to the earlier numbers of which magazine he contributed nearly fifty essays on political, military, and social subjects.

On his return to England Sir John Kaye devoted himself to the "History of the War in Affghanistan," a work which established his reputation as a historian. Of it the late Lord Strangford said, in the pages of the *Quarterly Review*, it was "a work as awful, as simply artistic, and as clear and lofty in its moral as an Æschylian trilogy." Sir John Kaye's next effort was a "History of the Administration of the East India Company," which was largely quoted in Parliament during the debates of 1853. He added to this a "Selection, with Notes, from the Papers of the late Mr. St. George Tucker," and a "Life of the late Lord Metcalfe," followed by the "Life of Sir John Malcolm." At this period the versatility of his literary labours was somewhat arrested by his appointment to the India House. To have been specially selected by the Court of Directors as Chief of their Political Department, in succession to John Stuart Mill, was no mean honour. But his new official duties were not allowed to obstruct needlessly his literary labours. The Sepoy War found in him its natural historian, and the "Lives of Indian Officers" became known as a text-book for every young Indian subaltern and civilian. Sir John Kaye's contributions to periodicals during this period were constant—quarterly, monthly, weekly, daily. A collection of some of his writings in the *Cornhill Magazine* was published only last year as "Essays of an Optimist." As a tribute, doubtless, to his literary merit, he was, without application and without ballot, made a Fellow of the Royal Society. Sir John Kaye's official services at the India Office, through many changes and vicissitudes, are well known. His career has been spent in assisting to infuse a kindly and statesmanlike spirit into the policy controlling the millions of

India. He was created in 1871 a Knight Commander of the Star of India; and for his official and literary services to India the Marquis of Salisbury and the Council of India have given him a liberal provision for his declining years.—*Times*, October 19th, 1874.

[The *Week's News*, of October 24, adds to the above sketch, that Sir John Kaye was the valued editor of *The Overland Mail* newspaper from its commencement in the year 1855, until the year 1868, and that for many years he was also editor of *The Homeward Mail*.]

SIR JOHN KAYE'S SUCCESSOR

(LIEUT.-COLONEL BURNE, C.S.I.).

Lieut.-Colonel Owen Tudor Burne joined the 20th Foot in May, 1855, and served in the latter part of the Crimean campaign. He embarked with the 20th for India in 1857, and served as Brigade-Major to the Oüh Field Force, &c., during the Mutiny campaign, including fifteen actions, and the siege and capture of Lucknow. He was three times mentioned in despatches; and was specially mentioned for his gallant conduct at the above siege, for which he received the rank of Brevet-Major. He served four years as Adjutant of his Regiment. In 1861 (when a lieutenant), he was specially selected by Sir Hugh Rose (Lord Strathnairn) as Military Secretary to the Commander-in-Chief. He returned with him to England in 1865, and served in Ireland during the Fenian disturbances. Major Burne was selected by Lord Mayo to be his Private Secretary, and left with his Lordship for India in 1868. He held the appointment till that nobleman's death in 1872. He returned to England in May, 1872, after acting for some months as Private Secretary to Lord Napier and Ettrick, K.T., who became, *pro tem.*, Viceroy and Governor-General. The Major was nominated a Companion of the Star of India early in 1872, appointed Political A.D.C., at the India Office, in August, 1872, Assistant in the Political and Secret Department in the beginning of 1874, and succeeded Sir John Kaye, K.C.S.I., as Political Secretary, on the 16th October, 1874. Major Burne was actually with the lamented Earl of Mayo at his death at Port Blair, 8th February, 1872. He did not purchase any steps; they were all given to him for distinguished services in the field, except the Lieut.-Colonelcy, which he obtained on the 23rd July, 1874, by seniority in the list of Army Majors. In the foregoing remarks, we have the recital of a distinguished career ; and, as the gallant Colonel is only in the prime of life (about the same age as Sir John Kaye when he became Political Secretary), he has a splendid field for action in view; and we have no doubt that time will show he is, in every respect, " the right man in the right place."

THE LAST COURT OF DIRECTORS.*

(1858.)

[The last Meeting of the Court of Directors of the Honourable East India Company was held 1st September, 1858.]

CHAIRMAN:

Sir Frederick Currie, Bart.

DEPUTY-CHAIRMAN:

William Joseph Eastwick, Esq.

DIRECTORS:

Charles Mills, Russell Ellice, William Butterworth Bayley, John Shepherd, Martin Tucker Smith, M.P., Esqrs. ; Sir Henry Willock, K.L.S., Sir James Weir Hogg, Bart., Colonel William Henry Sykes, M.P. ; Elliot Macnaghten, Ross Donnelly Mangles, M.P., John Harvey Astell, Henry Thoby Prinsep, John Pollard Willoughby, M.P., Esqrs. ; Lieutenant-Colonel Sir Henry Creswick Rawlinson, K.C.B., Lieutenant-General Sir George Pollock, G.C.B., Major-General Sir Robert John Hussey Vivian, K.C.B.

* Having alluded in the sketch of Sir John Kaye to the transfer of the East India Company's Government to the Crown, the two records here given will be of interest.

THE FIRST COUNCIL OF INDIA.
(1858.)

[The first Meeting of the Council of India took place 3rd September, 1858.]

SECRETARY OF STATE:

The RIGHT HON. LORD STANLEY, M.P.

(Who, succeeding Lord Ellenborough, was also the last President of the Board of Control.)

UNDER-SECRETARIES OF STATE:

Henry James Baillie, Esq., M.P.
Sir George Russell Clerk, K.C.B.

ASSISTANT-UNDER-SECRETARY OF STATE:

James Cosmo Melvill, Esq.

COUNCIL:

Sir Frederic Currie, Bart. (Vice-President).
Charles Mills, Esq.
John Shepherd, Esq.
Sir James Weir Hogg, Bart.
Elliot Macnaghten, Esq.
Ross D. Mangles, Esq.
William J. Eastwick, Esq.
Henry T. Prinsep, Esq.
John P. Willoughby, Esq.
Lieutenant-Colonel Sir Henry C. Rawlinson, K.C.B.
Major-General Sir Robert J. H. Vivian, K.C.B.
Sir Henry C. Montgomery, Bart.
Sir John L. M. Lawrence, Bart., G.C.B.
Colonel Sir Proby T. Cautley, K.C.B.
William Urquhart Arbuthnot, Esq.

SIR GEORGE POLLOCK, G.C.B., G.C.S.I.

LINES SUGGESTED BY THE FIELD-MARSHAL'S FUNERAL IN
WESTMINSTER ABBEY, OCTOBER 16, 1872.

After a well-spent life, work nobly done,
Nature exhausted, mourned by troops of friends,
Our Indian hero sleeps. But scanty honours
Graced such a wonderful career, for, Pollock!
With all who wish our Eastern Empire well—
And who so dead of soul not so to wish?—
Thy name shall live for ever! India,
When terrible disaster, deadly ruin,
Made all look black, and Afghan treachery
Was to the fore, and peace had left the land;
When faith in England's power began to shake,
And Russia's eagle, ready for his prey,
Hailed the impending storm; then came a star—
A "bright particular star"—which settled o'er
The head of Pollock, born to fight and save!
Type of the Anglo-Indian General he,
Type of the Anglo-Indian gentleman,
Type of a race who shall to time unborn
Be linked with India's welfare and true glory!
"The last of earth" calls forth a solemn meeting;
Now, in the Abbey—honoured resting-place—
Must he be laid, where glorious dust abounds.

Hark! the procession comes—what solemn music!—
Statesmen and soldiers following in the train;
Knights of the Bath and Star of India ranged
Beside the worthy freight now borne along. *
Conspicuous among the Stars of India,
Lawrence,† whose energy in time of need,
In later days, did much to crush rebellion;
And Kaye, the bounteous labours of whose pen
Have given historic truth to mighty deeds
Performed by Pollock—dreadful Khyber forced,
Brave Sale relieved, and conquest of Cabûl—
A page which England will not soon let die.
The solemn service o'er, a last sad look
We take at the old warrior's resting-place,
Thinking what Antony said of noble Brutus—
"His life was gentle"—life to what poets style
"A green old age"—the elements of good
All "mixed in him;" while some friends, loath to part,
Muse o'er the Khyber Pass—then glide away.

I. A.‡

* The pall-bearers consisted of three Knights Commanders of the Bath and three Knights Commanders of the Star of India.

† The Right Hon. Lord Lawrence, G.C.B., G.C.S.I. (late Viceroy of India.)

‡ "Indian Artilleryman."—The above "Lines" are from the *Broad Arrow*, 26th October, 1872.—See also Appendix IV.

FALCIERI:

AN INDIA OFFICE SKETCH; A CONNECTING LINK WITH LORD BYRON.

"His motley household came—not last nor least,
Battista, who, upon the moonlight sea
Of Venice, had so ably, zealously,
Served, and, at parting, thrown his oar away
To follow through the world; who, without stain
Had worn so long that honourable badge,
The Gondolier's, in a Patrician House
Arguing unlimited trust."
ROGERS' "Italy." (Bologna.)

THE men in London who connect the past romantic and poetical age with the distracting, busy present, are fast dying out; so we like to come across those who are still living. It is known to few that a remarkable man now holds the post of one of the senior messengers in the India Office. Giovanni Battista Falcieri is the man on whose shoulder Lord Byron died at Missolonghi, at seven o'clock in the evening, on the 19th April, 1824. He is a fine-looking, hale old man, of seventy-four years of age, and speaks with the highest respect of his noble master. In fact, any one who dared speak against the great poet might excite the indignation of Falcieri to a dangerous extent; and we doubt very much if even such Byronic detractors as Mrs. Stowe would altogether be safe. Falcieri used to swim with Lord Byron; but he was not with him till long after the famous feat of swimming the Hellespont.* The old chasseur tells with infinite pride that, while wearing a costume (uniform?) similar to that of his master, he would be occasionally saluted for his lordship. "Tita" is the Italian abbreviation of his name; and on an informant remarking on the difference of climate between England and Italy, he replied that he had not visited Italy for nearly forty years. He came over with the corpse of Lord Byron—afterwards returned to Italy—and, on his re-visiting England, was eventually appointed to service in the Board of Control Office, from which, on the Indian Government passing

* 3rd of May, 1810.

entirely to the Crown, through the influence of Sir John Cam Hobhouse (Lord Broughton), Falcieri was appointed to the India Office, where he is to be found daily, with every promise of reaching " a green old age "—one of the few connecting links between the times of Byron and our own.

The writer penned the above very brief sketch of a faithful servant upwards of two years ago, * and great was the delight of Falcieri when he read it in a popular journal; but greater still was his satisfaction when he received a letter from America quoting the same as a record of interest—the paragraph had been copied into an English illustrated weekly paper, which has a circulation in America—and requesting more information about the famous " Tita " of Lord Byron.

Alas! now "Tita" has gone after his famous master. He died on Tuesday, the 23rd of December, 1874, at 60, Seymour Street, Portman Square. † For upwards of a year the old man had been absent from his messenger duties in the India Office, in the vestibule of which (nearest to St. James's Park) he sat, under his friend Mr. Badrick (the polite and intelligent Head Office Keeper), arranging and stamping letters, answering in broken English the questions of distinguished and ordinary Anglo-Indians, and, in spite of his reticence, lighting up at the very mention of the names of Shelley and Lord Byron. His habits were strictly abstemious; but, like poor humanity in general, Falcieri could not long carry on a "conflict with the frosts of age." A stroke of paralysis was the first monitor; and then, towards the close of last year, congestion of the lungs set in, to which he rapidly succumbed; and "Tita" was no more! During what seemed his convalescence, Falcieri occasionally hobbled down to the Office, where the present writer talked with him about a month before he died. He was born in the year 1798, just ten years after Lord Byron, making him, at his decease, seventy-six years of age. He was buried at Kensal Green on the 29th December, Mr. Badrick, and one of the senior messengers of the India Office (Mr. H. Girard), following their respected old friend to the grave. Surely, such a distinguished member of the useful corps of messengers had never died before; distinguished, not on account of himself, but of him who admired the faithful " Tita," and died on his shoulder; the mighty genius whose chief characteristic, like that of

* November, 1872. The additional notes and brief reminiscences now given, were written in January and February 1875.

† A *Times* Correspondent (January 9th) is in error when remarking that Falcieri died at Ramsgate.

the ocean he so loved to describe, was restlessness; and, of whom our most brilliant essayist wrote (coupling Lord Byron with Napoleon):—"Two men have died within our recollection, who, at a time of life at which many people have hardly completed their education, had raised themselves, each in his own department, to the height of glory. One of them died at Longwood; the other at Missolonghi." * Although very far from being an Anglo-Indian, yet having so long breathed the same atmosphere as Anglo-Indians, for this reason, but chiefly on account of his illustrious master, whose works, next to those of Shakspeare and Scott, have excited more interest in India than those of any other writer, we think Falcieri worthy of a place in our little volume. The interest caused by the death of Falcieri, which was evident from the care taken to collate what was at hand regarding him in the principal London journals, is another reason for the writer's endeavouring to give something new about him; and we agree that "the minutest associations connected with Byron should be precious to his countrymen, and in Tita Falcieri there disappears a most interesting relic of the Byronic legends." The following authentic sketch is given, with but few alterations; and, on perusing it, perhaps, the readers of Rogers' "Table-Talk" will bring to memory what Mrs. Barbauld said to the "banker poet," that *she* thought Byron wrote best "when he wrote about the *sea* or *swimming* :"—

THE late Giovanni Battista Falcieri (better known to the friends of Lord Byron as "Tita") entered the poet's service in 1818, being then twenty years of age, as gondolier.† He was afterwards his personal attendant and chasseur, attending his lordship in his equestrian and swimming exercises, and also with the carriage. Falcieri was accustomed to speak with pride on the richness of his uniform—a cocked hat with a plume of feathers; scarlet coat, richly embroidered with gold lace; pantaloons, also similarly embroidered; Hessian boots, with tassels; sword and sash completed his equipment when out on special occasions in attendance on his lordship. He appeared to enjoy the reminiscences of their swimming excur-

* "Macaulay's Critical and Historical Essays :"—" Moore's Life of Lord Byron."
† The beautiful lines from Rogers which head this sketch, as "D. R." well remarks in a note to the *Times* (6th January), "exactly show the faithful character of the man." Rogers, in a note, says :—" The principal gondolier (*il fante di poppa*) was almost always in the confidence of his master, and employed on occasions that required judgment and address."

sions very much, when his lordship and he would go out at night-time, each with a light in one hand, elevated over their heads, while they swam with the other; and he also mentioned an occasion when two gentlemen, swimming with his lordship and himself, one after the other gave in, but Lord Byron and Falcieri kept on. They had swam some two or three miles, when Lord Byron turned to Falcieri to ask him if he felt disposed to go farther, which he was quite willing to do. On one occasion they lunched in the water. The table and provisions were tied together, and carried by Falcieri on his head; when they swam for some distance they then placed the board to form a table, drew the cork of the bottle, arranged the viands, and having partaken of lunch as much as they required, his lordship threw himself on his back, and with his foot kicked over the remains into the water. [So the admirers of Childe Harold now learn for the first time that he and his faithful "Tita" actually lunched *in* the sea!]

Falcieri went with his lordship to Greece, and (as before stated) was with him when he died at Missolonghi. He then came to England with the body. The coffin was brought over in a cask of spirits, and Falcieri never left it; indeed, he has said that if he had done so, the sailors would have pierced the cask to obtain the spirits; and when the body was placed in a house in Great George Street, Westminster, he slept on the coffin. He attended the funeral at Hucknel. Those among the more curious endeavoured to elicit something from him concerning Lord Byron, but to no purpose. His answer invariably was, "Me not know," or "I can't tell." He was unacquainted with English at that time. Such was his fidelity during his long stay in England, that nothing would ever induce him to betray any secret with regard to his late master. Among those desirous of hearing something important from him were distinguished persons of the higher classes; but their requests were of no avail.

He had in his possession the passports of the gentlemen who were with Mr. Shelley when he was drowned off Leghorn. Falcieri started with the party in the boat, but an English vessel was "laying-to," and the party stopped to converse with the captain. Soon after Lord Byron had sent Falcieri with the party in the boat, he required his services, and sent another boat to recall him; otherwise he would have been with Mr. Shelley when he was capsized, and the "strong swimmer" might have saved the poet of the "starry verse."

After the burial of Lord Byron, Falcieri went out in the

service of Sir John Cam Hobhouse and Mr. James Clay, as courier. On his return to England, he was engaged as valet to Mr. Isaac D'Israeli—the celebrated author of the "Curiosities of Literature," and father of the Premier—where he remained until the death of his master. Sir John Cam Hobhouse then gave him (we believe at the solicitation of the future Prime Minister) an appointment as messenger at the Board of Control, whence he came to the old India House in Leadenhall Street, and eventually to the India Office. It should be mentioned that, during his service with Mr. D'Israeli, Count D'Orsay produced a portrait of the late Lord Byron, which was shown to the personal friends of his lordship, and by them was pronounced a perfect likeness; but it was afterwards thought advisable that "Tita" should see it, to give his opinion. He was therefore sent from Bradenham, in Buckinghamshire, and he considered it an excellent likeness, with the exception of the hair, which was not quite the shade. As he had a piece of his lordship's hair, he sent it to Count D'Orsay; and it was found, as Falcieri had said, of a different hue. The alteration was made, and it was thought by Falcieri to be the best portrait he had seen. As a compliment for this, Count D'Orsay presented him with a valuable ring, set with emeralds. This ring he valued very much; and although too small for his finger, he would not have it altered. [*Here ends* his friend's manuscript.] Falcieri, at the present writer's request, brought this ring one day to the India Office, along with Shelley's passports, which appear to have been entrusted to his care. The ring was really a beautiful one, and the old man took it carefully from the box, and handled the treasure with a genuine pride. Even after the poet's death "Tita" had done something for his illustrious master, correcting the mistake of a brilliant Count —one of the social stars of the day—and clever artist. On another occasion Falcieri brought an admirable photographic likeness of himself, doing him full justice; he being represented wearing an Albanian cap, and, with his amiable visage and superb white beard, looking as no Government messenger ever looked before—which portrait he gave to the writer, as a keepsake.

Falci (as he was sometimes called) seemed to know a good deal about Shelley; and he would relate to us, with some graphic power, the story of the poet having set sail from Leghorn for Lerici, " in that treacherous boat which (some fifty-two years ago) sank, with all on board, to the bottom of the Mediterranean." He had also an anecdote of Shelley, which may not yet have been given to the world. While the poet of the "Sensitive Plant" was living by a lake, he went to an adjacent hill, where the nurse appeared with the baby, which he took, and quietly laid down, and, sending the nurse away, became so much absorbed in the book which he was reading that at length he went home, forgetting the child. On being asked where it was, he remarked that he had laid it down by the hill. Falcieri was immediately despatched to the spot, and found the morsel of humanity, with eyes wide open, quite happy and safe. The place was much infested with snakes, and "Tita" expressed his surprise that the child had not been bitten. Whatever may be said of Anglo-Indians, they seem more careful of their young children in India than Mr. and Mrs. Shelley appear to have been of theirs in Italy!

It is not at all improbable that Falci assisted to get up Lord Byron's famous dinner at Pisa, when Shelley (Shakspeare's stanch defender), Rogers, and Trelawney were the guests. We can fancy him standing behind his noble master's chair, while Childe Harold unjustly ran down Shakspeare (for whom Byron, like Sheridan, seemed to have little admiration), wondering, at the mention of the immortal name, who Shakspeare really was! But we must now pass on; there being still something to say about "Tita" and Lord Byron.

Falcieri being asked if he were a better swimmer than his lordship, replied, he did not know; for they "never out-ran each other,"—a truly respectful answer. "Tita," in his early days, appears to have been rather of a pugnacious tendency. On one occasion, in Venice, when some police came to take him up for some offence, he looked at them and smiled, telling them they had better not venture. They attempted to take him, and he threw three of them into the street, while the other four took to their heels. The Commandant of Police went to Byron, and Byron went to the Grand Duke. His Highness remarked that it would be "all right," as the men "were being attended to in hospital!" If all the mad pranks played by Lord Byron and his "Tita" in the "glorious city in the sea" were known, what amusing incidents would be found among them! and yet time and circumstances so alter us, that the old man generally seemed as if he had never played a prank in his life. With greater men than Lord Byron's faithful servant it has been, and will continue to be, the same—steady in ripe manhood and old age, after many young days of frolic and folly. Dupleix, long before he thought of dethroning the Great Mogul, taking India from us, and reducing Madras and Calcutta to their original state of fishing towns,* ran about the streets of the French settlement of Chandernagore (Bengal) with a fiddle in his hand, while an umbrella was held over his head, to the amusement of his companions! "Childe Harold," before he awoke one morning, and found himself "famous," had played many strange games; "fantastic tricks before high heaven," and, had he lived to the age of seventy, he might have almost been as demure-looking at times as his servant, Falcieri. Regarding the two notices of him which appeared in the London journals,† full justice is attempted to be done to the departed India Office messenger, and some most interesting incidents are brought forward; there are also a few mistakes of no very great importance. Falcieri's first meeting with his dead master's friend, Mr. John Cam Hobhouse (afterwards the well-known "Sir John" and Lord Broughton), appears to have taken place when that gentleman took him into his service in London, as a courier, preparatory to again setting out on his travels.

According to Mr. Murray's "Chronology of Lord Byron's Life and Works," the poet left London "on his travels, accompanied by Mr. Hobhouse," on June 11th, 1809; so we find Falcieri with Mr. Hobhouse fifteen years, or more, after that memorable setting out of the two friends in the morning of life. In one of the journals it is said that "subsequently he officiated as *valet* to old Mr. Isaac D'Israeli, the author of the 'Curiosities of Literature,' and father of the present Prime Minister of England." As has been already noticed, he did serve under Mr. D'Israeli, in whose household he received much kindness. Falcieri well recollected the celebration of the occasion of the Prime Minister's first entering Parliament,‡ when he drank his health. It is quite correct that Falcieri, in 1852, obtained, through Lord Broughton's§ influence, a situation as messenger in the Board of Control Office. In the East India Register for the above year, he appears as John Falcieri, the second among three. India was transferred to the Crown in September, 1858. In the first half of 1859, however, we still find "G. B. Falcieri" as "office messenger" at Cannon Row, where a portion of the India Office Secretariat Department were employed, under the Assistant to the Secretaries, and Keeper of the Records, T. Nelson Waterfield, Esq.∥ Falcieri served the Crown, but

---
* Orme.
† *Telegraph* of 5th, and the *Times* of 9th January, 1875.
‡ M.P. for Maidstone, 1837.
§ President of the Board of Control.
∥ Father of the present Secretary in the Department of Statistics and Commerce, India Office.

not the East India Company (as messenger to Sir George Clerk *) for a short time at the old India House in Leadenhall Street, which was vacated in September, 1860, on the occupation of the Victoria Hotel, Westminster, as a temporary India Office. The present stately building in St. James's Park was first occupied in September, 1867. In addition to clearing away some doubt expressed by the journalist, these facts may be of use for reference hereafter.

The correspondent of the leading journal, Mr. Richard Edgcumbe, writes :—" To the admirers of Shelley, Tita will also have some interest, since he is the gondolier who rowed ' Julian and Maddalo ' past the madhouse at sunset." He also gives an account of the death of Lord Byron, and the description (from Count Gamba's Narrative) would seem to be strictly correct. Falcieri told the present writer that Lord Byron died on his shoulder; and the truth of his assertion at once becomes apparent from the following "last scene of all," in a brief, though " eventful history :"—

"It was after a consultation of the physicians," says Gamba, " that, as it appeared to me, Lord Byron was for the first time aware of his approaching end. Mr. Millingen, Fletcher, and Tita had been standing round his bed; but the first two, unable to restrain their tears, left the room. Tita also wept, but, as Byron held his hand, could not retire. He, however, turned away his face ; Byron meanwhile looked steadily at him, and said, half smiling, ' *Oh ! questa è una bella scena !* ' He seemed to reflect a moment, and having released the hand of Tita with orders that Captain Parry might be summoned, a fit of delirium ensued." " In the 'hour of death' Tita stood beside the poet, and finally forsook his country to follow his master to the grave."

It is impossible not to feel a respect for Falcieri, so prominent an actor in this touching scene. Here was the mighty genius who loved nature more than man, who was in poetry what Rousseau was in prose, but who, as a great writer and divine† remarks, " never aimed to better a world which he utterly despised ;" here he was, while dying, holding the hand of his faithful servant, whose presence probably suggested that image of " eternity "—the sea—in which they had so often swam together ; and the fact of Lord Byron in his last moments placing his head on his faithful servant's shoulder to die, showed that the poet, in his noble, generous nature, esteemed at

* Sir George took his seat as Governor of Bombay, May, 1860.
† Dr. Chalmers.

least *one* man, of the city which Childe Harold so loved from his boyhood *—the gondolier of Venice—Giovanni Battista Falcieri! We are glad to be enabled to conclude this sketch by recording a most gracious act—that of Mr. Disraeli recommending the widow of Falcieri to Her Majesty for a pension from the Civil List, which she has now obtained.

NOTE.

Mr. Edgcumbe informs us that "the father of the present Prime Minister took the faithful *cassiatore* into his service," where he remained till "the death of his benefactor in 1848. The Premier then took him into his service, and, in due course, interested himself so far in his behalf as to get him an appointment as messenger to the India Office, to which post he was appointed by *Sir S. Holsham!*" (Sir John Cam Hobhouse, or Lord Broughton?) Falcieri's pension was two-thirds of his pay, or about £93, and not £140 (the full amount) as asserted. Mr. Edgcumbe has introduced the following amusing anecdote among his incidents in the life of "Tita" Falcieri; and we can vouch for the correctness of the concluding remark, having seen his writing (a fair enough hand for a foreigner) in the India Office :—" Mr. Moore, the poet, in his reminiscence of a visit to Lord Byron at Venice in the year 1819, alludes to Tita as the *segretario* in whose charge he was placed by his noble host. 'So you keep a secretary?' exclaimed Moore when he heard the title of his protector. 'Yes,' replied Byron, laughing, 'a fellow who can't write.' It is but an act of justice to the memory of Tita to inform the reader that this apparent deficiency in his education had been made up long before his death, for I have in my possession some remarks made by Tita, written in a legible hand."

* "I loved her from my boyhood ; she to me
Was as a fairy city of the heart."
"Childe Harold's Pilgrimage."

ANGLO-INDIAN PERIODICAL LITERATURE.*

"So might we talk of the old familiar faces."
CHARLES LAMB.

I.

It was not long after the terrible emotion caused by India's severest trial, "The Sepoy Mutiny," had subsided, that, while holding an important position in Central India, I had the honour to form one of a small band who were anxious to improve the various grades of Europeans resident at the station. The means were a series of lectures. As coming under the head of *subsidiary education*, they seemed particularly well adapted to the country; for, in the East, where intellectual stagnation, even among true Britons, is so apt to become lamentably frequent, should men only wish to have their memories refreshed (supposing them to be "too clever by half," to require any "subsidiary" knowledge), what better plan than a system of lectures can be devised to stimulate them to keep up an acquaintance with what they once knew of the various branches of science and literature? Again, the thought occurred to us that lectures, to many of our hearers, would not only be subsidiary, but actual, primary education. For my own part, having long held it to be indisputably true that "Periodical Literature is a great thing," that it is a potent instrument in the education of a people, it was selected for the subject—English and Anglo-Indian—on two occasions, when I attempted to give, with the help of a rather limited library, and the assistance of a few genuine old Indians—stars of a world gone by—some account of its rise, progress, and importance.

Having opened our campaign in July, 1859, Nagpore became the second great province,† in which, during the month, lec-

---

* This and the three following papers appeared in the *Dark Blue* for July, August, and September, 1872, under the heading of "Periodical Literature in India."

† On the 2nd July, a series of lectures was opened by Sir Bartle Frere, Chief Commissioner of Sind, in the Government English School at Kurrachee.

tures for the diffusion of useful knowledge had been instituted. Looking back to upwards of forty years, the Peishwa, the Nagpore Rajah, and Holkar, were all rising with one accord against the English. The Pindarries and Mahrattas were distracting the land.

On the very ground where we had now raised our humble standard to give an occasional hour's intellectual entertainment to those who sought it, during that critical period host was encountering host; the "fatal hill" of Seetabuldee resounded with the clang of arms, and the thunder of the "red artillery;" and Nagpore fell—another trophy to the Saxon race ! The remarkable events in Central India during that important time have been ably and graphically chronicled in the "Life of Sir John Malcolm"—a biography which will never die—by one of the brightest ornaments of our Indian Periodical Literature,* to whom allusion will be made in due course. And now the present writer must be pardoned for commencing his subject—which professes to treat of periodical literature in India only—with a piece of egotism. My first serious attempt in the walk of our indigenous Indian literature was made public through the pages of that popular vehicle, the *Calcutta Review*, some twenty-seven years ago ; and any literary ardour and energy I then possessed were thereby roused into a decisive state of action. In the preface to the little work under review it is remarked : "Literature in India may be said to be in a state of inaction [1845] with the exception of *one* Review, which, leviathan like, plays about in the torpid pool." Again—"The *Calcutta Review*, undoubtedly the best work (Anglo-Indian) we have ever had, we are afraid is not sufficiently patronised in *our* Presidency (Madras). We have frequently asked if such a person had seen the last number of the above Review, when the reply would be, 'I have heard of such a work, but have never read it ; upon my soul I've no money to throw away, and in fact I've not much relish for works published in India : besides, who can write here ?'—Who can write here ? *that* is the question !"

In this same number of the *Review*, it may be mentioned, a

* Sir John William Kaye, K.C.S.I., founder of the *Calcutta Review*; and who, true to his love of periodical literature, was present at the Newspaper Press Fund Dinner in London, 12th May, 1872 ; on which august occasion also the chair was filled by His Grace the Duke of Argyll, Secretary of State for India, who, amidst the most important official duties, in addition to writing several works, has found time to communicate with various periodicals (including newspapers) on subjects of vast importance.

volume of "Prose and Verse," from the Calcutta press, was noticed: the book was written by Captain A. H. E. Boileau, of the Bengal Engineers, who had taken up the mantle which had been worn, and worn so well, by Dr. John Grant, Henry Meredith Parker, H. Torrens, R. Rattray, Captains Macnaghten and Richardson, as the supporters of Anglo-Indian Periodical Literature in days gone by; and who, now a colonel and commandant in his own corps, lectured to us on "Topography" on our opening night. The Colonel's various scientific attainments, and his Lectures on Iron Bridges were still well-known in Bengal. The familiar, good-humoured face comes vividly before me, while writing this sketch. I behold him as he is pacing along with his bearer behind him—that Oriental functionary being always ready to receive the huge *lathie* (stick), as long as a hop-pole, carried by the Colonel from door to door, in manner quite patriarchal—his blue frock coat, with faded light-blue Bhurtpoor ribbon of '26, buttoned up to the throat, even in the hottest weather; and, as he goes, pouring forth to those who sought it his boundless stock of information. He was a genuine type of the old Indian school—generous to a fault, and abounding in anecdote. The Colonel's appearance in the lecture-room, after the severe official labours of the day, made every one happy; and, like Falstaff, he was not only witty in himself, but "the cause of wit in other men." Proposing to teach his audience how to take some measurement in the easiest way—gained from his vast experience in surveying—seizing the chalk and commencing—" You see the triangle, A B C," gave promise of a rather dry lecture; but soon the subject became deeply interesting from the introduction of a well-timed anecdote or illustration from his personal history; and all went home delighted. Not among the least worthy of old Indians departed, will appear this General (in that rank he died a few years since)—a sort of chief among "the old familiar faces"—one whom Charles Lamb would have delighted to take by the hand; and who, from the morning of life to its close, did battle in the East for the cause of knowledge and mental recreation in the small army of India's periodical writers.

Shortly after being criticised, I had the audacity to become an occasional Calcutta reviewer, when I began to carefully watch periodical literature in its various aspects, both at home and in India; and I became more and more convinced of its power and utility in the education of a people.

The number of the *Calcutta* (December, 1845) to which

allusion has already been made, is a very varied and interesting one, containing six leading articles, and four "miscellaneous critical notices"—the former consisting of elaborate essays on "Indian Buddhism, its Origin and Diffusion," "The Cape of Good Hope," "The Urdu Language and Literature," "Rammohun Roy," "Married Life in India," and "The Mahommedan Controversy"—the number almost a library in itself; and among the "notices," one of a "Charge delivered to the Grand Jury of Bombay by the Honourable Mr. Justice Perry" (Sir Erskine, and now (1872) Vice-President of the Council of India), and another of an anonymous pamphlet on the "Education of the People of India : its Political Importance and Advantages." The reviewer sums up his notice of the latter brief essay by remarking : " Undoubtedly, a *sound* education, widely diffused throughout the native community, of all classes and grades, must be regarded as one of the primary instruments of its effectual amelioration;" and as a set-off against "many disappointments and drawbacks," we are informed that the well-written "article in the present number, on *Rammohun Roy*— whose life embraces the commencement of that great social and moral revolution" through which India is "now silently but surely passing"—is the "*bond fide* production of a native Hindu."

The foundation of a well-conducted periodical literature in India, carefully translated into the vernacular, until English becomes (as it one day must) universal, I have long thought, would produce the germs of a mighty revolution, especially in what is now in a decided transition state—the Hindu mind; and the Mahomedans too, or those of any persuasion who take an interest in their rulers, would have easy access to a knowledge of our present political power, and that in days gone by, of our rational amusements and mental recreation, and of our scientific and literary attainments—all borne to the mind's eye with the idea of a highly Christianised civilisation. Such a hope could not have been entertained at the time of the publication, in 1780, of *Hicky's Gazette*, the first Indian newspaper.* This great event in the history of periodical literature in the East is duly recorded by the historian of Bengal with the importance it so well merits :—

"On the 29th January, 1780, the first newspaper ever published in India made its appearance in Calcutta." A newspaper could not have been started at a better time. The hands of Warren Hastings were indeed full, for he was employed during

* *Calcutta Review*, No. II., August, 1844, p. 314.

the next four years, chiefly out of Bengal, in managing the affairs of Benares and Oudh, in a war with the renowned Hyder Ali, the Rajah of Mysore, "and in negotiations all over India." But Mr. Hicky, and the society of which he wrote, afforded far from good examples for the improvement of the native community. "The whole picture of Anglo-Indian society, at this period, was a very bad one, and," remarks a Calcutta reviewer, "society must have been very bad to have tolerated *Hicky's Gazette*"—a strange contrast with the highly-polished and newsy *Pall Mall* of our time. Infamous slander is the chief material of which the first Indian journal is composed, and even Warren Hastings, the first Governor-General, and the dignitaries of the Supreme Court, came in for their share; while colonels, missionaries, and beautiful young ladies just arrived for the marriage mart, are all mercilessly dealt with. At length Mr. Hicky thought it "a duty incumbent on him to inform his friends in particular, and the public in general, that an attempt was made to assassinate him last Thursday morning, between the hours of one and two o'clock, by two armed Europeans, aided and assisted by a Moorman!" Such was the first Indian editor, the amusing chronicler of the gay and grave doings of a great age long passed away, the scene of whose labours was Calcutta, where, at that time, there was only one church, and deep drinking was considered a rational amusement. It may be interesting, while thinking of the improvement which has taken place since Hicky's time in our Indian newspapers, to look also at the improvement in civil and military salaries since then—not a bad theme for a reflective mind. When Sir Thomas Munro arrived in India, as a cadet, in 1780, his pay was five pagodas (17½ rupees, or 35s.*) a month, with free quarters, or ten pagodas without. Five pagodas and free quarters was the way generally followed. "Of the five pagodas," writes Mr. Munro, "I pay two to a Dubash, one to the servants of the mess, and one for hair-dressing and washing; so that I have one pagoda per month to feed and clothe me." Mr. Shore (afterwards Lord Teignmouth), a civilian in the Secret and Political Department, on his arrival in India, in 1769, had only eight rupees a month;† but the "writer," as the young civilian was then always styled, was, in those days, allowed to trade under certain restrictions. The mention of such eminent men suggests others of great celebrity in India, who, during the latter portion of the eighteenth century, even supposing no

---

* Taking the Sicca rupee, say £2 a month.
† *Calcutta Review*, No. I., May, 1844, p. 17.

difficulty existed in paying for the newspaper or periodical, could not get the article of the intellectual quality they desired. It was a dark night, even in England, for the broadsheet. The sunny days of a penny *Daily News*, *Telegraph*, *Globe*, or *Standard*, and a halfpenny *Echo*, were yet far remote. The future Sir John Malcolm, and Lord Metcalfe—of whom the biographer of the former has also written so well, and who was born in Calcutta, in 1785, or two years after the great soldier and political "Jan Malcolm, Sahib" arrived in India —during their early labours must have gained but little assistance from the Indian press, of which Sir Charles Metcalfe was afterwards styled the Liberator, and on whose account the noble Metcalfe Hall, on the banks of the Hooghly, was erected by the citizens of Calcutta to perpetuate his name.

Under the administration of Lord Cornwallis, or from 1786 to 1793, the tone of social morality in India became much improved. The *Calcutta Review* informs us that the *India Gazette* of 1788 has an editorial congratulating its readers on the fact "that the pleasures of the bottle, and the too prevailing enticements of play, were now almost universally sacrificed to the far superior attractions of female society." It was the old story, now told in India, which had long been told in other parts of the world, and of which the editor of the *India Gazette* must have been an admirer, while bewailing bachelor life in Calcutta:—

> "Still slowly pass'd the melancholy day,
> And still the stranger wist not where to stray.
> The world was sad!—the garden was a wild!—
> And man, the hermit, sigh'd—till woman smiled."

Or, perhaps, the ideas of the lively Moore regarding the "superior attractions of female society," would have been more palatable to the editor of the *India Gazette* than those of the more sober Campbell, as in the well-known verse of the Irish melody :—

> "Oh! 'tis sweet to think that where'er we rove,
> We are sure to find something blissful and dear;
> And that when we are far from the lips we love,
> We have but to make love to the lips we are near!"

But such a "defence of inconstancy"—such a piloting off and bidding "good-bye!"—may be unjust to an age in India when the precocious youth, the "girl of the period," and the periodical of sensational tales, had not yet appeared in England.

It is strange to think of what such men as Hicky and the

above-mentioned editor would write about the law of progress, could they now behold Young Bengal in his railway carriage or steamer, with his *Friend, Englishman, Phœnix*, or *Pioneer*— all ministering to his social wants. Shades of Caxton, Watt, and Stephenson, the reality is a stern one!

On the 29th of May, 1818, under the administration of Lord Hastings, the first efforts to improve the native mind by education, and by periodical literature in the shape of a native newspaper, were made. The journal appeared from the Serampore Press, and was styled the *Sumachar Durpun*. Lord Hastings took it into Council, and allowed it to be circulated at one-fourth of the ordinary postage. About the same period the Calcutta School-book Society was formed. Thousands of natives began to learn the English language, and there was every sign of National Education struggling to be born. There is not space here to enter into even a brief account of the restrictions on the Indian press, after the departure of Lord Hastings; of the ejectment of Mr. Buckingham by Mr. John Adams; of the comparative freedom of the Indian journals during the last two years of Lord Amherst's administration; of the attacks on Lord William Bentinck for carrying out his masters' (the Court of Directors') orders, and the consequent renewed restriction on the press; or of its liberation by Sir Charles Metcalfe in September, 1835. About the year 1832 there were several Bengali newspapers, also a Bengali magazine.

Let us now turn to the stars of Anglo-Indian periodical literature, some of which went out while giving fair promise of more glory, and to those whom to know was an honour, who, in their maturer years, thought sometimes with pride of the delight their writings gave while life's morning was opening on a brilliant Indian career.

I shall here bring the editorial *We* into operation, which was first adopted by the Printer, "the ostensible director of the paper," * in 1640; just eighteen years after the first printed newspaper appeared in London—the *Weekly News* of Nathaniel Butter.

Of course the mighty Oriental (Hindustani) HUM (*We*) has existed from time immemorial. The first work we shall turn to is the "Bengal Annual," of which the number for 1833 lies before us. This was a very successful publication while it lasted, and very superior in literary merit to some of the English Annuals. It was maintained for a few years at first without any engravings, but latterly with embellishments from

* Andrews.

Europe, which probably caused its abandonment as being too costly for India, and consequently unremunerative. Its principal contributors were Henry Meredith Parker, of the Bengal Civil Service; Captain D. L. Richardson (editor); John Grant, Apothecary-General; Lieutenant A. H. E. Boileau (the familiar face before mentioned), and numerous others, all of whose names are given in the respective volumes, which contain no anonymous productions. W. T. Robertson, C.S., R. H. Rattray, Lieutenants Macgregor and Westmacott, the Hon. Sir John Malcolm, Mrs. Hough, and Miss Anna Maria Mowatt, in addition to the names above mentioned, figure in a list of about fifty contributors to the "Bengal Annual" for 1833.

The volume, standing entirely on its literary merits—typography very good, bound in red (not morocco), with gilt edges, not a single illustration—opens with "An Oriental Tale," by the highly accomplished and versatile Henry Meredith Parker. This being the fourth number of the "Annual," which would make its foundation date from 1830, the London critics had ample time to decide on the merit of the Eastern stranger. The thing, to exist well, must be decidedly Oriental, was the unanimous voice, from which there is no appeal. When men go to India to seek their fortunes, and women to the marriage-mart, to carry out what Dr. Johnson styles the great end of female education, to get husbands (an idea now exploded, but which the learned Doctor might have thought more sensible than soliciting "Female Suffrage" at home!) said the critics, when they take up the pen they must leave their British character behind them and give us something of the marvellous, and Oriental-picturesque that we do not know. To please such a fastidious race, the "Oriental Tale" came forth; and it was thought so worthy of giving a flavour to "Bole Ponjis," that it appears in Mr. Parker's collected writings under that title, published in 1851. Remarks from the *Monthly Review* and *Morning Herald* head the contribution, the former probably written by some lineal descendant of Smollett's friend, Mother Griffiths; and they may be accepted as curiosities of literature:—

"To us, at this side of the Ganges, (which side?) subjects entirely Indian, or at least Asiatic, would be in general much more acceptable than those which we can easily obtain in our northern climate."—*Monthly Review.*

"The 'Bengal Annual' comes from about our antipodes (really!)— from the Calcutta Press, and is printed upon Indian paper. It would be well if the Eastern character had entered a little more into its contents."—*Morning Herald.*

The tale is full of fun and rich humour. Mounted on the pedestal of purpose, the tale-teller shouts forth: "Joseph, a duwaat (ink-stand), filled with the blackest ink of Agra, and 40,000 new Persian cullums (pens). Good! A fresh chillum; saturate the tatties with goolaub, scatter little mountains of roses, chumpah, and baubul blossoms about the room; bring me a vast serai of iced sherbet, pure juice of the pomegranate, you understand, and now here goes!"

And now commences an Oriental tale with a vengeance :—

"The snakes were prodigiously lively—thermometer stood precisely at 138° Fahrenheit in the sun, but was some degrees lower in the shade. There is an uproar! A tiger and a buffalo, coming to drink up the last quart of water which lies in a little patch of marsh, have got themselves into a sufficiently absurd situation: a playful boa has embraced them both. He, poor good-natured creature, quite unconscious of their dissatisfaction, has judiciously wrapped his tail round a pretty extensive clump of teak trees, and with the spare end of his body is uncommonly busy cracking the ribs of his companions, which go off like so many muskets, and otherwise preparing them in the most approved manner amongst boas for his supper. I said the snakes were prodigiously lively."

And so on, from the cracking of a tiger's tooth, fairly shivered by the heat, down to the adventures of Kubbadar Cham, Major Mimms, and his beloved Nealini. The escape of the dark-eyed Nealini and the redoubted Mimms from the pile which had been fired to burn them, is told with great humour; and the author, near the end, asks, "Who does not recollect the parties of the accomplished Lady Mimms at her mansion in Portland Place; her golden pawn-box; her diamond hookah; the emerald in her nose, and her crimson silk trousers?" And again: "Who does not recollect General Sir Godfredo Mimms, K.C.B., with his side curls and his pig-tail?" &c., &c.

With reference to the "side curls" thus mentioned as worn by the gallant Mimms, he may have worn them before he became a knight; and English readers will be inclined to allow a touch of fact to the above picture when they learn that, not very many years before the present writer went to India, a Commander-in-Chief's Order appeared in Madras, forbidding young officers to wear "side combs," as giving an "effeminate appearance" to officers in the Army; which most sensible Order, by the way, was said to have been written by His Excellency's admirable and gifted lady! Not a few who rose in the Madras Army will recollect this order.

The Calcutta reviewer of "Bole Ponjis" says truly of Parker's writings: "There is many a transition from grave to gay, from lively to severe; but the prevalent characteristic of them is humour, which occasionally, as in the "Oriental Tale," becomes broad and open-mouthed, but which is generally of that chastened and tasteful kind which was probably more appreciated in former times than in these days."*

II.

HAD Thomas De Quincey and Professor Wilson (Christopher North) served in India, what splendid contributions to Anglo-Indian periodical literature might have been expected from two such writers! How the Professor especially, in a country so stupendous, darkly mystical, and pagan, whose very ruins have an aspect of sublimity about them, would have added to what De Quincey, his friend and critic, styles, with reference to his periodical papers, "a *florilegium* of thoughts, the most profound and the most gorgeously illustrated that exist in human composition!" And what lights and shadows of Anglo-Indian life could Wilson have painted! That grief and joy are sisters, Christopher North in the "Noctes"—as the philosophical Adam Smith did before him—has sternly insisted on: "And this warld, ye ken, sir, and nane kens better, was made for grief as well as for joy." † How true it is that their very lives depend "on one and the same eternal law!" In India, perhaps, the sisters lie nearer to each other than in England. There would seem to be an intensity of feeling, even in the little occurrences of common life, in the company with which we spent the evening last night, and in "those frivolous nothings which fill up the void of human life," unknown elsewhere.

The exuberance of joy, the excess of grief—say, in the one case, from the exhilarating morning ride; to the sportsman, from the pleasure and excitement of the wild-boar hunt; to the soldier, from the prospect of service and distinction; to the student, from the various phases of life in the "gorgeous East;" or from the brilliant, social, evening gathering at the band;— and in the other, from the not unfrequent suddenness of death; from the feeling of exile; from the necessity of what has been styled "the grand Indian sorrow"—parting with one's children;—these and a hundred other joys and sorrows are truly intense in the Indian land.

* *Calcutta Review*, No. 32, December, 1851.
† *Noctes Ambrosianæ*, or, Nights at Ambrose's."

From gay to grave, then, is a most natural step; and before parting with the "Bengal Annual" we shall present our readers with nearly the whole of a little poem, forming a strange contrast with the humorous "Oriental Tale," cited at the conclusion of our last paper:—

THE NEW-MADE GRAVE.
By H. M. PARKER, Esq., C.S.

> The grave! for whom?
> What traveller on life's solemn path hath won
> The quiet resting place? whose toil is done?
> Who cometh to the tomb?
>
> Is it the sage,
> Who, through the vista of a life well past,
> Looked calmly forward to this lone, this last,
> This silent hermitage?
>
> Is it the brave,
> The laurelled soldier of a hundred fields,
> To whom the land he nobly warred for yields
> A peaceful, honoured grave?
>
> Doth the matron come,
> Whom many bright-eyed mourners of her race
> Will weep, when looking on her vacant place,
> By the hearth of their sad home?
>
> When the day dies,
> Not unannounced comes the dark starry night;
> To purple twilight melts the golden light
> Of the resplendent skies.
>
> And man, too, bears
> The warning signs upon his furrowed cheek,
> In his dimmed eye, and silvered hair, which speak
> The twilight of our years.
>
> But, oh! 'tis grief
> To part with those who still upon their brow
> Bear life's spring garland, with hope's sunny glow
> On every verdant leaf.
>
> To see the rose
> Opening her fragrant glories to the light—
> Half bud, half blossom, kissed by the cold blight,
> And perish ere it blows.

In our humble opinion, "the twilight of our years" is a beautiful idea simply rendered.

"The Draught of Immortality, and other Poems," by the same writer, is the title of a volume published in London in 1827. It reminds us at once of the famed *amreeta* cup in the "Curse of Kehama"—a poem condemned early in this century by the Edinburgh reviewers because they did not understand its mythological beauties—of which Kehama drinks, hoping to gain a blessed immortality; but Siva, the destroyer, has doomed him "to live and burn eternally." The graceful Kailyal drinks, and becomes a thing of immortal bliss; and father, daughter, and Glendoveer (good spirit), are now all enjoying happiness in the Hindu paradise. By writing " Kehama," Lord Byron said that Southey had "tied another canister to his tail"—the first canister being " Thalaba," severely handled in the *Edinburgh* in 1802. "By the way," writes the admirable Heber, some twenty years later, "what a vast amount of foolish prejudice exists about Southey and his writings." Few had read a line of his works, but all were inclined to criticise him; and now the "Kehama" is best known to the English public through the " Rejected Addresses:"—

" I am a blessed Glendoveer:
'Tis mine to speak, and yours to hear." *

Parker always received more kindness from his reviewers than the voluminous and versatile poet laureate. " The Draught of Immortality," by our great contributor to Anglo-Indian periodical literature, sometimes reminds us of Moore in " Lalla Rookh." The former has only twenty pages; the latter is an elaborate volume; but as the critics praised the " extraordinary accuracy of Mr. Moore, in his topographical, antiquarian, and characteristic details," even Sir John Malcolm saying the poet wrote " with the truth of the historian "—this same " Tom Moore," Byron's friend, let it be remembered, never having visited the glorious East—we are inclined to think that Parker, who knew and could describe Oriental scenes so well, could have written, had he turned his mind to it, the next best Oriental poem in the English language to " Lalla Rookh."

And now we proceed with our sketch. The *Meerut Universal Magazine*, commonly called " M. U. M." from its initials—though, as a facetious friend observed, it was by no means *mum* in its character—was an exceedingly able periodical, got up principally by the late Sir Henry Elliott and Mr. H. Torrens, who also founded and contributed largely to the *Meerut Observer*. The latter journal was established in 1832, and is supposed to have been the first newspaper published in the Upper Provinces. Captain Harvey Tuckett—afterwards famous in the black-bottle duel with Lord Cardigan, to whose regiment (the 10th Hussars)

* " The imitation of the diction and measure, we think, is nearly almost perfect; and the descriptions as good as the original."—Note to " The Rebuilding, by R. S.," from the *Edinburgh Review*.

he belonged—was also a contributor to the Meerut journal, and the initials "H. T." not unfrequently caused confusion. Here we may say that two of the most distinguished Bengal civilians that ever lived were Indian editors; and the three writers, Torrens, Elliott, and Meredith Parker, were not only three of the most brilliant men that ever did honour to the Civil Service of the East India Company, but three of the greatest, in the face of many obstacles, that ever did credit to our Anglo-Indian periodical literature. In general ability, for writing on any subject, Mr. H. Torrens appears to have seldom been surpassed by those to whom literature was not a profession. He was a classical scholar, had made himself master of most of the European languages, and had won a name in Oriental literature. He had not so large a share of purely poetical inspiration as his friend Parker, but he had quite as much quickness and versatility of mind. He seemed rather to have resembled Sir Henry Elliott in his mental acquirements than his other contemporaries. Writing just after the intelligence of Sir Henry's death at the Cape, Mr. Hume remarks:—"In their love for Eastern learning they were alike, and so they were in versatility of talent. Both were accomplished scholars, and the charm of the society in which they moved."* Mr. Torrens, amidst all his official labours and anxieties, found that which only great minds are able to find for everything—TIME. Parker was another example of this admirable faculty; and that "great utilitarian," Lord William Bentinck, who admired him (H. M. P.) for his versatile genius, was forced to admit "what he had hitherto considered impossible, that literary attainments and excellence in dry official routine were qualifications which admitted of a happy combination." In addition to his other works, Torrens wrote "Remarks on the Scope and Uses of Military Literature and History," published in January, 1846, in the weekly *Eastern Star* (with the daily *Morning Star*, edited by Hume), and afterwards as a volume; and the *Calcutta Review* declared that the work was written with "great ability and clearness of analysis: evincing in the author intellectual powers of a high order, no less than extensive acquirements." In a welcome to the R. W. Br. Burnes, K.H. (1840), Mr. Torrens has the following graceful verse, which may be acceptable to "brothers of the mystic tie," or to "the sons of light," as Burnes' kinsman, the great poet, also styles them, and who are

---

* Biographical Memoir, by James Hume, Esq. (p. 108), published with "Writings Prose and Poetical," by Henry Torrens, Esq., B.A., vol. i.

more numerous and zealous in their good work in India than is generally supposed :—

"Had you wandered among us all penniless poor,
With no hope on the ocean, no home on the land,
Oh! the key that you wot of had opened each door,
And each brother stood by you with lip, heart, and hand."

It has been already remarked that the *Meerut Observer* was probably the first English newspaper published in the N.W., or Upper Provinces. The "Agra Ukhbar" *(Agra News)* was another receptacle about the same time, and several years later, for, in addition to brilliant leaders, all sorts of small periodical writing, such as growls from subalterns and apothecaries, and complaints from parties proceeding to the hills, composed of such valuable materials to every society, as beautiful young ladies with their admirers, disappointed widows, and manœuvring mothers!

Having touched on such delicate ground, at the risk of being considered slightly out of strict chronological order—for we should ere this have been with Captain David Lester Richardson (the famed "D.L.R."), and the *Calcutta Literary Gazette*—we proceed to remark that the "Mountain Wreath" was got up at Mussoorie, in 1834, by the brothers French, of the Civil Service, Captain Arthur Broome, of the Bengal Artillery, and others (including Lieutenant A. H. E. Boileau), and was illustrated with drawings, running only to two or three numbers, and was never put in print, though some of its articles were equal to the general run of those in the "Bengal Annual." Mountain air, if anything can, should rarefy the intellect ; and this is, perhaps, the reason why the leaders in the principal London journals are so much more brilliant in and immediately after August than before. Catching a fine trout, or shooting a brace or two of grouse, is the best of all medicines for a worn city editor. How he would enjoy a day's recreation, even without the grouse and trout, in the magnificent valley of the Dehra Doon! Mussoorie 7,000, and Landour 8,000 feet above the sea, are almost close together, on the northern side of the Doon. The views from these sanitaria for Europeans are very beautiful, corresponding in this respect with the famed Neilgherries (blue mountains) of the Madras Presidency. No level ground, and the houses built upon terraces cut out of the solid rock, it really is to be wondered at why the " Mountain Wreath " was not a decided success ! What sublime ideas could some of our London poets attain—the vapid " Fleshly School " included—by writing with the eye resting on the north upon "successive tiers of mountain ranges, terminating in the snowy peaks of the Himalaya!"* We shall dismiss the "Mountain Wreath" with a little anecdote of one of its contributors, which is not unknown to several officers of the old Indian army. It may be styled

WAITING FOR A GOVERNOR.

Two young officers, one being the periodical writer, called to pay their respects to the Lieutenant-Governor of the North-West Provinces. Only those who have been in India can fully estimate the high position of such a functionary. His Honour happened to be absent at the time of the visit; but, after some time, returning, the grey-bearded *chuprassie* announced that there were two gentlemen waiting to see the *burra sahib* (great master). Gazing with his searching eyes on the middle of the reception-room, "Where are they?" inquired his Honour, in the purest Persian. "*Dekho, sahib!*" ("See, sir!") exclaimed the faithful Mussulman, pointing to two corners of the room, in one of which was our periodical friend standing on his head, his uniform making the attitude more ludicrous; and in the other stood his brother officer, in a similar position, both seemingly determined not to be deprived of amusement while waiting for a Lieutenant-Governor!

Should this Anglo-Indian sketch fall into the hands of the philanthropic Earl of Shaftesbury, his Lordship may bring to memory the conclusion of his speech on the second reading of the Acrobat's Bill (July 4) :—"At one of the schools with which he was acquainted, there was a boy who, in consequence of having undergone this training, could not do his lessons unless he went and stood on his head in a corner for three or four minutes every now and then." (Laughter.) Perhaps the accomplished officers just cited † thought the act requisite to give the necessary composure to ask for an appointment as well as to amuse! But, whether from necessity or a love of the ludicrous, we see in life, every day, men as well as boys playing "fantastic tricks before high heaven."

Let us now turn to the *Calcutta Literary Gazette*, which brings us to think of the literary labours of Captain D. L. Richardson. This periodical was established upwards of forty years ago, was

---

* To complete the picture of such a magnificent field for the poet :—"On the south, the Dehra Doon, more than 4,000 feet below, appears with its fields, forests and rivulets, and beyond the Sewalik range, as far as the vision can reach, are seen the fertile plains of Upper India."

† Both of them rose to high rank and position.

tolerably successful for some years, when it declined and became merged into the Saturday edition of the *Bengal Hurkaru* (messenger), the old Calcutta journal, which had previously swallowed up and attached to its popular name the old *India Gazette*. The original was printed after the fashion of its English prototype; but though containing very able and interesting articles, it does not appear to have paid as a literary speculation; and it perhaps weakened its resources by declining to insert anonymous articles even when authenticated by their authors. The *Literary Gazette* seems to be an unfortunate name for a journal. There is something not sufficiently defined about it. Jerdan did a great deal for the London journal, which he founded; but when he left it, the change of hands was manifest, till at length it disappeared from the scene, and became merged in some other paper.

Richardson's literary fame commenced with the "Literary Leaves." His "Selection from the British Poets," with notices biographical and critical, were compiled and collected for the use of the Government Educational Institution of Bengal. In the work, partly written from this, entitled " Lives of the British Poets," there are what a Calcutta reviewer says pervade the " Literary Leaves," " a fine taste and acute observation, combined with a polished style and a most candid exercise of the critic's office." We recollect the literary " Chit-Chat," while it was being published in the " Literary Gazette " of the " Hurkura," in 1847; just seventeen years after Richardson became a giant in Anglo-Indian periodical literature, fourteen years after the publication of his " Ocean Sketches and Other Poems," and twelve after that of his chief work, the " Literary Leaves."

To give some idea of his work as an editor, the following is a correct enumeration of his labours in this respect :—

"Bengal Annual," from 1830 to 1836............ 7 Vols.
" Calcutta Literary Gazette," from 1830 to 1835 6 „
" Calcutta Magazine," from 1830 to 1833 ...... 10 „

Total................ .. 23 Vols.

As a volume, the lively and earnest " Chit-Chat " was reviewed, with his other works, in the " Calcutta " of September, 1848. And a most elaborate and learned review it is—one hundred and twenty pages on the " Literary Labours of D. L. Richardson." The reviewer brings out Macaulay in an arrogant light, hinting that " D. L. R." wished the " mighty member of the Council," the Whig and Edinburgh Reviewer, the "monopoliser" of all conversation, the idol for the hour in Calcutta, to write for him. What a catch he would have been! But fancy the brilliant man of genius, who had read every book and knew everything, fancy him "condescending to write one line for a 'Calcutta Annual,' or a 'Literary Gazette!'"

During the appearance, every Saturday, of the "Chit-chat," "Agellius"—a writer whose will was perhaps greater than his power to become a star in Anglo-Indian periodical literature—published a series of "Saturday Sketches" in the "Literary Gazette of the Hurkaru." Among them were the "Author in India," the "Missionary," the "Cantonment Beauty" (this would make a capital title for a novel!), the "Apothecary," the "Eccentric Captain," the "Indian Editor," &c.—the whole an attempt to sketch some of the principal portraits in the chequered drama of Anglo-Indian life. He also wrote in the same journal "A New Review of an Old Poem—Southey's 'Curse of Kehama!'"

Let us now turn to a goodly tome, "The Calcutta Monthly Journal and General Register of Occurrences throughout the British Dominions in the East, forming an Epitome of the India Press. For the year 1838."* This remarkable volume, in size reminding one of Lord Macaulay's famous description of Dr. Nares' work on "Burleigh and his Times"—which book "contains as much reading as an ordinary library"—commences with an admirable biographical and critical sketch of D. L. R. and his works, by Mr. (now Sir John) Kaye, who was a true friend of Richardson's to the last, when friendship and kindness were most required. The remarks concerning the difficulties under which a writer labours in our Indian community are of great value:—"Almost everybody in Calcutta knows the names and perhaps the persons of each writer in the different periodicals. . . . One person will not think much of a writer who happened to be, many years ago at college, inferior to him in scholastic attainments; another will recognise in a particular writer a junior officer, and will not admit of intellectual, where there is not military precedence; a third will say that A. is un-educated, or B. quite a boy, or C. too fond of society—and thus deny their right to set themselves up as public instructors. But all this is exceedingly unfair, exceedingly mortifying, and exceedingly embarrassing. The writings, not the writers, should be canvassed." No man—civilian, military officer, or merchant—who ever came to India, had, perhaps, so much right to utter such opinions as Mr. Kaye,

* Third series, vol. iv.

who founded the *Calcutta Review* six years afterwards. Every word is truth, and defies question. It is most interesting to get some earlier glimpses than we have yet given at the life of such a man as D. L. R.

According to the sketch we wish to introduce to our readers, David Lester Richardson was born in the first year of the present century. When only eight years old, he lost his father,* a Colonel of the Bengal Establishment, who contributed to the "Asiatic Researches," and was an excellent Oriental linguist. D. L. R. entered the Company's service in 1819, and first appeared as a poet in 1820, "when he began to send his verses to the *Calcutta Journal*, which was then under Buckingham's editorial management."

Soon after arrival in Europe, on medical certificate (in 1825), Richardson, through the publication of "Sonnets and other Poems," became admired in London as a poet. Regarding this difficult style of writing, Mr. Kaye says that most of the sonnets are "exquisitely finished and full of genuine poetry. We think that, with the exception of Milton's and Wordsworth's they are equal to any in the language." As a proof of his volume's popularity, it was included in a well-known diamond edition of the British poets, Richardson being "the only *living* bard whose works are included in the collection" (1827). About this time the Indian subaltern established in the Metropolis the *London Weekly Review*, expending thereon a large portion of his patrimony, which was considerable. His uncle, Colonel Sherwood, of the Artillery, had often said to him, "You are the richest Ensign in India; if you go home you will return a beggar." The Colonel's prediction was in a fair way of being verified. D. L. R. edited *The Weekly Review* (of which he was sole proprietor), "in conjunction with Mr. St. John, author of the 'Anatomy of Society,' 'Margaret Ravenscroft,' and some works of Oriental travel. Hazlitt, Bowring, Roscoe, Moir, Pringle, and many other eminent writers were amongst the contributors to this journal." So, no wonder, when he wrote in such splendid company, that the proprietor of this most talented and "most honest weekly periodical" should one day become such an ornament to periodical literature in India. In 1828, Richardson sold *The Weekly Review* to Mr. Colburn, and "began to think he had better return to his old profession in India." When it was known that he was about to return, his literary associates gave him a farewell dinner, at which Thomas Campbell, the poet, presided. Martin, "the poet

* He was lost on his passage home to Europe.

painter," and General Miller, who had distinguished himself by his "more than chivalrous services" in South America, were present; and the poet of "Hope," and some of the finest and most stirring odes in our language, considered the meeting as "an occasion of offering their sincere congratulations to their friend and guest, on the literary reputation he had already so creditably achieved, and their fervent hopes that his departure for India, which he had resolved upon, for reasons perfectly consistent with the spirit and manliness of his character, would furnish no bar to his fair and promising prospects in literature."

We cannot part with Mr. Kaye's sketch of D. L. R. without remarking on the excellence of the criticism contained therein. He tries to do his author full justice, and evinces what are styled the characters of taste—delicacy and correctness at every turn:—"'The Ocean Sketches' are bright Turner-like sea-views—they are beautiful, and dazzling, and highly-coloured; they attract the eye at once, but we cannot linger on them—they awaken scenic remembrances, but not heartfelt associations, and therefore they do not dwell upon the mind. The spirit of humanity pervades them not. They are gorgeous views without a figure in them, and therefore they lack vitality. This is a fault, which, we acknowledge, lies more in the subject than in the execution of the pictures, but we *have* a fault to find with their execution. 'The Ocean Sketches' are overladen with epithets," &c.

Again, the reviewer, alluding to Richardson's "Home Visions" being realised when once again he trod the shores of Old England, gives utterance to the following natural reflections, with which every Indian officer with a soul must at once agree :—"Oh! is it not worth a few years' exile—a few years of heart solitude in a strange land—to feel the exulting spirit, the bounding pulse, the access of animal life, the buoyancy, the hopes which stir within us, when we plant our foot upon the strand of merry England, and feel its mild airs breathing on us once more?" This feeling is increasing; men no longer consider India as their home. Even the proposed hill colonies will not do away with the joyful expression—so dear to every true Briton—"This is my own, my native land!"

The most famous literary competitor with Richardson was Dr. Hutchinson, Secretary to the Medical Board, and author of the "Sunyasse," a poem which, although possessing fine touches of feeling and fancy, was attacked with "all the virulence of offended criticism."[*] But the Doctor's merits, says a Calcutta

---

[*] *Calcutta Review* for December, 1845.

reviewer, were not "fairly tested." With reference to Richardson's prose, Mr. Kaye records his opinion that "in grace of diction and felicity of expression, few writers have surpassed D. L. R." A small extract from the essay "On Children"— quoted by the biographer and critic—will at once convince our readers of the truth of this remark :—

"CHILDREN.

"The changing looks and attitudes of children afford a perpetual feast to every eye that has a true perception of grace and beauty: they surpass the sweetest creations of the poet or the painter. They are prompted by maternal Nature, who keeps an incessant watch over her infant favourites, and directs their minutest movements, and their most evanescent thoughts. . . . . It is a sweet enjoyment to watch the first glimmering of the human mind, and to greet the first signs of joy that give life and animation to the passive beauty of an infant's face, like the earliest streaks of sunshine upon opening flowers. But, alas! this pleasure is too often interrupted by the sad reflection that the bright dawn of existence is succeeded by a comparatively clouded noon, and an almost starless night. Each year of our life is a step lower on the radiant ladder that leads to heaven, and when we at last descend into the horrible vault of death, our best hope is that we may rise again to a state resembling the happy purity of our childhood."

In this same number of the *Calcutta Monthly Journal*, we have ten biographical sketches (including that of D. L. R.), each lord of human kind being honoured with a capitally-etched portrait for the august occasion. James Sutherland; Lieutenant J. W. Kaye, Hon. Company's Artillery; Sir Edward Ryan; John Pearson, Esq., Advocate-General; Sir J. P. Grant, Puisne Justice, Calcutta; the *soi-disant* Raja Pertaub Chund; John Ross Hutchinson, Esq.; Longueville Loftus Clarke, M.A., F.R.S.; Alexander Ross, Esq., late President of the Council of India—all pass before us in rapid succession, as brilliant members of a society which—originally springing from the middle classes—has seldom been equalled upon earth. In the *Journal*, also, we have a few glimpses of the "great literary Lycurgus, Mr. Macaulay." We learn that, while in Calcutta, he undertook to prepare a work of selections from our prose writers, to correspond with a similar work on our poets, by Richardson (then Professor of Literature in the Hindu College); but, having sketched out the design, he left it to be completed by Sir Edward Ryan."* Again, some observations having been

* The present First Commissioner of the Civil Service Commission, in London, who was formerly Chief Justice in Calcutta.

made relative to the personal hostility which the press manifested towards Mr. Macaulay, the *Bengal Herald* replied that the press "says nothing about him in his personal capacity, nor cares about him in his personal capacity." The *Calcutta Monthly Journal*—naturally indignant at the strong feelings of hostility towards such a man—being assured that the line of distinction had *not* been drawn between his personal and his official character, says :—" We appeal to the experience of everyone who has been in the habit of reading the papers, whether for three years the whole artillery of the press—from the great guns of the *Hurkaru* and the *Englishman*, to the little swivel of the ' Gyananneshun '—has not been directed against him with a degree of vehemence and perseverance unexampled in the history of the Indian press." Such conduct towards a master-mind, one who could rise from the " Black Acts " to examine the moral and intellectual character of Bacon, is wholly unjustifiable.

There are just two other sketches in this volume to which we shall allude briefly, and these are James Sutherland, who, in 1827, became editor of the *Bengal Hurkaru* ; and John William Kaye, who was also its editor, crowning his periodical literary labours when he projected and founded the *Calcutta Review*, in 1848, some time after the elaborate criticism on his works in the *Monthly Journal*. Mr. Sutherland, at the early age of fourteen, went to sea, and spent seven years in the Navy as a midshipman. He served in a dashing frigate, the *Acasta*, commanded by Captain Ker, a famous "tartar," from whom the " Sea-Fielding," Captain Marryatt, in " Peter Simple," may have drawn the portrait of "Captain Savage." In 1815, the *Acasta* was paid off; and Sutherland, not long after, became a "Country Captain," and a zealous contributor to Anglo-Indian periodical literature. His first connection with the Indian press was in 1818, when he joined Mr. Buckingham (who had also been a sailor) in the office of the celebrated *Calcutta Journal*. As many other sensible men have done before him, he married, again went to sea, speculated, lost ; and when, early in 1823, Mr. Buckingham was " so tyrannically ordered out of the country," he again joined the staff of the above journal as reporter and contributor. Sutherland played a most conspicuous part in all the press squabbles of that most interesting period in Calcutta, when men thought they were beginning to die for want of what Junius styles "the air we breathe"—the liberty of the press ! In 1836 he resigned the editorship of the *Hurkaru*. Sutherland had also managed the *Bengal Herald* at the same time, in which journal appeared some of his best articles, literary and political. Here are a few remarks * on

"CAPTAIN MARRYATT.

"EDITOR.—He has neither the learning, nor, perhaps, the graphic power of Smollett in delineating the human character, but he is a delightful writer, and I have heard men of your profession say that some of his descriptions in 'Peter Simple' surpass anything in the same line in the works of any living writer, not excepting Cooper, the American—the club-hauling, for example. What say you ?
"NAUTICUS.—I entirely agree in that estimate of his literary character. He is the best nautical novelist of the day, out and out ; and I doubt his inferiority to Smollett, except in learning. . . . . His Peter Simple is a character, I will engage, drawn from the life, nay—I have actually known such a character, and some of his miseries while he was yet a Johnny Raw, are such as probably every naval officer has felt."

No one had a better right to criticise a sea-novel than Mr. Sutherland. Alas ! we shall never have another tale of the sea : the force of education and the iron-clads have rendered such a thing impossible. We now turn to contemporary biography, while its subject was of the military service. Mr. Kaye arrived in India in 1833, having been appointed to the Bengal Artillery, and soon (1834) became a regular contributor to Richardson's *Calcutta Literary Gazette*, in which he wrote the first of a series of papers, entitled "The Essayist." The subject is "The Pen and the Pencil ;" and the powerful critic *in esse* is immediately displayed by some discriminating and ingenious remarks which would have done credit to Hazlitt himself. There is time for both poetry and painting in India, and it is pleasant to see their relative advantages and pleasures so well set forth by an Indian officer. Which is the more likely to be, "not for an age, but for all time ?" is, after all, the grand question. All his essays in this series are written in a most pleasing style, evincing great knowledge, and causing us to wonder how the Artillery Cadet at Addiscombe found time to read up aught save mathematics and fortification. Mr. Kaye appears to have been born with all the feelings of a genuine author, which is proved by his just and striking remarks on " Excitement of Publication—Disappointment of Genius." Besides the essays to the *Gazette* he contributed many poetical effusions, a story entiitled the " Double First,"—in which the character of " Everard Sinclair," one of the principal personages of his novel of " Jerningham," is developed—and " Gasper Henric," a tale in twelve chapters. All

* Written between 1834 and 1836.

these were written within the short space of six months; and when the climate of India—and particularly Calcutta—is considered, such literary industry is truly wonderful. In the rains of 1834 he had no less than three severe attacks of fever, and in the same year he returned to England. On arrival in Europe, in Jersey, he printed, for private circulation, a small volume of poems, some from the *Literary Gazette*, to which he had been such an ornament—all of which evince decided poetical talent. His "Invocation to the Spirit of Beauty" would have done credit to the imaginative Shelley. Mr. Kaye's " Jerningham ; or, the Inconsistent Man," was published in June, 1836 ; and, we read, his various works of fiction " elicited the highest praise from some very able critics."

Striking specimens of the beautiful and pathetic—especially in " Margaret's Song "—are to be found in " Jerningham."

A brief specimen must suffice from the "Song," which is quoted in full in the *Calcutta Journal*:

" I pine—I wither—I am dying—a captive in a great prison house. I shiver with cold ; I am girt about with ice. I wander here and there, but all is dark and desolate. My soul harmonizes with eternal nature. How can I be joyous in this place, where everything around me is so drear? I speak in the language of my country ; it is my only solace—I have none beside it. I am a wretched outcast. Why was I not cut off in my infancy? It is better to die in Italy than to live anywhere else in the world."

"Doveton ; or, the Man of Many Impulses," is considered by the Calcutta critic, " both in design and execution, an extraordinary production." It is an allegory "in which certain qualities of the mind are embodied in the characters." It is enough to say of this work that it received high praise in the *Court Magazine* from the female Byron—the Honourable Mrs. Norton. We have no space to cite other works by Mr. Kaye up to 1838, but we feel it a duty to remark on the extraordinary powers displayed by one who could write graceful essays and verses at nineteen and twenty, and striking romances before the morning of life had fled ; and who in later years became the stern Calcutta reviewer of facts and fallacies, the historian of wars, and the biographer of eminent men * whose like, take them for all in all, we shall not look upon again.

We cannot dismiss the *Calcutta Monthly Journal* without alluding to the Free Press Dinner at the Town Hall of Calcutta. The liberation of the Indian Press by Sir Charles Theophilus Metcalfe, as before remarked, dates from the 15th of September, 1835. On the present occasion Sir Charles, having been invited

* Metcalfe, Malcolm, Sir Henry Lawrence, Neill, &c.

as the guest of the evening, the annual celebration was postponed to the 9th of February (1838). As dates are of consequence in our sketch we should also mention that the date of annual celebration is here given as the 15th of December. Mr. Longueville Clark presided, and Mr. Henry Meredith Parker was in the vice-chair. One hundred and ninety-six gentlemen sat down to dinner. Sir Charles sat at the head of the table between the Chairman and Mr. R. D. Mangles. The many toasts and speeches were grand and suitable in their character; but, as belonging to the profession of arms, we prefer giving an extract from that of the Vice-President, Mr. Henry Meredith Parker, with whom we have already made our readers acquainted :—
" Gentlemen ; my toast is the British Army. (Cheers.) I know there has been discussion infinite touching the politics of the British Army. Whether it was Whiggish or Toryish, Reformatory or Conservative—whether it loved a Free Press or did not love a Free Press—for my own part, I will own to you candidly that I don't care a fig what its politics are, or what its feelings are, on the question I have hinted,—it is sufficient for me to know, that through long years of peril and gloom the British Army fought and bled, that the hearths and altars of their country might not be polluted by a foreign foe. (Cheers.) It is sufficient for me to feel that it placed between a terrible enemy and our pleasant fields and native homes the iron barrier of its indomitable valour. (Cheers.) I can no more bring myself to care for the politics of our brave soldiers than I can care for those of that glorious chief who led them crowned with victory from the Rock of Lisbon to the gates of Toulouse, and from the wood of Soignés to the towers of Notre Dame. (Cheers.)" C. P. Prinsep, Esq., in a pithy speech, gave " Trial by Jury, the bulwark of the Freedom of the Press." Mr. Stocqueler (Editor of the *Englishman*), a well-known Indian periodical writer, was then called on by the Chairman to sing :—

"In the glorious old days of the glorious old Bess
(Though she scarce would have suited the present, I guess !)
The chronicles say that a newspaper first
On the wondering eyes of our forefathers burst.
 Sing Ballinamora, Ora,
 Huzza, for the Press is now free !"

The newspaper here alluded to was published in England in 1588, by the authority of Queen Elizabeth, at the time of the Spanish Armada. Its object was "to allay the general anxiety, and to hinder the dissemination of false and exaggerated statements." After holding forth the hardships of Indian editors—the glorious "jackals for India of the British lion!"—Mr. Stocqueler sang:—

"Aye, and still by her friends, through the world shall be loved
His name, who that badge of our slavery remov'd;
And year after year shall resound in this hall
The glory of METCALFE, who freed us from thrall.
   Sing, &c., &c., &c."

The Chairman—one of the most gentlemanly-looking men who ever came to India—well remarked on this great occasion, what few will venture to deny:—"In those countries where the Press is most free, is knowlege most diffused. It not only imparts instruction, but excites to learning; and the man who is opposed to the freeing of the Indian Press must be the foe to enlightening the natives. (Loud cheers.)" In short, there are two hundred millions in India to be instructed through Education and the Press; and, if those who wield such powerful weapons do not exercise their calling discreetly, they will have much to answer for.

At this stage we shall remark that, after the expiration of the East India Company's trading charter, in 1834, some of our best Indian newspapers came into existence. The *Bombay Times* in 1836-37, established a great reputation, under Dr. Buist, its highly accomplished editor. Mr. Knight succeeded Dr. Buist. changing the title of the paper to the *Times of India*. The *Friend of India*, in 1837-38, grew rapidly into notice, under John Marshman, son of the eminent missionary; and even now has, perhaps, the largest circulation of any Indian Journal. Marshman, Smith, Townsend, and others less known to fame, despite a few crochets, struggled to make the Serampore journal in every sense the *Friend of India*. The *Hurkaru* has already been mentioned; but "old Hurky" exists no longer.

The *Englishman*, under Mr. (afterwards Sir Macdonald) Stepenson (who succeeded Stocqueler); the *Star*, under James Hume (who wrote the famous letters in the *Eastern Star*, by an Idler), flourished in Calcutta.* In Madras, the *Athenæum*, projected and founded by Pharoah (1837-38), and the *Spectator*, by James Ouchterlony—who, after fairly starting the paper (now defunct), was succeeded by Glover in the editorship—were our earliest South of India journals. The *United Service Gazette* (now defunct) was a favourite among the military, thirty years ago, when it was under the management of Captain Langley,

* Mr. Butcher was also, if we recollect right, connected with the *Star*.

formerly an officer in the Madras Cavalry. India at the present time is well supplied with newspapers; and the *Friend of India*, the up-country papers, such as the *Pioneer* and *Delhi Gazette*,* the *Indian Daily News* (Calcutta), the *Madras Times*, the *Times of India*, the *Sindian* and *Our Paper* (both published at Kurrachee, in Sind), the *Rangoon Gazette* and *Times* (both published at Rangoon, in Burma), the *Ceylon Observer*, *North China Herald*, *Penang Argus*, and other journals, keep us well acquainted with what is going on in Queen Victoria's splendid Eastern dominion. The wonderful rapidity with which Indian news is anticipated (taking from the freshness of the overland summaries) by the telegraph, is enough to make our forefathers leap from their graves, when we consider that formerly (1811) it took ten or twelve months to get an answer to a letter or a dispatch from India; and now the Viceroy can send a message to the India office, in London, and be quite sure of its arriving safely there, perhaps (on account of the difference of the time in the two countries) even before its leaving the City of Palaces!

> " A word—and the impulse is given;
> A touch—and the mission has sped!
> Hurrah! 'tis the best conjuration
> That science, the wizard, has done!
> Through me nation speaks unto nation,
> Till all are united in one."

III.

The foundation of the *Calcutta Review* is quite as important an event in the history of our indigenous Indian literature as that of the far-famed "Edinburgh" and "Quarterly" at home. Sydney Smith, the original projector of the "blue and yellow," and Sir Walter Scott, the Ariosto of the North, who started the "Quarterly" as its Tory rival, doubtless would have greatly admired the idea of founding a Review in the City of Palaces, where the love of a high order of critical literature seemed at a discount, and the spirit of man

* The *Delhi Gazette* under Mr. Place, and the *Moffusilite*, when edited by its founder, John Lang, attained very high positions in Indian newspaper literature. The *Neilgherry Excelsior*, edited by Mr. Kenrick, and the *South India Observer*, under that veteran champion of the Press, James Ouchterlony (formerly of the *Madras Spectator*) are the chief up-country papers in the Madras Presidency. The up-country ("Moffussil," or district) papers in India are generally weekly and tri-weekly; the dailies are confined to the Presidency towns.

in general was very far from divine. The *Tenui musam meditamur avena* motto, originally proposed by the English reviewers for their journal—" We cultivate literature upon a little oatmeal"— seemed about to give place to one announcing its cultivation on a little curry and rice, which humble but popular repast, to the *Calcutta's* staff, amidst so many disadvantages of climate, promised to be permanent. But energy in this matter, as in everything else, had its glorious triumph. It had occurred to Mr. Kaye, then residing in Calcutta, to establish a Review, similar in form and character to our great British Quarterlies, but entirely devoted to Indian subjects and Indian questions. It was indeed a bold and seemingly hopeless experiment; "and," writes Mr. Kaye, " success astonished no one more than myself." And, again, speaking of one of the greatest on the roll of India's heroes and statesmen, he says, " That it did succeed is, in no small measure, attributable to the strenuous support of Henry Lawrence." Truly, the hour had come and the man ; or, perhaps, we should say the men! The *Calcutta* was precisely the organ for which Lawrence had been wishing, " as a vehicle for the expression of his thoughts;" and although, up to the time of its projection, he had never seen Mr. Kaye, his kindly heart and vigorous pen were at once placed at the disposal of one who had been a brother officer in the Bengal Artillery, and under whose "peculiar care" the coming Review was first to see the light. Lord Ellenborough had selected Lawrence to fill the highly important post of Resident at the Court of Nepaul. He had to "wait and watch" rather than "interfere." As soon as he heard that the *Calcutta* had been started, he " promised to contribute to *every* number."* But before this time the great "political" had contributed to some of the up-country journals, especially to the *Delhi Gazette,* in which appeared the " Adventurer in the Punjaub," a most interesting series of papers afterwards published in London, by Mr. Colburn. To the same journal another distinguished soldier and political of the Indian army—Lieutenant (afterwards Sir Herbert) Edwardes, eventually " Calcutta" reviewer—also contributed, under the strange but comprehensive signature of the " Brahminy Bull."

The first number of the Review was too far advanced for the editor to avail himself of Lawrence's aid. To this number Dr. Duff contributed one article; Captain Marsh, of the Bengal Cavalry, an earnest-minded and singularly-gifted man, contri-

* "Lives of Indian Officers." By John William Kaye, author of the "History of the War in Afghanistan," &c.—(1869)—p. 113 to 116—"Sir Henry Lawrence."

buted another; *and the editor wrote all the rest.* The latter remark evinces energy and literary heroism on the part of the editor, seldom equalled, and which only those who know something of India and its literature can fully appreciate. To come out in the month of May—the hottest in Calcutta—to do battle with ignorance, and probably superstition, required as much courage as to lead a forlorn hope! And, doubtless, such an idea crossed the mind of the statesman at Nepaul (whose father, Lieutenant Lawrence, had commanded the left column of General Baird's forlorn hope at Seringapatam),* while gloating with intense delight over the first number of the Indian " Quarterly." May, 1844, then, we consider, beyond all question, the most important month and year in the history of Indian Periodical Literature. Well might each reader in such weather, with thermantidotes going, and punkahs in full swing, exclaim with our friend, Mr. Parker :—

" But all in vain I sigh for lands
  Where happy cheeks with cold look blue ;
While here in the shade the mercury stands
  At ninety-two."

The contents of the first number must be cited to give a finish to our sketch. " 1. The English in India—Society past and present. 2. Lord Teignmouth. 3. Our Earliest Protestant Mission to India. 4. Ouchterlony's Chinese War. 5. The Condition-of-India Question—Rural Life in Bengal. 6. The Ameers of Sindh. Postcript:—The Massacre at Benares. Miscellaneous Notices." The motto is from Milton, more benign than the terribly critical *Judex damnatur, cum nocens absolvitur* of the " Edinburgh : "—" No man who has tasted learning, but will confess the many ways of profiting by those, who not content with stale receipts, are able to manage and set forth new positions to the world ; and were they but as the dust and cinders of our feet, so long, as in that notion, they may yet serve to polish and brighten the armoury of truth : even for that respect they were not utterly to be cast away."

To the second number Henry Lawrence contributed " a long and very interesting chapter of Punjabee history"—recent history of the Punjab ; the other contributors, besides the editor, being Mr. Marshman of the *Friend of India*, Dr. Duff, and his colleague, the Rev. Thomas Smith. After this, Lawerence's contributions became more numerous. He generally " furnished

* " Thus wrote, in the first year of the present century, Colonel Alexander Beatson, historian of the war with Tippoo Sultan, and of the famous siege of Seringapatam."—KAYE.

two or three papers to each number of the Review." Mr. Kaye also tells us that he once undertook to supply to one number "four articles, comprising 116 pages." The historian, biographer, and critic, writes that " his contributions were gravid with matter of the best kind—important facts, accompanied by weighty opinions and wise suggestions." Like other great men, Lawrence was always deploring, and not without reason, his want of literary skill! Yet the editor generally considered his contributions as the most popular in the Review. His article on the "Military Defence of our Indian Empire" evinced that knowledge which every true soldier ought to possess. He continued to the end of his life to contribute at intervals to the now well-established periodical, and was, when the rebellion of 1857 broke out, employed on a review of the "Life of Sir John Malcolm" (in our opinion one of Mr. Kaye's greatest works), which he never lived to complete.*

We shall now give some brief extracts from the *Calcutta Review*, from articles by Kaye, Lawrence, and Edwardes. The first three are from the editor's contribution on "The Ameers of Sindh :"—

"The Sindh Ameers, it is said, violated treaties. It would seem as though the British Government claimed to itself the exclusive right of breaking through engagements. If the violation of existing covenants ever involved, *ipso facto*, a loss of territory, the British Government in the east would not now possess a rood of land between Burhampooter and the Indus. . . . . But the real cause of this chastisement of the Ameers consisted in the chastisement which the British had received from the Affghans. It was deemed expedient at this stage of the great political journey, to show that the British could beat some one ; and so it was determined to beat the Ameers of Sindh. It is true that two victorious armies had marched upon Caubul through the eastern and western countries of Affghanistan, and carried everything before them, but it was deemed expedient immediately to withdraw those armies. . . . . Far be it from us to say that British rule may not, in time, become a blessing. If we were not hopeful of better things—if we saw before us nothing but dreary stagnation—if we believed that the evils, of which we have endeavoured to give some intelligible exposition, were irremediable evils—evils inextricably and eternally interwoven with the whole fabric of Hindustani society, we should not have launched this review into being."

The last remark is significant as connected with periodical literature in India; so before turning to the "Howard of the Punjab"—the noble artillery colonel, Sir Henry Lawrence—for something striking, let us look for a moment into "Contemporary

---

* Two elaborate reviews on the "Life of Malcolm" afterwards appeared in the *Calcutta*.

Biography,"* where, beside the name of J. W. Kaye is written : " English historical writer ;" that he served in the Bengal Artillery from " 1835 to '45 ;" that he entered the Home Civil Service of the East India Company in 1856, when he was appointed secretary to the Political and Secret Department, which highly important post he now holds in the India Office ; and that he is the author of " The History of the War in Afghanistan," " Christianity in India," " History of the Indian Mutiny," and other works.

Sir John is, *par excellence*, the literary Knight Commander of the Star of India.†

The contributor, like the editor, was decidedly opposed to annexation. In his article on the " Recent History of the Punjab," Lawrence writes :—

" We are among those who believe that the ocean, the Indus and the Himalyas, will some day be our boundaries ; but we have no desire to see that day hastened by events over which we have no control—much less to see interference forced upon the Punjab. We have now a good position on the frontier. Let it be still further strengthened with troops and material; let our own territories be rendered safe from insult, and the means be at hand of readily redressing any injury that may be offered ; and we shall not soon find ourselves tempted to aggression."

The following remarks are admirable ; and in these unsettled times, both in India and England, we may take a lesson from them :—

" NATIONAL RESTLESSNESS.

"To be strong but placid in our strength, is the condition which we should endeavour to preserve. Restlessness often indicates, or seems to indicate, weakness : and nothing is more contagious than excitement. To be prepared is one thing ; to be always making preparations is another. The former neither rouses the fears nor stimulates the presumption of our neighbours; the latter often operates in both directions, for whilst it betrays uneasiness, it suggests an apprehension that such uneasiness is dangerous."

Germany, at the present time, conscious of her strength, is betraying wonderfully little " restlessness " after conquest.

Our last extracts are from " The Sikh Invasion of British India," which appeared in the *Calcutta Review* for September, 1846, by the admirable Sir Herbert Edwardes. Before the terrible victory of Ferozshah—the Indian Waterloo—took place, a bloody battle was fought on the 18th of December, 1845, at Múdkí. The weary foot-sore troops had dragged themselves on

---

* " Contemporary Biography," by Frederick Martin. London : Macmillan & Co. 1870.—Sir John served from 1833 to 1845, *not* from 1835, as stated in this work.

† Mr. Marshman is C.S.I.—a most worthy companion.

to this position, which they reached at noon—"and what a welcome sight met their view! Beneath the walls of a fort spread a wide clear tank of water; and the reader who has not the memory of that long march of twenty-one miles, with heavy sand under foot, and the air disturbed by the dust of 15,000 men, cannot paint the eagerness with which men and horses rushed to the bank, and tried to slake a thirst which seemed unquenchable."

"Young ladies! languishing on your damask couches, you never sipped eau sucrée or lemonade out of a crystal goblet that was to be compared to a greasy chako full of muddy Múdki water. Between two and three o'clock . . . . Major Broadfoot again galloped into camp with the news—this time true enough—that the enemy was advancing in force in front."

Having finished their breakfasts, the whole army, after a march of unusual severity, "turned out, as if fully recruited, to the battle." We remember the following passage being much admired in India at the time of its appearance. It is very graphic, and would have done credit to the pen of Sir William Napier, and our best military writers:—

"A PICTURE AT MUDKI.

"Once more the Governor-General, with a courteous bow, that would have done honour to St. James's, waved his dashing staff over to the brave chief of that brave army, and then fell back upon the infantry. The artillery was in the centre of the front line, and the cavalry on either flank, the main body of the infantry in contiguous columns behind, and a reserve in rear of all. A mile and a half at least from their own camp did the British advance in this order before they came under the fire of the Sikh guns; but then the "long bowls" came bounding in among them with deadly aim, and that peculiar *whirr* which makes the young soldier "*bob*" his head.* Now tumbrils begin blowing up, and artillery men dropping from their saddles; the mutual roar of cannon reverberates over the plain, and smoke obscures the vision. Closer and closer approach the hostile armies; and a staff officer, almost simultaneously from right and left, gallops up to Sir Hugh† with a report that the Sikh cavalry in clouds are turning both his flanks. Right

* The present writer recollects General Godwin saying to the young gunners at the capture of Rangoon—"Don't 'bob' your heads, men: you'll never hear the ball that hits you!"

† [General Sir Frederick Haines, K.C.B., Commander-in-Chief Madras Army, was Lord Gough's Military Secretary, and was present at the battles of Múdki and Ferozshah: in the latter engagement he was severely wounded. Again, he served in the Punjab Campaign (1845) with distinction. He served also in the Crimea; and it has been well and truly remarked, that "these services represent the hardest fighting that ever took place in India, and the hottest of the greatest European war in which Great Britain has been engaged during the present half century."]

and left he launches his own cavalry upon them ; right and left their brilliant charge makes the enemy's horse give way. The British infantry deploy and advance rapidly in line."

Without any disparagement to our brave neighbours, it may be said that the Sikhs, during their invasion of British India—one of the most critical periods in Indian history—fought with more system and united determination than the French did in the Franco-German war.

Dr. Duff, the Great Indian Missionary and eloquent writer and speaker, contributed to the earlier numbers of the *Calcutta* some splendid articles on the Khonds of Goomsur ; and the present writer, under the doctor's encouraging patronage, had the honour, among a few reviews and notices furnished to our Quarterly, to give the public some account of the "Tributary Mehals of Orissa, and Recent Operations against Ungool."

In the *Calcutta Review* also appeared the first regular account of British connection with the famous temple of Jagannâth in Orissa, written from official documents. Why will we still persist in calling it Juggernaut? In *jagan*, "the world," and *nâth*, "lord" (in Sanskrit), how do we find such a horrible word? Orissa, from the famine which some years back nearly ruined this remarkable province, drew forth the sympathy of both India and England ; and the instructive work just published by Mr. Hunter will do much to keep up an interest in its welfare.

We cannot take farewell of the *Calcutta Review* without thinking of Mr. Marshman's notes on the rivers of Bengal, and how he made the banks of the Hooghly interesting to us all, from vivid descriptions and memories of the past. And now we shall merely say to the favourite periodical, which has instructed and amused us so often in India, Go on and prosper!

Lang's *Meerut Review and Magazine* was announced for publication in August, 1846. Editing the *Mofussilite* at Meerut, killed it at its birth. Mr. Lang had really not time to pay attention to the *Review*. " Of the success of such a periodical in the North-Western Provinces," he wrote in the above year. " We have no sort of doubt ; we have not the slightest hesitation in saying, that a profit, of *at least* 6,000 rupees (600*l*.) *per annum*, might be derived."

At the end of the year 1848, there were seventeen lithographic presses established in the North-West Provinces, from which newspapers and other periodicals in the native languages were issued, independent of such as were conducted by the Christian missionaries. Of these journals three were in the Persian language, the Palace newspaper of afterwards treacherous Delhi being one; three were in the Nagree character, and the rest were published in Oordoo. The Mussulmans were the chief patrons of periodical literature in the North-West. As the Mahomedan has always been famous for giving a flowing title to his Emperor, or Empress, or their children—" Throne's Ornament," " Light of the World," " Light of the Seraglio," and such like, so we find one of the North-West periodicals enjoying the title of " The Chief of Newspapers ; valuable to good people, but a scourge to the wicked." Proceeding to Calcutta, we find the *Hindu Intelligencer*, at that time edited by a Hindu, though written in English, sneering at the " Juggut Bondhu Patrika," a journal conducted for and by the junior students of the Hindu College, " who render into Bengali, with *raw attempts*, the essays and lessons they read in their class studies ;" so we may yet hope for a native Lord Kames, or a Hindu Gifford or Jeffrey. The *Friend of India* gave a curious piece of information about this time—that the main object of the native journals, published in the native language, " by natives who have not embraced Christianity," is to subvert the popular system of idolatry ! In 1848-49, the Bengali publications of Calcutta were sixteen, at a monthly subscription varying from one rupee (2*s.*), to two annas (3*d.*). We must reserve for a concluding brief paper some matter we have yet in store on periodical literature in Bombay, Madras and Ceylon, particularly Anglo-Indian, which, through presenting our various thoughts and actions to the native mind, in the most truthful and attractive fashion, will surely, among Her Majesty's Hindu and Mahomedan subjects, produce what is so much desired—a healthy state of public opinion.

IV.

To book-hunters especially, a very interesting character is to be found in British India in the shape of the book-wallah or book-hawker—a sort of literary pedler who wanders about from town to town and from station to station with much patience, and an apparent love of books and periodicals which such glorious old book-worms as our Roscoe and Charles Lamb would have greatly admired. Without this dispenser of heavy and light literature in our splendid Eastern dominion, we may doubt if India would be as secure as it is. Through the travels of the book-hawker, many antidotes to poisonous writings are administered ; educated natives purchase English philosophical treatises, mathematical works, and old magazines—all with equal composure; the poorer Hindu or Mahomedan, with Lord William Bentinck's famous remark ringing in his ear—" Education is the first want, education the second, education the third want of India!"—dives into the box or bundle (to the astonishment of the patient cooly or native porter who carries it) for a grammar or spelling-book; while the *burra sahib*, his wife and daughter, seated in splendid mansion at tiffin (lunch), or it may be enjoying a siesta, with the thermometer 100° in the shade, startle at the sonorous voice exclaiming from the door, or beside the refreshing *kus-kus* tatties,*—" Book-hawker, Sir!"

We shall now give two brief anecdotes of this important *periodical* visitor in India. The first may be styled

THE TWO SHAKSPEARES.

"It was towards the close of sultry day—we shall not say how long ago—that we were sitting beneath the porch of our humble dwelling ensconced in a comfortable arm-chair, and engaged in musing on the various vicissitudes of an Indian career. We were startled from our harmless reverie by the drawling tones of a voice, which said, close to the chair, ' Master, want any book?—very good book for master.' Turning round suddenly, we beheld, standing at our side, a middle-aged Borah, with dark turban and not unpleasant countenance. He held a book in each hand, and immediately behind him was a cooly, who had just thrown his box or basket, covered with a blanket, on the ground.

"Master, want Shakspeare?" resumed the book-wallah, "Shakspeare very good book."

"Aye," said we musingly, "Shakspeare was a great man. No writer, ancient or modern, ever came near him in the delineation of human character or the human passions. He is the poet of all ages, the poet of nature, fancy's child : ' exhausted worlds, and then imagined new!'—who can write like Shakspeare? In every sense, ' his head was the palace of the passions.' But, anxious to see what edition of our favourite author was proffered on this occasion, we snatched the book enthusiastically from the hawker's hand, and found it to be—*horrible dictu!*—' Shakespear's Hindustani Dictionary!'"

The next is from "Colonel Davidson's Travels"—the gallant officer weighing nineteen stone, and having "a strong predelic-

---

* These most necessary mats or screens outside the door in India, being kept wet, with the hot wind blowing on them, causes the *kus-kus*, of which they are composed, to emit a most grateful perfume.

tion for the good things of life in general, and of tomata sauce in particular"—where, according to his Calcutta reviewer, the colonel encounters a wag, and here we have a sketch of

THE CORPULENT COLONEL.

"Riding past this (Baboo's) ghat one morning, I heard a loud call in my ear, and turning round, discovered that a Bengalee book-hawker wished to enjoy my conversation. He ran up quite breathless, and opening his wallet, took out a little octavo half-bound in Russia volume, which he placed in my hands with an air of triumphant satisfaction. 'Lo, Sahib! lo! Take it, sir, take it.' I took and opened the book, and the first glance displayed an old fat lady in a chair. Its title was 'Wade on Corpulency.' I had never before seen, although I had heard of, the work. I saw another similar etching, and at last laughed heartily. 'What do you want for this?—how much?' 'You know best, sir.' 'No, I don't; what is its value?' 'You ought to be the best judge of that, sir,' said the nigger, laughing in my face. I immediately looked round to ascertain whether he had not been directed by some wag to bring it to me as a joke, but I could not see any one." The Calcutta reviewer well thinks the fellow ought to have received "a rupee on the spot."*

Whether or not the book-wallah (lit. book-keeper) ever rises to the dignity of a native editor of a newspaper or magazine, or occasionally gives a lecture for the benefit of some of his benighted countrymen, we cannot say; but there can be no doubt that, by hawking about good books, he assists ambitious editors and all young Mahomedans and Hindus who are inspired with the vanity and glory of literature.

We have already alluded to the native journals of the northwest; but to give a correct idea of the extent to which the periodical press exercises an influence over the natives in those parts would require the pen of the *Friend of India*, who in November, 1848, published an excellent paper on the subject. The editor of the "Zoobdut-ool Ukhbar" (written in Persian), we read, does not often hazard his own opinions, or lay himself open to attack, but is very cautious, and clothes in flowery language any expression of dissatisfaction which he may publish. No scurrilous matter found place in this respectable Agra journal, the information in which used to be generally correct, "and for the most part gathered from the English and other

* *Calcutta Review*, No. 1. p. 256.

papers." The following information regarding this "chief of newspapers "* is of great importance, especially when we consider the nature of our hold on India. Its advocacy of the views of educated natives on religious and other subjects, in opposition to the Europeanised opinions which are now becoming so extensively disseminated by means of various periodicals, is seldom of a direct and open character ; " but the editor being a staunch, though cautious Moosulman, is not backward to avail himself of opportunities for insinuating opinions agreeable to the Moosulman population." What an argument we have here in favour of everything being done that can be done to establish a sound and healthy system of education in India! The longer we live the more we are convinced that the love of knowledge is strongly implanted in every nature.

In Bombay they have Parsee editors and vernacular journals, one of which used to be the "Apakhytar" *(Independent)*. In 1859 the dawn of intelligence in Bombay became decidedly manifest among the native community. In the *Times* of 10th September, it was announced that Dr. Bhawoo Dajee intended to give a lecture in the Town Hall on the travels of Fa-hian and Hiouen Thsang, two Chinese Buddhist ecclesiastics, who visited India in the fourth and seventh centuries of the Christian era respectively. Light was to be thrown on a dark period of history by Dr. Dajee. The lecture, we believe, was a success. The first traveller, Chy Fa Hian, is alluded to at some length by the late Colonel Sykes, in his valuable work (or, rather, elaborate paper), published in the Journal of the Royal Asiatic Society, 1841, "Notes on Ancient India."

By the *Homeward Mail* of July, 1872, we learn some particulars regarding the "native press of Bombay," which, according to a correspondent of the *Gujerat Friend*, far from showing any disloyalty to the Government, is wonderfully tame, and is simply a second edition of the daily journals. " In the Anglo-vernacular journals there is no great talent displayed, though Bombay is richer than any other city in India in the excellence of its daily papers, under the editorship and proprietorship of Englishmen. Of course the natives are inferior to Europeans in journalistic talent, for it is a very difficult task to become an able journalist—more difficult, perhaps, than to pass the Civil Service Examination. The Calcutta Anglo-vernacular press is

* Alluded to at the end of our last paper ; the high-flowing title in Persian being "Zoobdut-ool-Ukhbar-Tuhfut-ool Ukhyar-o-mikrut-ool-Ashrar." This used to be the only indigenous paper in the N.W.P. not connected with the Government colleges and schools.

superior to that of Bombay, in consequence of the wider spread of education in Bengal." The native editor is at present in his infancy; but the time is not far distant when he will act as a mental lever on the benighted millions of India, and, Archimedes-like, or rather excelling him, having found a rest, move the Eastern world. Even the next twenty or thirty years may see some self-made, energetic Gordon Bennett, proprietor and editor of a Hindu or Mahomedan *Herald,* sending his Stanley, or fearless "special correspondent," far beyond the ranges of the "cloud-capt" Himalayas, to bring back to civilised parts some lost daring British traveller, who, with the great Livingstone in his mind's eye, has gone forth to explore distant lands, peopled by the Mongolian or other varieties of mankind of which we know little or nothing, and where may be wealth untold—gold, coal, precious stones, beyond the possibility of human calculation. Should such a consummation ever be effected, and the discovery tend to enrich our Eastern dominions, and consequently Great Britain, how England would rise from her wretched apathy towards India; what debates concerning her welfare would take place in Parliament; and how soon would Britain's greatest glory—the cradle of science, which possessed a grandeur of its own ages before Athens and Rome promoted the arts of civilised life and literature, and now containing one-sixth of the human race—receive due attention and consideration! But let us begin at once, and not delay the study of India till some internal convulsion brings us near the dreadful word—LOST!

At present there are said to be fifty-nine native newspapers published in the Bengal Presidency, which considerable number of native organs is considered a good sign—"so many opinion-ventilators running through it." In July of the present year a new Indian magazine was about to be started in Calcutta, under the promising title of the *Bengal Magazine.* It professes to be a monthly review of Indian politics, society, and literature. The editor, Rev. Lal Behari Dey, has, it is said, "secured some of the best native writers as contributors to the new magazine." There is decidedly a love of periodical literature in India, and the curious traveller will not be long in the country without ascertaining the fact. While serving in Orissa the present writer has looked over a small Oorya periodical, entitled "Gyánáruna; or, Dawn of Intelligence," published under the superintendence of the missionaries at Cuttack; and while marching with artillery through far-famed ancient Madura, in Southern India, he has purchased from an intelligent Hindu a well got-up paper entitled the *Morning Star*. It was published in English and Tamil by the American mission at Jaffnah (Ceylon), and consisted of articles by the missionaries, with short sketches and correspondence by the native converts. The writings of the latter were generally good. The natives of India evidently think like ourselves in the matter: "Without a periodical literature we should be in this dilemma—either to be silent, and let what small insight we may have attained die with us; or else, resolutely undertake tasks for which we are not fitted."

We commenced this sketch by alluding to lectures at Seetabuldee (Nagpore); and now we read that in the present year there are to be vernacular newspapers for the Central Provinces —the Chief Commissioner having determined "to supply the want of a vernacular newspaper in the districts under his rule." The *Central Provinces News* and the *Gazette* are henceforth to enlighten the natives in this historic quarter of India; the former journal being printed in "Hindi, Urdu, and Marathi."*

Periodical literature will ever have one good effect among the intelligent natives of India, that of making them travel. In May of the present year, several well-educated Madrassis started for England, somé for pleasure, and others to study for the bar; and our countrymen at home may not fully be aware that a good native pleader is a gentleman not to be despised. As a sort of finish to these glimpses of the new dawn of Hindu and Mahomedan intellect, chiefly as regards native periodical literature, we shall give an extract or two from the native opinions or ideas regarding the murder of the late Viceroy (8th February, 1872), when, as the *Calcutta Englishman* well said, "it must have been a severe trial to those who had known him so intimately, and been so much in his company, to see the manly form laid low, and to know too bitterly that they had no power to raise a timely hand to avert 'the deep damnation of his taking off.'"

LORD MAYO.

The Bombay "Jam-i-Jamshed" wrote :†—"Everywhere we see signs of sorrowfulness. The public have left off their business, and they seem to ask what the motive was of the scoundrel in committing such a horrible act. . . . . He is not fit for a single moment to live in this world." And *Native Public*

* The head master of the Nagpore School was to be editor.
† *Homeward Mail*, March 11, 1872.

Opinion says :—" That so noble a life should be ruthlessly cut short by the assassin's knife is as appalling a tragedy as any that the records of human crime present." And then the journalist goes on to express " the deep and cordial sympathy which all loyal subjects of the Queen, be they European or native, feel for Lady Mayo, under this cruel bereavement." Such ideas at least show a healthy state of native periodical literature, and may well take a place beside a fine passage from *Indian Public Opinion* (February 13), by one of our own countrymen :— " Not climate, not overwork this time. That clear, firm intellect was never more securely seated on its lofty throne ; that herculean figure never firmer in the saddle, more commanding at Durbar, more conspicuous in brilliant assemblies, more lordly and magnificent everywhere." *

It must be kept in view that the early development of native intellect, according to our ideas of what civilisation should be, or the process at work of a transition state of the Hindu mind, only dates from the beginning of the present century ; so, let us look at the picture as we will, some good has been done during the last seventy years. And this remark leads us to think over Carey, Marshman, and Ward, the missionaries of Serampore, a trio almost matchless in zeal and the glorious attempts to conquer ignorance and superstition ; and in sternness of purpose not unworthy to take a place beside the fine old Roman triumvirates. Purpose was the secret of success with the above three great men ; and their success shows how little birth is to be considered in the great battle of life. William Carey was a bad cobbler ; but he possessed the determined spirit of Whitfield in England, and Xavier in Asia, so much so that we find the divine and philosopher, Chalmers, talking of him, in a flood of philanthropic eloquence, as the man " from whose hand the generations of the East are now receiving the elements of their moral renovation." Marshman was the son of a weaver and Baptist minister. William Ward was a carpenter. At the very commencement of the present century, after overcoming the most serious obstacles, they were

* [The late Earl of Mayo (Richard Southwell Bourke), well known in England as Lord Naas, before his succeeding the fifth Earl, was born 1822. He was educated at Trinity College, Dublin, the city of his birth, and became M.A., 1844 ; M.P. for County Kildare, 1847-52 ; Chief Secretary for Ireland, March to December, 1852 ; and again February, 1858, to June, 1859 ; M.P. for Coleraine, 1852-53 ; M.P. for Cockermouth, 1857-68 ; for the third time Chief Secretary for Ireland, with a seat in the Cabinet, July, 1866, to September, 1868 ; appointed Viceroy and Governor-General of India, in succession to Sir John (Lord) Lawrence, September, 1868.]

all three settled at Serampore. They set up a Press. Dr. Carey translated the Scriptures, and Ward printed the translations, the printer also preaching in Bengali when time permitted. Dr. and Mrs. Marshman opened schools; and their popularity was soon proved by the receipt of sometimes as much as 4,000 rupees in one month for tuition. Everybody (Europeans, East Indians, and natives) sent a son or two to Serampore. We have already said the missionaries published the first native newspaper; they also published the first periodical work in India. They established the first native schools, organised the first college for native catechists, printed the first books in the Bengali language, and founded a vernacular library.* In fact, they were the great pioneers of knowledge *versus* ignorance in India, during the early part of the nineteenth century. Ignorance is the greatest enemy we have here to contend with. In a fair stand-up fight we can see our foe, lay our guns, and dispose our troops; but in India, where treachery is generally combined with ignorance, we never know when the enemy is at hand. Doubtless, it is nearly the same in all countries. But ignorance of our power and resources is a more serious matter in India than elsewhere, perhaps only exceeded by British ignorance of the vast country, its history, geography, wants, and our great responsibility towards it. Probably, in history, we are a little better up than formerly. There is no longer doubt as to Holkar *not* being a Mussulman; but we are afraid there is still a chance of at any time, in a debate which might require an allusion to the early conquest of our Indian empire, hearing a desire expressed (as was really the case in the last century) to learn whether or not Surajah Dowlah (Sir Roger Dowler?) were a baronet!

We have not space to say much regarding the religious periodicals of India. The *Madras Native Herald* used to be very well written, and was great on the question of "Educational training" for the general population of the country. It is deemed self-evident that the efficiency and success of a system of general *education* for the Hindus will mainly depend on the character of the *inspectors*, *teachers*, and *books*, to be employed in carrying it on. . . . . "We do not demand that inspectors (European) should be ministers of religion; but we deem it indispensable that they should be

---

* See article in the *Calcutta Review* (1859), brought about by the appearance of a "Life of the Three Missionaries," by John Marshman Esq., C.S.I., son of the great Indian missionary.

truly religious men." In another number of the *Herald* (for 1848) we have a glance at passing events, and a comparison between a fearful tragedy just enacted in Paris and what was going on in the "great heathen city of Madras." Alluding to the *Cheddul*, or Swinging Feast (at Jagannáth it is styled the Dole Jattra), the writer says : " This brutal exhibition is not only destructive of all true religious feeling, but a nuisance and an offence to common decency. To offer, in the name of devotion, half-stupified wretches, hooked up by the backs and suspended to a cross-beam whirling on a pole sixty feet from the ground, is an insult to the enlightened understanding of mankind, and proves that two of the features of Hindu superstition are *childishness* and *cruelty*."—The Calcutta *Christian Intelligencer* and *Christian Advocate* may be mentioned among the influential Anglo-Indian religious periodicals. We have two numbers of the former magazine (1858-59) before us ; one containing the "Fall of the East India Company," our former munificent masters, who gained and ruled a mighty empire—an empire comprising, as Mr. Bright tells us, "twenty different nations and twenty different languages ;" while both numbers have most interesting "Recollections of Daniel Wilson, Bishop of Calcutta." The periodical writer here gives us a few good anecdotes of the admirable Bishop. His outset as a preacher at home was by no means favourable. " When Richard Cecil, whose curate he afterwards became, first invited him to preach in his church, the young preacher no doubt made the best display he could when in the pulpit of one who was himself so eminent as a preacher. On rejoining Cecil in the vestry-room, young Daniel Wilson, either inquiring how his sermon had been appreciated, or else appearing desirous to know, Cecil is related to have said, ' Well, of all the bad preachers I have ever heard, for both matter and manner, you are one of the worst.' " Now, for the commencement of the Bishop's career as a preacher in India :—" After, say the story-tellers, the first novelty of the new Bishop's style, manner, doctrine, &c., began to wear off, the somniferous influence of a tropical climate began to re-assert itself; and the Bishop often looked round from the pulpit on a drowsy and nodding congre-

---

* Regarding the vital question of Christianity in India, in a review of Mr. Kaye's work (1860) it is remarked that the Rev. Mr. Long had urged strongly the necessity for native missionaries. The "Calcutta " reviewer says :—" We believe that if Christianity is ever to take a hold on the people of India it will be by native agency." In the same number we learn that the end of the seventeenth century saw the first Protestant Church erected in Madras.

gation. 'This,' he exclaimed, 'will not do; I must at least have the people awake to hear the gospel I bring them.' And hence, it is said, he on design adopted the homely, abrupt, eccentric manner of address, the odd anecdotes, strange illustrations, and personal recollections which at times marked his preaching."

One of the Bishop's peculiarities was "a rather overweening estimate of *big people*, persons of rank and position." He would excuse the offence given to minor lights in the way of indifference, by saying, with the greatest simplicity, "But, my dear friend, he is a *Member of Council!*" The Governor-General was regarded by him as a species of divinity, and others with rank as *Dii minores*. Thinking so much of a Viceroy, what the good Bishop would have thought of Her Majesty's Secretary of State for India, had he been spared to have an interview with His Grace in the palatial India Office, it is impossible to say.

The Bishop eschewed all needless show and style; the furniture of his palace was of the humblest kind, and his table was marked by extreme plainness; but, let it be remembered, he gave two lakhs of rupees (20,000*l*.) to the new Cathedral in Calcutta, where he now sleeps, having nobly done his work. To the above anecdotes, furnished us by periodical literature, another one may be added, the truth of which may be vouched for, as the remark was made to some men of the present writer's corps during the Bishop's inspection of the Artillery Company at Moulmein, in British Burma. The men were much struck with the "bold and plain-speaking truthfulness" of their exalted "friend," and particularly when he said, "Now, I tell you what it is, men, every dram of arrack * you drink more than your allowance, you drink down damnation along with it!"

We shall now proceed to another station in Burma, and very briefly introduce a little periodical to our readers, the *Toungoo News* (*pro Deo et Ecclesia*). It was edited by the learned American missionary, Dr. Mason, author of " Fauna, Flora and Minerals of Burma," founder of the Karen Institute, and who, with his excellent wife, laboured for many years among the Karens (of Pegu), a remarkable people, who preserve in their books† the fossilised skeletons of our faith. Being simply

* The spirit distilled from rice, or the various kinds of palm, of which the allowance used to be two drams a day; afterwards one dram, if beer was taken.

† Some account of their traditions will be found in "A Narrative of the Second Burmese War."

Deists, without any idolatry or multitude of false gods, it is easier to engraft Christianity on such a foundation than on the Hindu; and religious periodical literature, in their own and the English language, is a most useful instrument among them. The first number of the second volume (1865) commences with an account of the Pali alphabet.

When Europeans first visited India, they noticed some remarkable stone pillars, scattered in different parts of the country, with inscriptions cut on them. These were sometimes found in three various characters. In the process of time, the languages of two were discovered, "but the most ancient characters defied every attempt to decipher them."

Five centuries ago the learned Brahmans of a Mahomedan sovereign could not decipher the inscription on the pillar at Delhi. A native historian wrote; "Round it have been engraved literal characters, which the most intelligent of all religions have been unable to explain."* Early ignorant European travellers thought the writing to be Greek, from the association in their minds of Bactrian coins and Alexander the Great, from which they were ready to pronounce any Indian inscription to be in the Greek character. "From the days of Sir William Jones," writes Dr. Mason, "the eyes of all the antiquarians in India had been directed to these inscriptions, but they were directed in vain." . . . . The first attempt to render any part of them was made by a Bombay scholar, who, in 1834, translated the first thirteen letters :—"In the two ways (of wisdom and works?) with all speed do I approach the resplendent receptacle of the ever-moving radiance." In 1837, James Prinsep walked up to the inscriptions and read them off to a wondering world, with as much apparent ease as Daniel did MENE, MENE, TEKEL, UPHARSIN, to the bewildered Babylonian monarch: "Thus said King Devanampiya Piyadasi!'" Remarking on the Pali alphabet, Prinsep says: "There is a primitive simplicity in the form of every letter, which stamps it at once as the original type whereon the more complicated structure of the Sanskrit has been founded." And he adds what has never been controverted: "I consider it the primeval alphabet of the Indian languages." As "all the ancient alphabets west of the Indus have been traced to the Phœnicians, and all east of the Indus have been derived from the Pali," it may be interesting to give a note or two on the language of Burma, where, if the learned Chief Commissioner, Sir Arthur

* *Journal of Asiatic Society of Bengal*, July, 1837, Supplement; Supplement, 1864; October, 1834; and March, 1838.

Phayre, had met Prinsep, there might have been some addition to the flood of light which, we trust, Sir Arthur is yet to furnish us with on Buddhism and Chin-India. There never was a better time for English students to learn something about such a land. The "intercourse of West and East," is rapidly bearing fruits. In truth, to use the words of a popular London journal, "The lands of Buddha and Brahma have entered what we call the paths of progress." We have now in England for the first time Ambassadors from Burma, Western China (the Panthays), and Japan, anxious to see our wonders and learn about our commerce and science; and fifty years hence, if Japan has gone far on the road towards becoming "an Oriental England, if Burma and Western China have not done the same, Great Britain will have much to answer for. More periodicals should at once be started to furnish information regarding these important parts of the world, with which we are so closely connected. The Burmese Embassy has already drawn much attention to the land of the Golden Foot of Ava, and the following brief notes on their language may be added to what has already been said about the Pali :—The common language of Burma is called the Burman, and is written from left to right in characters of a circular form. "The language in which all their religious books are composed is called the Pali, and is written in the Sanskrit character. The Burmese use the Palmira leaf, and for common purposes the iron style; their religious and other books of value are written with lacquer, or sometimes with gold and silver, and the leaves are splendidly gilt and ornamented." *—After the capture of Rangoon we found some manuscript leaves and other books in less elegant taste than the above; and no doubt many a Pali periodical escaped our notice.

We now proceed to make up for this digression from our sketch, which may be excused on account of the attempt to make it a vehicle of instruction, and for directing attention to Indian affairs.

Among the scientific periodicals of India we used to have the *Madras Journal of Literature and Science*, a *Journal of the Indian Archipelago and Eastern Asia*, and the Calcutta and Bombay *Journals of the Asiatic Society*. The Asiatic Society of Bengal (which used to be the great feeder of the "Royal" in London) was founded by Sir William Jones. Their meetings are held in one of Calcutta's noble mansions, and the prophecy of Sir William—the motto of their Journal—has been tolerably

* The Rev. A. R. Symonds, M.A.

well fulfilled : "The bounds of its investigation will be the geographical limits of Asia; and within these limits its inquiries will be extended to whatever is performed by man, or produced by nature!" In the grand room you will behold busts of Sir W. Jones, Colebrooke, Horace Wilson, and James. Prinsep, the greatest lights of our Oriental literature. We had also an *Indian Journal of Art, Science, and Manufacture*, which was published in Madras. It contained some able articles on Geology and Native Manufactures. The labours of Dr. Hunter in pottery, and for the improvement of native taste, have also been set forth in periodicals.—Nothing has yet been said about Medical periodical literature in India, a most potent instrument for the advancement of this supremely necessary science. A medical journal, to which the graduates of the Medical School at Hyderabad * (Dekhan) contributed, used to be published in Hindustani. An English *Medical Journal* was once attempted in the North of India, but it met with little encouragement. We know not the name of the Anglo-Indian Wakley who gave us a *Lancet*, but certainly the Indian *Lancet* was published at Lahore in August, 1859; and it appeared thrice a month. We once had hopes of Madras having a *Law Times*, but we are not aware if they have been realised; however, cases of importance which came before the Indian Courts of Judicature used to be regularly published. Madras, which has now emerged from its darkness into a marvellous and, we trust, lasting light, must do something more than hitherto for Indian periodical literature. Calcutta has had, and still has, its "Quarterly," the early numbers of which even went through three or four editions. Bombay had her "Quarterly" twenty years ago : why it ceased we know not; we presume through want of patronage, but still the effort deserved credit.

But Madras is nowhere in the race, and yet her journals have always been edited by men of considerable talent. From the very fact of a *Calcutta Review, Bombay Quarterly*,† and *Sporting Review* having existed in India at the same time, it is evident that with able and, above all, energetic editors, and the amount of talent we know to exist in the civil and military services, from which might be got a powerful staff of contributors—who would be nothing if not *punctual*, as well as critical—periodicals to suit all tastes might be set a-going and prosper.

* Under Dr. Smith.

† Mr. Anderson (now Sir Henry, Secretary in the India Office) wrote in this "Quarterly." [See Notes at end.]

Some thirteen years ago, while musing over the uncertainty of the fate of Indian periodicals, we read in the *Bombay Times* an account of a "Sunderbund tiger-hunt, by young Nimrod," in which the death of the tigress, measuring 9ft. 4in., was told with much feeling; and in the next paragraph the death of the *Indian Sporting Review* was announced, and its subscribers were asked to rally round its heir and successor, the *Indian Field* (newspaper). The *Calcutta Sporting Review*, under "Able East," was much admired in India and elsewhere by the Nimrods of the day. Older Indians than the present writer also tell us of a Bombay *Sporting Magazine*, in which some "Letters from John Dockeray, a Yorkshire jockey, to his brother in Tadcaster," were of a first-rate character—full of vigorous writing and dry humour. It will thus be seen that in order to counteract the apathy and rouse into activity "the slumbering energies" of the educated Indian community, every stimulant that could excite was resorted to in the way of periodical literature. That the energy of "the leaders of public taste," under so much indifference and so little sympathy, should have died away was natural enough; but we trust that the energy will burst forth again stronger than ever. We should have liked in this sketch to have said more about Madras; but it may be mentioned that, in 1840, we had a *Madras Miscellany*. The now defunct *Metropolitan*, of London, flattered the bantling by facetiously declaring that the sun of Madras "rarified and sublimated the intellect." But, as the Turkish poet sings, "Nature said it was too sweet to last!" "Pickwick in India"—written by a most intelligent Madras officer, now holding a high scientific appointment—was generally acknowledged to be clever; but it wanted the idea of originality. We once read in the "Miscellany" a whole chapter upon a tiffin! What would Crabbe, "Nature's sternest painter," have said to this? Even Sydney Smith, with all his love of wit and fun, would have declared that a tiffin—a good one— is a very good thing, especially with a glass of cold beer; but however essential it is to the stamina of the body, it cannot be said, at the outset, to be favourable to that of a magazine.

As near the Madras presidency, and of old joined to the Peninsula, let us now proceed to the utmost Indian isle, Taprobane, and glance at the periodical literature of Ceylon. It commenced with a "Religious and Theological Magazine," nearly forty years ago, having been published at Colombo in 1833. The "Colombo Academy Miscellany," and the "Friend," were both to be found in Colombo in 1837. The "Protestant

Vindicator," the "Colombo Magazine," the "Ceylon Magazine," and the "Ceylon Miscellany" were all to be found between the years 1839 and 1842. The "Investigator" flourished in Kandy in 1841; and between 1840 and 1844 were to be seen two papers, chiefly for the natives—the *Lanka Nidhana*, published at Colombo, and the *Morning Star* (as before stated) published at Jaffna. The first of these periodicals appeared at a time when the reading community consisted of "civilians and military, fewer far than at present, and of a very small number of clergy." The Rev. B. Bailey was its able conductor, and before the days of Overlands and general coffee-planting, he furnished the society of Colombo with readable and instructive essays, as well as Bible biographies. The average life of Ceylon periodicals used to be two years; but the "Friend," which owed its origin to the ubiquitous Wesleyan missionaries, existed ten. This excellent periodical enabled the Singhalese, who acquired a tolerable knowledge of English at the schools, to become acquainted with our European books and magazines, liberal extracts from which were freely given. The "Lanka Nidhana," or "Lamp of Ceylon," was a Singhalese publication of a similar character to the "Friend." The "Colombo Magazine" was edited by a gentleman in the Ordnance Department, who, escaping from the heavier occupation of indents and piling of shot and shell, contributed tales, essays, poetry, and anecdotes to its pages. This journal was the first to rouse the desire for a local periodical literature, which, let us trust, may one day be permanently established in Ceylon. The "Ceylon Magazine" had Dr. Macvicar and Mr. Bailey among its contributors; but in 1848 the *Morning Star*, of Jaffna, alone glimmered as the sole survivor of the periodicals above-mentioned. Writing on this Ceylon periodical decline, the *Calcutta Review* informs us that "the romance of life bowed down its head before the strong reality of the prices current. Quotations from the classics were replaced by quotations from the coffee market;" and even at present we believe the local newspapers do the literary periodical as well as the chief commercial business. But in many other places besides Ceylon the "quick pulse of gain" is beginning to beat too high for men to think of anything but making money.

We have sometimes wondered why, in such a military country as India, where the reality of soldier-life is ever apparent, no firmly established army journal or magazine exists. This is a want that should at once be supplied, and if discreetly edited, would doubtless effect much good. During the second Burmese war an "East India Army Magazine and Military Review" from Calcutta, reached our tight little force at Toungoo. It was most ably conducted, and furnished a supplementary paper to a narrative of the campaign in Burma, 1853.*

The forests of India—especially before the coal of the country is developed—being of such vast importance, we must not omit to announce that, in April last, the Punjab Forest Department were about to start a periodical. It was, doubtless, the result of a conference, wisely recognised by Government, at which "essays were read, experiences related, difficulties solved, and much valuable information given and received." An Indian paper prudently suggested that "matter which would be of interest to the *shikaree* (sportsman), as well as the tourist, might be added to the subjects of the proposed periodical, which would render it popular, not only departmentally, but also with the public, and tend to make its financial success more certain."

In the "Annals of Indian Administration," published at Serampore, India has an excellent magazine, to show at a glance what the Government is doing for the good of India and Burma; and in a number before us (September, 1866) we find forest conservancy in Oudh and British Burma concisely related; the Government of India declaring that forest administration in our portion of Burma was in a "very satisfactory state." Lighthouses, education, police, geological survey, with a number of other subjects, are also to be found commented on in this useful State periodical. It is difficult to get the English people to understand that, in spite of shortcomings which, where such a large portion of humanity is concerned, must every now and then occur, the India Office at home and the Indian Government are (especially at the present time) working hard for the good of our splendid dominion. Periodical literature in the country should do its utmost to aid this good work; and we trust and believe that there is a grand future for it in India. For anything we know, the pens of Native editors may now be working towards a mighty consummation which, a few hundred years hence, may, as a sort of companion to Lord Macaulay's New Zealander, afford the interesting spectacle to the world of a once chief of the native Indian press (as if he had copied a leaf out of the book of the great M. Thiers, who owes so much of his well-won fame to having been a journalist) governing a mighty Indian Republic, and, with

---

* "The Second Burmese War"—Pegu—p. 422.

flowing robes and ready pen, sending forth severe monitors *
from Bombay, Madras, or the City of Palaces! But without
indulging in any such dreams, there is yet much to be done in
the way of encouraging the "potent instrument" everywhere
in India. Our very hold on the Empire, in some measure,
depends on the proper management of it.

Among the Anglo-Indian community, a well-conducted periodical literature is a pearl of great price; and, at the conclusion of this rapid sketch, we are glad to notice that a new weekly journal has been started at Simla. It is styled the *Civil and Military Gazette*, and is designed to supply a void which has long been felt in that glorious region by "the very large proportion of the intellect, ability, and talent of India congregated at Simla six months out of the twelve." Madras and Bombay must be more than ever on their guard! We trust the remark is at an end, that such and such a periodical is "defunct for want of patronage;" the saying is a stain upon the Anglo-Indian social and literary character. The late Lord Cockburn —at a dinner given many years ago, in Edinburgh, to a famous artist—said, while talking of the goodness of one of Roberts' early patrons, he remembered hearing Henry Mackenzie, the Man of Feeling, say, when talking of a certain lord who should be nameless, "'Oh, he is proud of the blaze of Burns' light, when it shone in its full brightness; but,'" added the Man of Feeling, "'I am prouder still, because I was one of the few who fanned that flame when in its infancy.'" The prophetic historian of our disasters in Afghanistan, the acute biographer of Malcolm and Metcalfe, and the founder of the *Calcutta Review*, may, we think, among living writers, safely take to himself some credit of this kind; and so may it be with others—patrons of periodical literature, and promoters of knowledge in our Eastern dominion—at a time which may not inaptly be styled "Gyánáruna"—the dawn of general intelligence in India.

NOTES.

COMIC PERIODICALS IN INDIA.

Although, throughout the sketch just concluded, it has been attempted to blend an occasional touch of the comic with grave matter, while thinking of the twin genii, Grief and Joy, and of the force of the saying, "Il n'y a rien plus près du rire que des larmes," we find that no allusion has

---

* The *Moniteur Officiel* of Pondicherry—the Paris of the East—a great monitor during the Empire, may be mentioned in this sketch as an example of French periodical literature in India.

been made in the foregoing pages to the *Delhi Sketch-book*, which Indian *Punch*, in Lord Dalhousie's reign, was very good sometimes. *Momus* succeeded the *Sketch-book ;* but its chief fault was its bad lithographs, spoiling an excellent design. The *Delhi* was far different, and gladdened the Anglo-Indian world with as much zeal as *Punch*, *Judy*, and *Fun* evince at the present day for the amusement of London. In the *Delhi*, "the Royals in India" formed a capital series of sketches : Mrs. Corporal Flouncey objecting to take service with "the lady of a Sepoy officer," the quiet surprise of the lady, and the grim corporal in the background, being admirably brought out, was one of the best. "The War with Burma" formed the subject of some amusing verses in one number, and where the Lion flares "right up," and sends "two wise ambassadors, the Serpent and the Fox" (the actual names of a gun-brig and frigate, R.N., employed at the commencement of the second Burmese war), is told with some humour.

Two conundrums from an old *Delhi* may be given :—"Who was the greatest drunkard in Indian history ?—Asoka. Which is the most killing —Brown Bess or Miss Minié ?" Also a capital sketch of Anglo-Indian military life, in which the stern visage of Colonel Blowhard, in his Bengal muster buggy, and the harum-scarum look of Sprugg, on his tattoo at full speed, are drawn with admirable effect:—"Cornet Sprugg hath just joined his regiment—hath not had sufficient time or opportunity to set himself up in chargers, or purchase a buggy. Church being over, he mounteth a diminutive tattoo. Having previously divested himself of his sword and belts, he giveth the same unto his syce [horsekeeper] to bring after him. Blowhard, the man in authority, twiggeth him. C. O. [Cantonment Order] No. 2.—The practice of officers' servants being permitted to carry their swords is unmilitary, and is to be discontinued. The place for the sword is *always by the side* of the officers."

This number of the periodical was issued from the *Delhi Gazette* Press, which also sent forth "Saunder's Monthly Magazine for all India," with some good original writing and translations, in June, 1852.

"THE BOMBAY QUARTERLY REVIEW."

[To a learned friend we are indebted for the following authentic information regarding the projection of the *Bombay Quarterly*, which, as it brings some "old familiar faces" to memory, will be interesting to many Anglo-Indians.]

The project of publishing a *Quarterly Review* in Bombay was discussed in July, 1854, at a dinner given by H. L. Anderson, then Secretary to Government in the Political Department. There were present among others :—William Howard (afterwards Advocate-General), his brother, Edward Howard (afterwards Director of Public Instruction), William Frere (afterwards a Member of the Bombay Government), H. B. Frere (afterwards the Right Hon. Sir Bartle Frere), H. Conybeare (the Civil Engineer), Captain Marriott (afterwards Secretary to Government in the Military Department), the Rev. Philip Anderson, M. A. Coxon (Registrar of the Sudder Adawlut), John Connon (afterwards Senior Magistrate of Police), Herbert Giraud (afterwards Principal of the Grant Medical College), and C. J. Erskine (afterwards a Member of the Bombay Government).

The Rev. P. Anderson, the author of "The English in Western India," was chosen to be Editor ; and it was determined, after considerable discussion, that articles on other than strictly Indian subjects should be admitted. The *Review* was to be published by Smith, Elder & Company, who had at that time a branch firm in Bombay.

The *Review* was a fair success, the literary ability of some of the articles being of a high standard, especially those written by Edward Howard. One of these, on Thackeray's novels, was shown to Thackeray himself, and declared by him to be the best article he had ever read on his works. Edward Howard also wrote articles on "Oxford," "Music as a Social Recreation," and "Burton's Pilgrimage to Mecca." Pelly (now Sir Lewis Pelly) wrote one on "Sind," Marriott one on "Ruskin's Works," Sir Bartle Frere one on "Rifle Musketry," the Rev. Philip Anderson one on "Erskine's Life of Baber," and several others founded on the old records of Government, which he intended, when completed, to be published as a second volume of his "English in Western India." His namesake, Henry Anderson (now Sir H. L.), wrote two ; one on "Kaye's Life of Sir Charles Metcalfe," and the other on "Competitive Examinations for the Civil Service." Dr. Peet, the Principal of the Grant Medical College, wrote two ; one on "Education in Western India," the other on "The Moon and her Libellers ;" the late Kinloch Forbes, author of the "Ras Mala," one on Kaye's "Life of Sir J. Malcolm." These are all I can at this moment recollect.

The death of the Editor (the Rev. P. Anderson), and the occurrence of the Mutinies, brought the *Review* to an early close. Of the original projectors, six are dead—the two Howards (the one by a fall in the hunting-field, and the other by a railway accident), Connon, Taylor (of Smith, Taylor & Co.), M. A. Coxon, and the Editor. The rest survive.

[Sir Henry Lacon Anderson, K.C.S.I., alluded to in the foregoing notes, is now Secretary in the Judicial, Public and Revenue Departments, India Office, London. He was Secretary to the Government of Bombay in the Political, Secret, Educational, and Judicial Departments.].

SPORTING LITERATURE IN INDIA.*

THAT a thirst for adventure, and a love of excitement and danger, may be engendered in the hearts of the rising generation of Englishmen, is the earnest wish of a well-known Indian officer, who writes with great practical experience and ability on the "Wild Sports of India." Experience in shikar—particularly in hunting and killing the large game with which India's forests abound—is a great thing, and has doubtless tended to rear more genuine "captains" in the "nursery"† than anything else; for, talk as we will, a good soldier is generally a keen sportsman, or, we should rather say, the keen sportsman has in him the materials for a good and distinguished soldier. The ever-ready tact, the nerve firm and unquailing, the talent for constant resource, a constitution like that of the "Iron King" of Sweden, our own "Iron Duke," or Napier of Sind; to be weather-proof, even—as the late gifted Meredith Parker might have expressed it—while snakes are "prodigiously lively," and tigers' teeth are cracking from the sun: all these requisites are essential for great success in sporting as in military life. Doubtless, we owe much of the brilliant success which has attended so many Indian officers in their profession to a love of field sports, which has kept them "fit for their duty as soldiers, both in body and inclination."

Colonel Shakespear goes so far as to style hog hunting "the very first sport in the world." In danger and excitement it perhaps only comes short of tiger shooting, especially when such is rashly performed on foot, instead of from the back of an elephant. Then there is good sport in the destruction of other less fierce four-footed game and the endless varieties of the feathered tribes—in the latter particular also to aid the sciences

* From *The Field*, London, April 26th, 1873.
† "India, the nursery of captains."—LORD LYTTON.

of ornithology and gastronomy. Horse racing, too—the love of which goes with Englishmen all over the world—is deeply rooted in Anglo-India; and thus, with their profession, the attractions of female society, a pipe, a little reading, and an occasional longing for old England, "runs," and has long run, from year to year, "the world away" among numbers of our countrymen in the glorious Empire of the Sun.

That there should have been from time to time separate periodicals in India for recording sporting exploits was only natural. The enthusiasm with which Englishmen enter upon every description of sport in India induced Mr. Stocqueler, when editor of the *Bombay Courier* in the year 1828, to start the "Oriental Sporting Magazine." Its principal contributor was Captain D'Arcy Morris, of the Bombay Army. He wrote some admirable parodies of Moore's "Loves of the Angels," which he called the "Tales of the Tinkers"—"tinker" being a term of reproach applied to bad sportsmen—and some spirit-stirring songs, one of which lives to this hour; "The next grey boar we see" will be popular in India as long as a boar remains to fall to the spears of the huntsmen. The great success of this magazine, to which Sir James Outram and Mr. Chamier, M.C.S., contributed, induced Mr. Stocqueler to start a similar one in Calcutta in 1834, and during the nine years of his editorship its success was immense. During the last two or three years of its existence it was supplemented by a miscellany, and the combination of the two elements rendered the magazine popular with all classes. The first talent in the country contributed to its pages. Besides innumerable sketches of tiger, lion, elephant, boar, deer, and jackall hunting, shooting in all its branches, racing, boating, cricket, and other registry, many articles were inserted in relation to the zoology of India. Among the sporting writers were Sir George Harvey, K.C.S.I., Mr. Charles Butcher—an Indigo planter, a poet, and a capital shot—Sir Alfred Larpent, Mr. Bailey, and many other distingished civilians. Mr. Brian Hodgson, whose works on the fauna of India have a world-wide reputation, and Major Brown, of the Bengal Infantry (Gunga), were constant writers on the deer and game birds of the up-country. Dr. John Grant the Apothecary-General, a man of rare and diversified literary attainments, Henry Meredith Parker, Captain Robert A. Macnaghten, Captain Percy Eld, Major Backhouse (of the Artillery), Lord Exmouth, Dr. Parry, and Captain Walter Hore, all men of marked ability, contributed largely on an infinite variety of subjects; and Mr. Stocqueler himself not unfrequently added to his editorial duties by writing humorous sketches. The magazine was profusely adorned with engravings illustrative of sport chiefly commissioned from England. It is not unworthy of note that the now popular "Tale of a Tub and a Tiger" first appeared in the "Bengal Sporting Magazine," whence, writes Mr. Stocqueler, the sketches were plagiarised and the story paraphrased by the late T. H. Bayley.

Bearing on the subject of Indian sporting literature we are indebted for most of the following notes to a choice spirit of a world gone by—a distinguished officer and fellow of "infinite jest and most excellent fancy." The very mention of the names contained in them may tempt some Anglo-Indians of the old school in London to exclaim, like Aytoun, while singing the praises of his redoubtable old Scottish Cavalier,

"Oh ! never shall we know again
Of hearts so stout and true ;
The olden times have passed away,
And weary are the new."

Never, never, more ! Change has done its work. Never again can we hope to see such famous "letters" as those "from John Dockeray, a Yorkshire jockey, to his brother in Tadcaster," which first appeared in the *Bombay Sporting Magazine*. An able and amusing little article, said to be from the pen of the editor of that periodical, gave an admirable idea of the English stage coachman of the olden time. The manner in which he was represented as entertaining his friend on the box with the popular song of "Young love among the roses," intermixed with professional addresses to his team, was extremely amusing.

Some of the poetical contributions were of a degree of merit very superior to the ordinary run of poesy of that description to be met with even in England, in periodicals of far higher pretension. We doubt if the song commencing "The boar, the mighty boar's my theme," and ending with the chorus

" So here's to all who fear no fall,
And the next grey boar we see,"

has ever been surpassed as a sporting lyric ; in short, we have little or no hesitation in saying that a more spirit-stirring canticle has seldom, if ever, been chanted at *shikar* party or " our mess." And, in a different style, the beautiful imitation of Moore's "Harp that once through Tara's hall," commencing

" The spear that once o'er Dekhan ground
The blood of wild boar shed,"

is worthy of a place in poetical literature far above that of ordinary parody.

Of gun and rifle celebrity some forty-five years ago, we particularly hear of Tiger Shirreff, Tiger Apthorp, Vivian, Humffreys, Boddam, and Backhouse, the famed Bengal foxhunter.

Boddam (Madras Cavalry) heard of Lord Kennedy's famous match, and he resolved to emulate it. He accordingly did the distance from Arcot to the Tinnery tank, Wallajahbad—forty or more miles—driving, riding, and walking, and returning in the same manner, bringing back with him fifty-two couple of snipe, in the incredible short space of twelve hours, within which time he was dining at the mess.

Killing a tiger on foot was by no means an uncommon occurrence in the old days. Such men as Apthorp,* Humffreys (who was killed by a tiger), Shirreff, and Christie, with others of our own time, are hardly to be trifled with either in the forest or on the battle field. We observe that the last named gallant colonel has recently left Madras for England; and we much regret that the Presidency tiger-slayer's exploits have never been fully detailed in a Madras sporting periodical.

Well-known heroes of the turf of a past age in India are summed up in the names of Shepherd, Hall, Gash, Parker, and Salter. They are equally renowned as jockeys. As hunters, whether with hound or spear, John Elliott and Backhouse are never to be forgotten. But we should mention that some of the chief turf men in Bengal were Stevenson, Bacon, Grant, and John White. Stevenson was the father of the turf in that Presidency, while Macdowell—well-known as Arab Mac—claimed the honour in Madras.† Duncan Mackenzie (who enjoyed the turf sobriquet of Mr. North), Edward Gullifer Showers, of the Artillery, and the two Macleans, were chief among the glorious old "Mulls" who in their day shed glory o'er the turf, as Cunningham (Cavalry) did in Bombay. As Nelson wished for a Gazette all to himself, so those turfites, with the other sportsmen already brought forward, might well have claimed an extraordi-

* We have just read that General East Apthorp, C.B., K.S.F., died at Tunbridge Wells, March 3, aged 69.

† ["Arab Mac" always kept some twenty or thirty horses in his stable; and the Griffin, or needy officer, wanting a "charger," knew where to go for the value of his money. Arab Mac's way of doing business was something in the following style: "Ye want a horse, Mr. Robinson; now here's a fine Persian" (or it might be an Arab) "which cost me 400 rupees. He's been in my stable a month; so I shall only charge ye 6 rupees for the Ghorawallah's (horsekeeper's) pay, 3¼ for the grass-cutter, 3½ for gram, and one rupee for shoeing, with a rupee for heel-ropes, and the horse is yours for 415 rupees!" This speech delivered with a strong Scotch accent, was highly characteristic of the kind-hearted Anglo-Indian sportsman.]

nary magazine or review to chronicle all their brilliant sporting achievements. And are not the pages of the Bombay (*Oriental*) *Sporting Magazine* adorned with the illustrious names of those equine sons of the desert—the last, alas! of the *genuine* ones—Pyramid, Chapeau de Paille, Feramors, Salonica, Paul Pry, Sackcloth, Hurry Skurry, and a host of others well known to its able editor ? Although far from wishing to be guilty of the too common folly of crying up the past at the expense of the present, still we cannot help exclaiming, so far as sporting in India is concerned, Where are now the horses? and, more important still, Where are the men ? The ghost of an Outram on Ariel, or of a Pottinger on Selim, answers, Where ? *Heu, quanto minus est cum reliquis versari quam tui meminisse.*

Colonel Davidson in his "Travels" gives some valuable information on Anglo-Indian gastronomy. This amusing, sprightly traveller, when he weighed less than nineteen stone, must have been a veritable sportsman. His discourse on the *cours gastronomique*, while officiating as *chef de cuisine* and excelling in making rich bread sauce for partridges, found its way into our most celebrated Indian periodical (the *Calcutta Review*); and, as we know some admirable Indian Nimrods who are very good cooks, the following extract, commencing in rare Johnsonian style, may be received with gratitude by our readers :—

"Bleak and barren indeed must that spot be where the eye of a sound-hearted and skilful gastronomist cannot discover matter for thankfulness ! For him does sad and solitary Ascension gather together her luscious and indescribable turtle ; for him the dark rocks and arid plains of the dry Deccan, produce their purple grapes, and cunning but goodly bustard ; for him burning Bundelkund its wonderful rock pigeon and ortolan inimitable; the Jumna, most ancient of rivers, its large rich kala banse and tasty crabs ; for him yields the long and marshy Teraee her elegant florican ; the mighty Gunga its melting mâhâseer ; the Goomtee its exquisite mullet."

Long may such gastronomists as the colonel be able to prepare a tiffin for Indian sportsmen ! and long may the periodicals exist which endeavour to chronicle their triumphs in ministering to the appetites of men who, as soldiers and statesmen, may deserve well of their country !

Having alluded to the pursuit of the "grey boar" as such splendid sport, and such hunting in India having formed the theme of so many exciting descriptions in magazines and newspapers, it may not be out of place, before taking leave of "a sounder of wild hog," to remark that the chief difference between hog hunting in Bengal, and in the Bombay Presidency and the "Hyderabad Deccan," is in "the nature of the ground ridden over, the length of the spear used, and the way it is carried," the difference of lengths and the system of using the weapon being accounted for "by the difference of grounds and the habits of the animal."* Let us then sing once more—

"So here's to all who fear no fall,
    And the next grey boar *they* see !"

* Col. Shakespear's "Wild Sports of India," p. 33.

APPENDIX.

I.
LORD PALMERSTON AND SIR ALEXANDER BURNES.

[The following extracts from correspondence between Lord Palmerston and Dr. Burnes, relating to his brother Sir Alexander, are of interest. After a few letters the correspondence ceased, his lordship remarking that the opinions expressed were " those which he entertained, and the observations which he made were those which presented themselves to his mind." Those opinions his lordship still entertained, and those observations he was "not prepared to retract."]

1.
J. BURNES TO LORD PALMERSTON.

40, Ladbroke Square, W., March 25, 1861.

MY LORD,

I beg to transmit to your Lordship the enclosed extract, from the report in the *Evening Standard* of Wednesday last, of your speech in the debate of the preceding evening, and to ask the favour of your informing me if it be correct. Should it be so, I would explain that, although Lord Auckland disapproved of my brother's money arrangements with Candahar, yet shortly after his proceedings were reported to England, your Home Government distinguished him by knighthood and a lieutenant-colonelcy; and that in announcing these honours to him, the Governor-General himself made the following frank avowal :—

" Simla, November, 5th, 1838.

"My dear Sir,—I cordially congratulate you upon the public proofs of approbation with which you have been marked at home. My private letters speak in high terms of your proceedings in Cabul; and I may in candour mention, that upon the one point upon which there was some difference between us—the proposed advance of money to Candahar—opinions for which I have the highest respect, are in your favour. I do not grudge you this, and am only glad that a just tribute has been paid to your ability and indefatigable zeal."

I would also point out—in reference to the statement that "Sir Alexander Burnes was taken to task for having communicated, while in Afghanistan, to the Indian newspapers, information with which he was entrusted on account of the Government, a reproof" (your Lordship is alleged to add) "of which Sir A. Burnes was well deserving,"—that the Parliamentary Blue Book, page 98, distinctly disproves the same, and shows that it was one of my brother's subordinate officers, and not himself, who had indiscreetly communicated the said information, thereby incurring his disapprobation as well as that of the Governor-General, who, if I mistake not, took advantage of the occasion to compliment Sir Alexander Burnes on his well-known discretion.

Should this newspaper report be substantially correct, your Lordship will doubtless see the necessity of making the explanation I have furnished, in the place where the statements were made, seeing that, as they stand, they can have but one effect—that of depreciating the character and services of Sir Alexander Burnes.

I have the honour to be, my Lord,
Your Lordship's most obedient Servant,

JAMES BURNES.

The Right Hon. Viscount Palmerston, K.G., M.P., etc.

" In a despatch written by the Governor-General of India he found fault with Sir A. Burnes for having entered into an arrangement with the Queen of Candahar, by which he committed the Indian Government beyond what he had authority to do. The Governor-General said he would not call upon him to make a public disavowal, but that he must take an opportunity of showing that the Indian Government were not prepared to make good the engagements which Sir A. Burnes had said that Government would enter into. So, with regard to Runjeet Singh, it had to be intimated to him that the policy of the Indian Government was not that which Sir A. Burnes recommended them to pursue. There was another dispatch omitted, in which Sir A. Burnes was taken to task for having communicated, while in Afghanistan, to the Indian newspapers, information with which he was entrusted on account of the Government. That was a reproof of which Sir A. Burnes was well deserving. He did not mean to say that these things were serious cause of blame to Sir A. Burnes."

2.

LORD PALMERSTON TO J. BURNES.

Downing Street, April 1, 1861.

SIR,

I am desired by Lord Palmerston to acknowledge the receipt of your letter of 25th March.

Lord Palmerston desires me, in reply, to say that what he stated in the House of Commons with regard to the first dispatch from Sir W. Macnaghten, conveying the disapproval of Lord Auckland, of some communications made by Sir Alexander Burnes to the Ameer of Candahar, was much to the same effect as what Mr. Dunlop had, in his speech, said on the same subject. Lord Palmerston will, however, when he returns to town, look again at the Blue Book, and turn to the subsequent dispatch to which you refer him.

I remain, Sir,

Your most obedient Servant,

EVELYN ASHLEY.

James Burnes, Esq.

[We may conclude with some remarks from a letter by the energetic political, regarding the distinctions he had won, alluded to in his brother's note to Lord Palmerston.]

"Shikarpore, November 12, 1838.—You do indeed convey to me news, for I had not the remotest idea of the honours (the lieutenant-colonelcy and knighthood) coming, though they are to me truly acceptable, not as empty honours, but as setting my mind at rest that my conduct in Afghanistan has been approved. You may imagine that this gratifies me the more when I was at issue on it with the Government of India, and had plainly told them that they would sacrifice millions hereafter instead of lacs now."

II.

VISIT OF DR. JAMES BURNES, K.H., TO THE COURT OF SIND.

(HIS CURE OF AN AMEER.)

THE visit of Dr. Burnes to a highly interesting, but, at the time, almost unknown Court, at Hyderabad on the Indus, made some forty-seven years ago, forms the subject of a narrative originally printed by the Government in India, and first issued from the Bombay press in 1830. The author little foresaw that his "visit to Sinde" (he spells the word with an *e*) would be followed by such a train of stirring events, in reference to the Indus, as would take place in the course of ten years (date of preface April, 1839). In 1831, the river was successfully navigated from the Ocean to Lahore, by his brother, Sir Alexander Burnes; during 1832-3 and 4, negociations were in progress, and treaties entered into with the Ameers, under Colonel (afterwards Sir Henry) Pottinger,* for the free opening of it as a channel of trade; and at the end of 1835, Messrs. Hedle and Wood—as if emulating Patrick Miller of Dalswinton, in Scotland—exhibited to the astonished natives of Hyderabad the *first steamboat* that ever entered the Indus. Our distinguished Anglo-Indian author thought that the extension of our power along the whole course of that river, would render it certain that, "ere long, the manufactures of Manchester, Glasgow, and Birmingham, will be as common in Bokhara, Candahar, and Samarkand, as in the chief cities of Europe and Anglo-Asia." About 1827-28, Dr. Burnes, residency-surgeon in Cutch, was requested by the Ameers of Sind (in a most friendly letter to the Resident) to proceed without delay to Hyderabad on acount of the sickness of Meer Mourad Ali Khan, one of the principal chiefs. The Knight of Hanover and accomplished Mason was to do for Sind what Boughton (1634) had done for Bengal in our early history of India, in which great country the members of the medical profession, whether in the case of natives or Europeans requiring their attendance and treatment, have done so much for humanity through their admirable skill and never-ceasing kindness. The passages quoted we trust will show Dr. Burnes' easy and graphic style as a writer:—

"By a rigid attention to diet and constitutional treatment, together with the application of the most simple dressings to

* Well known for his diplomatic services in China, and Governor of Madras, 1848-54.

the disease itself, all dangerous symptoms disappeared by the 20th of November (1827), that is, ten days after my arrival at Hyderabad. I will confess that I was myself taken by surprise; and it is hardly possible to describe the gratification and gratitude of the Ameers when I announced to Mourad Ali the propriety of his resuming, with moderation, his usual pursuits. The illness of one confines the whole family; and none of them, therefore, had breathed fresh air outside the fortress for many months. Preparations were immediately made for a hunting excursion, to which they all proceeded, and I was also invited. The Ameer suffered no inconvenience for some weeks from his disorder; while a dread of the consequences prevented his neglecting the regimen prescribed. But when this ceased, he was guilty of some acts of imprudence and excess, which brought on a slight relapse, but did not much retard his general recovery.

" The suddenness of a cure so unexpected, and which was to be attributed, in a great measure, to the removal of the irritating substances formerly applied, impressed the Ameers with the idea that there were no bounds to my skill in my profession; and some fortuitous circumstances contributed to strengthen the delusion. I had occasion to administer a small quantity of a powerful medicine to Mourad Ali, who declined taking it, even after the same dose had been tried on the luckless attendant I have mentioned [Burnes had been the subject of experiment for each nauseous dose, but resigned in favour of an attendant], till he was positively assured by me what would be the exact effect upon himself. I saw at once that this was in their estimation a grand test of my knowledge; and it was one certainly which perplexed me considerably. Having no alternative, however, I boldly hazarded a guess, which the event, luckily for my reputation, proved correct; and this circumstance, trifling at it may seem, excited so much the attention of the Ameers that they alluded to it often afterwards.

" But to nothing, in this respect, was I more indebted than to the sulphate of quinine; a remedy hitherto perfectly unknown in Sinde, and the effect of which, as it scarcely ever fails in stopping the intermittent fevers of natives, I could generally foretell with a degree of precision that astonished them. By means of this valuable medicine, I was enabled, shortly after my arrival, to cure, in two days, a favourite child of the prime minister, who had been suffering from fever for months together, with several other persons in the immediate service of the Ameers; and I would no doubt have gone on to raise my character higher, had not their Highnesses, the moment they discovered the effect of the quinine, seized the phial which contained it without ceremony, and ordered it to be sealed and locked up for their own proper use at a future period. Even afterwards, when I myself fell sick, no solicitations could induce them to part with a single grain, though I was dangerously ill; and when at my departure, I made a request for the bottle in exchange for another, as it was one which belonged to a valuable medicine chest, the proposal was at once rejected, evidently from an idea, that it might share with its contents some supposed talismanic virtue.

"Sinde would be a fair field for English quackery to flourish in. The Ameers never thought of doubting that I had the power of restoring the vigour of youth, provided I was disposed to do so; and Meer Sohrab sent me a letter from Shikarpoor, requesting me to bring to his senses one of his children who had been twelve years an idiot! Meer Noor Mahommed was disappointed that I did not possess the lamp of Aladdin or the wand of Prospero, to turn his mean and contemptible figure into the stately form of his brother Nusseer Khan. I was applied to by Meer Mahommed to remove a white speck from the neck of one of the beauties of his Seraglio, which had been born with her; and his Highness was evently displeased when my attempts proved unsuccessful. The circumstances of my interview with this lady are curious. It was proposed that I should meet her in a garden, with a wall about five feet high between us; but as I objected to this mode of examining a patient, she was brought to my tent, muffled up among a crowd of old and ugly females, her attendants. She was very beautiful, almost as fair as an European, and altogether a favourable specimen of the women of Sinde, who are superior in appearance to those of India. I saw several dancing girls, whose elegant forms might have graced the harem of the Caliph Walid.

"In proportion as Mourad Ali's health recovered, the kindness and attention of the Ameers towards me increased. During my stay at Hyderabad, for the succeeding two months and a half, every means were adopted by them that could afford me comfort or amusement. The vizier waited on me every morning and afternoon to accompany me to the durbar, where I passed six hours, and often more, daily in their company, and where they received me latterly in nearly the same manner as they did the younger princes. After the first or second visit, the ceremony of taking off the shoes, which was, I understand, rigidly insisted on during the two or three short interviews the late envoys had with them, was entirely dispensed with; and the whole arrangement of their court was changed, that a chair might be introduced for me. No entreaties could induce them to discontinue the extravagant system of entertainment for me and my people, which was kept up to the very last day I remained in Sinde.

"The conduct of a despotic prince regulates that of his followers. No sooner did the Sindian courtiers observe the disposition of the Ameers towards me, than they began to vie with each other in their obsequiousness. While I was at Hyderabad, I was visited, I believe, by the heads of all the tribes resident at court. Letters were read in my presence at the durbar, which were to be sent to the Sikhs and other allies, announcing Mourad Ali's recovery, and highly complimentary to myself, together with congratulatory addresses from Meers Sohrab and Thara, entreating that every distinction might be paid me. Persian verses, filled with the grossest flattery, were repeated daily, and appeared extremely satisfactory to the Ameers, who themselves took the trouble to explain to me the meaning of the difficult passages.

"The example of the rulers had a proportionate effect on the people of Sinde. The intelligence of Meer Mourad Ali's recovery passed through the country like wild-fire, and crowds flocked from all quarters, in the expectation of obtaining relief, many of them from incurable diseases. In every direction, around the garden which I occupied, there were encampments of strangers who had come from a distance. My gate was surrounded by petitioners from morning to night; and the moment I appeared abroad, I was assailed by the most piteous entreaties for medicine and assistance. All these demands on me I was obliged to attend to; nor is there any period of my life during which I underwent more continued labour than in Sinde. The Ameers gave me credit for my assiduity, and thanked me for expending, as they had been informed by report, four thousand rupees' worth of medicine on their subjects. I assured them of my readiness to do my endeavours, but did not conceive it necessary to add, that the utmost the Honourable Company was likely to suffer on the occasion was nearer forty rupees than the amount they had alluded to.

"The consequence of my unremitting exertions was a violent attack of fever, which confined me to my bed for several days. The kindness I then experienced ought not to be omitted here. The Ameers did indeed refuse me the quinine; but they were constant in their inquiries, and extreme in their expressions of anxiety. During the whole of a day in which I was delirious,

Wullee Mahommed Khan, whose good feeling I had gained by attention to his children, and frequent conversations with himself, never left my bedside; and when I recovered my senses, the first object which met my eye, was the respected old man kneeling in earnest prayer for my recovery. Such Samaritanism would do honour, and might be an example, to many of a purer creed and better education."

III.
OPINIONS OF DISTINGUISHED MEN ON SIR JAMES OUTRAM.

"Sans peur et sans reproche."

[A NUMEROUS and highly influential meeting was held on the 5th March, 1861, at Willis's Rooms, "to mark in a permanent manner their high sense of the great public services and eminent character of that distinguished soldier and statesman, Sir James Outram."]

On the platform were Lord Shaftesbury, Lord Harris, Lord Lyveden, Lord Keane, the Hon. Arthur Kinnaird, Sir John Lawrence, Sir Henry Rawlinson, Sir Robert Hamilton, Mr. Crawford (Member for the City), Sir Frederick Currie, Sir John McNeill, Sir Minto Farquhar, Sir James Fergusson, Sir Henry Havelock, General Malcolm, General Hancock, Dr. Norton Shaw, Colonel Holland, Colonel Sykes, Captain Eastwick, Dr. Burnes, K.H., &c., &c. Among others present on the occasion were :—Lord Clyde, Sir R. Arbuthnot, Mr. Ricketts, Sir James Colville, Sir F. Abbott, Sir Henry Montgomery, Mr. Charles Raikes, Captain Lynch, &c., &c. A considerable number of ladies, including Lady Keane, Lady Havelock, Lady Somerset, Lady Eastlake, Lady Green, Mrs. Bagnold, &c., were present in the front seats.

Lord Keane was sorry to state that the DUKE OF ARGYLL was unable to take the chair. His Grace's letter on the occasion contained the following tribute :—

" I trust I may be allowed to say with what warm admiration I have always regarded the character and services of Sir James Outram. The many great qualities which have been requisite for a successful career such as his in India are now much more generally appreciated than they once were. It is a matter of public importance that those who spend, and too often are called to exhaust, their powers in the service of our Eastern Empire, should receive, even in their lifetime, the public acknowledgments and honours they deserve."

The chair was taken by

LORD LYVEDEN.

THE person we are met here to celebrate is one of those characters which all Englishmen must admire—a real, thorough Anglo-Saxon, one of whom all of the race I am now addressing ought to be proud. (Cheers.) I had not the honour of his acquaintance in the earlier part of his life. The beginning of my acquaintance with him was somewhat singular, and at the same time so demonstrative of the character of the man, that I will mention the circumstance. It was in the year 1843, when the vote of thanks was proposed in Parliament to Sir Charles Napier and the army of Scinde, that I took occasion to mention the services of General Outram. Let no man suppose I am about to enter into the unfortunate controversy of that period; I am merely stating a matter of fact when I say that I endeavoured to urge upon the Government of that day the necessity of including in that vote of thanks the name of General Outram. I did so on account of his brilliant services in the celebrated defence of the Hyderabad Residency—that defence which was one of the brilliant achievements of that war, and characterised by Sir Charles Napier as "the extraordinary defence of the fearless and distinguished Outram."

I have glanced at the beginning and the close of General Outram's splendid career: others who will follow me will enter into more specific details of those brilliant actions which have distinguished his life. I ask you to consider who it is we are met here to honour—what has been his course of life, and what the results. Did he, as is said is always the case in this country, owe his advancement to interest? How did he stand at the beginning of the race? He started single-handed, with his merit and ability only to carry him forward. I do not know who procured him his first nomination, but I do know who gave him his first preferment. This time last year we met here to celebrate and do honour to the character of one of the finest and noblest of our Indian statesmen—Mountstuart Elphinstone. He it was who first saw Outram's merit and advanced him to promotion. It was to Elphinstone and to his own merit that he was first indebted for that first position which afforded him the opportunities he has so nobly improved upon. What were General Outram's peculiar qualifications for success? He had that singularly useful qualification to every Indian official, the power of ingratiating himself with the native chiefs and with the native people. (Hear, hear.) Of all men I have ever known in the Indian service, except, perhaps, Sir George Clerk, the present Governor of Bombay,* he had that faculty beyond them all. It was not only that he possessed an intimate acquaintance with them and with their feelings and habits, but a sympathy with them and respect for their rights. It was this that won their hearts, and it was through this medium that he achieved such wonderful results. I pray God that all officers going out to India may emulate him in that quality; for without sympathy and regard for the feelings and rights of the native population, it will be impossible for us to maintain our Empire in the East; while, if you can kindle and keep alive a spark of sympathy and good feeling between the native and European populations, you will be able not only to maintain that Empire, but advance its happiness and prosperity far beyond anything that has yet been accomplished. (Hear, hear.) This is the character we are called upon to-day to celebrate; for the manner of the celebration I leave to future speakers to detail to you. But I do hope that before you leave this room you will provide the means, by your subscriptions, to raise some memorial to him, not only in the one country, but in both countries to which his fame belongs. I do hope that you will raise such a memorial in the land of his birth—that land which has sent forth so many of her sons to distant parts of the world, challenging all others in enterprise, and carrying the fame of Britain to the most distant regions of the habitable globe. I do hope, too, that you will raise such a memorial in India—the country which has witnessed his brilliant achievements, where his name is known from Cape Comorin to the mountains of Thibet, and from the mouth of the Brahmaputra to the Indus—thereby setting a bright example to succeeding ages, and showing what may be done by men of honesty of character and nobleness of purpose in the path of duty. Not once or twice has the path of duty been the way to glory; and if, as is sometimes the case, that glory lead but to the grave, let us remember that that grave is environed with martial honours, covered with a civic crown, and bedewed with the tears of all upright men.

* [Appointed 1860, and in 1874-75 a distinguished Member of the India Council.]

SIR H. C. RAWLINSON.

HAPPILY, the invidious distinctions of past times are now swept away, and all officers, whether serving in the East or West, are equally the servants of Her Majesty the Queen; but if it had not been so, if the old gulf yet existed between the Royal and the Indian armies, still the case of James Outram would have been, and must have been, an exception. It would never have been tolerated that services of so noble and so national a character should have been localised as the exclusive property of an Indian presidency. No; James Outram's career belongs to England, and is the property of all time. (Hear, hear.) It is the career of one of England's best and bravest soldiers. (Loud cheers.) It forms a bright and spirit-stirring chapter in the national history, and will descend to after ages with other histories of England's worthies, as an inheritance of glory, wherever the English language may be spoken, and wherever the memory may be cherished of gallant actions and of generous feelings.

To recapitulate Outram's services would be to travel over ground with which you are already familiar; yet I cannot keep silence altogether. A bird's-eye view of a few prominent features in his career, such as we may suppose to be displayed to the wondering gaze of our children's children, will perhaps answer all present purposes. Firstly, then, will appear the young officer of stalwart frame, unflinching nerve, iron constitution, and of joyous heart. The jungle side, the parade-ground, have equal charms for him; he is a first-rate regimental officer, and the prince of Deccan sportsmen. And here I would observe in passing, with all possible respect for the system of competitive examination, that the examples of Elphinstone and Malcolm, of George Clerk and James Outram, would go far to shake one's faith in the necessity of an exclusive mental culture while the boy is being ripened into the man. The next scene in the drama brings forward James Outram as the pioneer of civilisation, reclaiming the Bheels of Khandeish from barbarism, restoring order and good government to the Myhee-Caunta. Then comes the magnificent episode of the first Afghan war. Outram is still the daring officer, foremost in pursuit, last in retreat; now chasing the Ameer of Cabul across the Indian Caucasus, now sharing in the danger of the storm of Kelat, and afterwards riding alone and in disguise through an unknown and hostile country for 400 miles to carry the first news of the victory to Bombay.

R

Of Outram's later services in India I need say but little. His defence of the Residency at Hyderabad, which is one of the most striking passages in the military history of India, has been prominently brought before you by the noble lord who has preceded me. It is an exploit almost lost among the more glittering trophies of Outram's long and varied career, but it would alone have made the reputation of any less distinguished officer. (Loud cheers.) But we must remember that " peace has her virtues as well as war," and that the fifteen years which Outram passed during this part of his career in the political administration of Lower Scinde, of Sattara, of Guzerat, of Aden, and finally of Lucknow, constitute, in reality, the most valuable portion of his public life. He himself, no doubt, with the true instincts of a soldier, would dwell with more complaisance on the brilliant success of his Southern Mahratta campaign, than the brief drama of the war in Persia; and finally, on the great crowning scene of his military career—the relief of Lucknow, and the defence of the Alum-Bagh; but in this estimate he would not be doing justice to himself. There were, in fact, great truths of civil government, which he enunciated and supported in every political situation that he filled—truths based upon eternal justice, and aiming at the vindication of right, irrespective of force or fraud, or convenience, or any other opposing influence, the full value of which is yet to be recognised in the future history of India.

EARL OF SHAFTESBURY.

INDIA had produced some of the greatest men to be found in the whole range of history. But how remarkable was it to see those mighty intellects, having run their course in India—some of them dying there and forgotten, and others coming back here, and (so far as their country was concerned) sinking into oblivion—men whose great knowledge, large hearts, and long experience would render them capable of giving valuable advice to the Government—put aside as though they had never existed at all, and other men, satraps in power, if they had only the dishonesty common to man, might have enriched themselves to any extent, returning to this country in a condition of almost absolute poverty. When they had an example before them such as he need not name, for it would be apparent to all who were present, those who knew these things and appreciated them should, when they had the opportunity, exalt with all the force they could the disinterested services of those remarkable men. (Hear.) Heartily did he pray for the welfare of India, and for those who were going out to administer her affairs—those alike who were going to the highest, and those who were going to the lowest, stations, under the new and (as it was called) improved system of government. Whatever might be thought of the old system of governing India, he for one could not have unlimited confidence in the new; and well would it be for India, well would it be for her teeming millions, well would it be for the cause of civilisation and for the honour and dignity of Great Britain, if, in the two generations next to come, they had in that Empire such gallant, noble, and disinterested men as Sir James Outram.

COLONEL SYKES

Moved that the following noblemen and gentlemen form a managing committee, to carry out the resolutions of the meeting [regarding an " Outram Testimonial "] :—General Sir George Pollock, G.C.B., Chairman ; the Lord Keane ; the Right Hon. the Lord Mayor, M.P. [W. Cubitt]; the Right Hon. Sir John M'Neill, G.C.B. ; Sir James Fergusson, Bart., M.P. ; Sir James D. H. Elphinstone, Bart., M.P. ; General E. M. G. Showers ; Major-General Sir R. J. H. Vivian, K.C.B. ; Major-General D. Downing; Dr. Norton Shaw ; W. H. Russell, LL.D.; J. W. Kaye, Esq. ; Major-General D. Malcolm ; Major-General H. Hancock ; Captain Sherard Osborn, C.B., R.N. ; Colonel J. Holland ; Lieutenant-Colonel Sir H. Havelock, Bart., V.C.

He observed that the chief characteristics of Sir James Outram were hatred of oppression and wrong in every form, and a total abnegation of self. As marking Sir James Outram's disinterestedness, Colonel Sykes referred to his refusal of the Scinde prize money, and described him as the Bayard of the East, *sans peur et sans reproche.*

DR. JAMES BURNES.

THE merit of his noble qualities, except what is due to the widowed and devoted mother who fostered his chivalrous spirit, belongs exclusively to himself, for he was cast upon the waters at the age of fifteen, and must be considered the architect of his own intellectual and moral character, as well as of his own success and glory—self-educated, self-elevated, in a struggle through a service by seniority, where nothing but pre-eminent merit or powerful interest (which he never had till he made it for himself) could obtain effectual preferment. That these noble qualities have won the esteem of men need not be told here; the present great assembly and the list of names connected with it show triumphantly how Outram has secured the admiration of his own sphere, whether connected with India or not; but it is needless to say that this feeling is not confined to his own sphere. Throughout life he has been the friend rather of those below than those above him—the friend of the private soldier; and many now present may recall the remarkable scene at the banquet given at Bombay to the noble 78th Regiment, on its return from Lucknow, when (after the other toasts had fallen coldly), on his health being proposed, the men started up *en masse* to do him honour, many of them in tears. He was far away, and though soldiers might admire a brave and successful commander, and civilians an astute diplomatist, none but a truly loveable man could have forced his way into the hearts of rude veterans, steeled by passing through the most horrible events the age has witnessed. (Cheers.) It is well we should know, also, what other nations think of him, and I have seen a letter from a distinguished general of our Royal army, now domiciled at Paris, which says, that, had he been a Frenchman, long ere this his statue would have graced many of the principal cities of France. As for the idea which has been pressed by some, that statues should not be raised to living men, it would be idle to meet it in a company where so many men of Indian experience are assembled. To say nothing of those erected at Calcutta to many while alive, we had at Bombay, Wellesley, Elphinstone, and Malcolm, all in cold marble long before they were dead; and in doing justice to Outram, there can be no reason why our wishes on this point should not be carried out here, and the highest of all honours, a statue, be dedicated to him. Englishmen are, I presume, English alike, whether in the torrid or the frigid zone, and as much entitled as the ancient Romans were to raise statues to their living heroes.

But to the resolution. The committee proposed is small, for a reason which will suggest itself to all practical men; but it is undeniably a fair type and representation of the unprecedented number of our countrymen who have come forward, even before official steps were taken, eager to do honour to one who has done honour to us all. Foremost stands appropriately the gallant veteran who forced the Khyber pass, supported by the noble lord, the son of the famous General who captured Ghuznee, himself a comrade of Outram, and the son and worthy representative of Havelock—a name to be imperishably identified with that of Outram in history; and here foreshadowing the statues of the "great twin brethren," which we intend shall

"Stand in the Comitium,
Plain for all folk to see!" (Cheers.)

To represent the diplomatic service we have Sir John M'Neill, so distinguished by his career in Persia and his independence in the Crimea ; while, in literature, we have Mr. Kaye and Mr. Russell, perhaps the most brilliant writers of the day.* Parliament appears in Sir James Fergusson and Sir James Elphinstone, the former of whom has taken so marked and interesting a part in the proceedings of this day; our great metropolis in its respected chief magistrate ; science in the person of Dr. Norton Shaw, the well-known popular secretary of the Geographical Society ; the navy in that of Captain Sherard Osborn, one of the class of which Nelsons and Dundonalds are made ; and the army by various esteemed generals, including Sir Robert Vivian and George Malcolm—the one an able member of the Indian Council (better known here, perhaps, as the commander of the Turkish contingent in the Crimea), and the other the son of a man whose great deeds forced an apathetic English public to admit that India did produce soldiers and statesmen ; with General Hancock and Colonel Holland, officers highly honoured in the service, and who, having filled for years the chief places in the staff of the army to which Outram belonged, are especially fit to judge of his merits, and to take a prominent part in doing honour to them. Such tried men must, I am confident, be acceptable to the promoters of this great movement, and I accordingly beg to support Colonel Sykes's nomination of them. (Much applause.)

A REMINISCENCE OF SIR JAMES OUTRAM.

THE present writer once only had the honour of being in the company of Sir James Outram. The interview is briefly described in the "Lighter Literary Recreations," attached to his work on "Orissa," &c., (p. 267, "Overland—Homeward-Bound ;" 12th June, 1849). But it is not mentioned in the traveller's diary that the Bayard of the Indian Army, at breakfast, about to indulge in the homely beverage of tea, aided by cold mutton and pickles (of which he had been ordered by the doctors *not* to partake), rather dispelled the romantic idea of Chivalry which had been formed regarding one whose proper food ap-

* Mr. Kaye, Dr. Russell, and General Hancock, were also honorary secretaries to the managing committee.

peared to be a "pasty of the doe," with a cup of Malvoisie, or red wine, to drink "through the helmet barred!" But brave knights, on furlough for their health—especially in Egypt—are very like ordinary mortals. The rambling subaltern had just been visiting and making notes on Pompey's Pillar at Alexandria:—"After an excellent bath, returned to the hotel, where I met Colonel Outram, 'the Bayard of the Indian Army,' at breakfast. There appeared to be no affectation of the 'great man' about him; the soldier and political agent boasts too solid an intellect for such unmeaning absurdity. The Colonel was on furlough in Egypt, on account of his health. In manner he evinced great urbanity; like all really great men, silent unless spoken to, and then concise though explanatory." His eye was remarkable; it seemed to look through you at once, as if, in vulgar phrase, "stock" having once been taken, there were little or no chance of his opinion regarding you being altered.

London and Calcutta have now their statues of Sir James Outram. The "Outram Memorial," by Mr. Foley—the lamented artist cut off in the flower of his genius—which was recently forwarded to the City of Palaces, represents, says a writer in the *Oriental*, "the intrepid Sir James on a fiery Arab steed, in the heat of action. Bareheaded and sword in hand, he appears to be urging his followers to the glorious strife." While this admirable work of art was in position, between the United Service and Athenæum Clubs, loungers in Pall Mall and the general public might be seen gazing on the statue with no common interest.

IV.

FIELD-MARSHAL SIR GEORGE POLLOCK, G.C.B., G.C.S.I.

IT is not so very long since we recorded the high compliment paid to the old Indian Army by the appointment of General Sir G. Pollock to the Constableship of the Tower. His sudden death at Walmer last Sunday morning (October 6th) recalls too vividly the picturesque, wintry scene which witnessed his installation in the post of honour which has proved to be the last earthly reward of his distinguished services. And yet we ought scarcely to regret that the gallant old soldier received his last marching order so suddenly. More than a generation has passed away since the exploit of arms which rendered his name a famous one in English history ; and old Time, which had silvered his hairs, had no power over his health and spirits, nor even over his reputation. It is pleasant to reflect that the kindly courageous old soldier, who forced the Khyber Pass, has marched through the gates of death with bands playing and colours flying, not as one who surrenders to the enemy, but as one who makes a gallant sortie.

Born in 1786, he entered the military service of the East India Company at the time when Lord Wellesley was Governor-General, and his brother Arthur had the command of the forces, a year before the Mahrattas were crushed at Assaye. He was commissioned as Lieutenant in the Bengal Artillery just when Lake and Wellesley were about to take the field, and all India was watching with eager expectation the movements of the British Army, which was carrying all before it. At the storming and capture of Deïg, in 1804, young Pollock was present ; and in 1805, during the gallant but unsuccessful attempts of the British army to carry Bhurtpore by assault, he was busy in the trenches. At the close of the year he was selected by Lord Lake to command the artillery with the detachment under Colonel Ball, which was sent in pursuit of Holkar. He held different staff appointments from this date down to the year 1817, when, in command of the Artillery with General Wood's force, he took part in the stirring scenes of the Nepaulese war. In 1818 we find him appointed Brigade-Major; and subsequently he held the Assistant-Adjutant-Generalship of Artillery, from the first institution of that appointment down to 1824, when, having attained the rank of Lieutenant-Colonel, he volunteered to join the army destined for Burma. He was now nominated by Sir Edward Paget to command the Bengal Artillery attached to the force under Sir Archibald Campbell, which was proceeding to Rangoon, and for his services in this compaign he received the Companionship of the Bath. From this time, with the exception of a three years' furlough, which he spent in England for the benefit of his health, he had different regimental and brigade commands, and established his reputation as being one of the best officers in the service.

In 1841, when Sir Robert Sale and a British force were shut up in Jellalabad, Pollock, then in command of the garrison of

Agra, with the rank of Major-General, was selected to take the command of the troops proceeding to Peshawur, in the place of General Lumley. As Sir John Kaye has observed in his "History of the War," the force sent on this critical service required the superintendence and control of an officer equally cool and firm, temperate and decided. The situation was desperate, and the position of Pollock, when he reached Peshawur on the 5th of February, 1842, and found that an immediate advance was impossible, was a most painful one. He knew that it was sound policy to wait; but Sale and McGregor were writing urgent letters calling upon him to push on without delay. A single incautious step was almost certain to be fatal; the enemy was flushed with success, the country almost impassable, the reinforcements slow to come, the demand upon his chivalrous sentiments almost importunate. It needed a cautious temperament and a cool determined judgment to resist the temptation to make a dash, but Pollock completely justified his reputation and kept his soul in patience. At last the wished-for moment arrived, and though he had now to disobey his government, he was no less firm in his purpose to advance than he had been to wait. His brilliant successes in the operations against the Afghan forces at Mamookail and Jugdulluck, and finally against all troops under Akhbar Khan, make one of the most glorious pages in our military history. Two days later he took possession of Cabul, and within a few days reaped the reward of his long and patient waiting by effecting the release of the prisoners, after the many months of their long and hopeless captivity. He was almost immediately joined by General Nott, and in the course of the following month led the whole of the united army safely back to the east of the Indus, and so to Central India, through those formidable passes which had so long delayed his progress. If he did not "save India" by this exploit—for indeed the time had not yet arrived, though it was fast approaching, when the salvation of India was in question—he at least restored our *prestige* in the East, and lifted the old flag from the mire in which it had been trodden.

Few men with the same modesty of temperament as Sir George Pollock have dared to act with equal firmness on their own responsibility. Quiet and unobtrusive in his manners, apparently without ambition, averse to display, and with little of the outward pretence to dignity, he was yet tenacious of his purpose, and no more capable of being turned from the path he had deliberately chosen than the most ambitious man alive. For his services in this memorable crisis of history, Sir George

APPENDIX. 249

Pollock received the thanks of both Houses of Parliament, and a pension of 1,000*l*. per annum from the East India Company. The freedom of the City was also conferred upon him, and on taking up his residence in England he became one of the Crown Directors of the East India Company. Finally, he was one of the first to receive the Decoration of the Star of India, and had the honour of succeeding Field-Marshal Sir John Burgoyne as Constable of the Tower. On the whole, there is not a more honourable record in the annals of the British Army than that which is headed with the name of Field-Marshal Sir George Pollock. [The foregoing very able article, nearly the whole of which we have presented to our readers, appeared in the *Broad Arrow*, October 12, 1872.]

V.

EXTRACTS FROM "ACTION IN EASTERN ASIA."
(July, 1874.)

[UNDER the above title, the writer published "a few words" on political and commercial action, with a view of rousing public interest in a portion of the East little known; but which, chiefly on account of the favourable reception given to a resolution (13th April) of the Halifax Chamber of Commerce (in which some fifty other Chambers concurred), in the matter of trade with South-Western China, by the Secretary of State for India (April 18th), promised to secure the attention of the wealthy and enterprising English merchants, to whom extending British trade to the vast and rich provinces of Western and Central China would be a profitable and, for their country, a grand achievement.]

1.

China should now occupy a position in the East among us second only to India. Sir Frederick Goldsmid has well remarked: "Never, in fact, since our earliest connection with the far East, have the immediate surroundings of British India presented so marked a combination of interest for its rulers and people as at the present moment. North and east we had to do with China, with which our relations are *rapidly developing from day to day*."*

* In a paper on "Roads in Central Asia," read at the Royal United Service Institution.

Touching on the race of the creeds and education in India, we recently remarked : " It will be interesting in a few years to compare the progress of education in British Burma with that of Indian provinces which have been very much longer under our our rule. It will be an intellectual race between the doctrines of Buddha and the incarnation Gaudama, and those inculcated by the Veda and the Koran, if, by opening up the commerce of South-Western China, English education should extend to new provinces."* In Chin-India, at least, education need never be compulsory. It will not be the fault of youth in that quarter if most interesting specimens of the Mongol variety of mankind should perish for lack of knowledge. They have an innate desire to learn and be taught (we speak from some experience in the matter); and should trade, through British enterprise, bring India far nearer to China than at present, we shall at no distant date be more fully informed on a vexed question with Orientalists —Have Buddha and Vishnu (or Jagannáth) a common origin ? It may be borne in mind that Buddhism came to China from India (65 A.D.), and that the Buddhism of India became the Lamaism of Thibet. The local differences of Buddhism form a remarkable study; but we must go back to trade, which the contemplative creed influences more than is generally supposed.

In 1870 Mr. Ormerod said that no apology was needed for introducing the subject of trade with China to the Chambers of Commerce. During the last ten years "sixty memorials, emanating from ten Chambers," had been presented in favour of the route sought to be surveyed. Before the American War there was a question of where the market was to be found for the goods to be produced. The French treaty and the enlargement of our business with France that followed it, added an impetus to the commercial movement, and now the result was visible in the cry of over-production which had of late years been so unfortunately predominant in the market reports of the manufacturing districts.† Manufacturers were continually crying, "There are too many of us ;" and " a few years ago," before the prohibitory tariff had been established in the Western States of America, Mr. Ormerod remarks, " There were two houses in Huddersfield whose exports to America annually amounted to near a million sterling, and now their trade with the States was merely nominal."

* "Administration of British Burma: with Notes on Trade with South-West China," p. 38.
† See "Eleventh Annual Report of Association of Chambers of Commerce," p. 46.

In the commercial dilemma already alluded to, it was boldly remarked: "Public opinion seemed to point to the vast Empire of China as a new market for our productions, and of that there could be no better proof than the fact that no less than ten distinct routes from the Brahmaputra to the Yang-tsze had been brought under public notice." Now we think that action has fairly been taken in the question of direct trade with Western China. The problem must soon be solved as to our being able to open up and develop new fields of commercial enterprise such as those contemplated. In an age when, what Elia styles "the quick pulse of gain" is beating at a fearful rate, and we meet keen competition at every turn, the subject becomes a most interesting study.

2.

A successful opening up of trade between India and Thibet would probably have a most beneficial effect on our commercial efforts in Eastern as well as Western Asia; it is to be hoped, therefore, that some useful action in Thibet may soon take place. Sir George Campbell has called attention to the importance of the subject in his last Bengal Administration Report. The Thibetans are said to be not adverse to intercourse with us: they rather seek it; but the pressure of Chinese exclusiveness upon them (enforced, as elsewhere, sometimes by military power) is very great. It is believed that if a route through the Sikkim country were opened, a ready sale might be found for "woollen, cotton, and linen goods from England, and indigo and tea from India; while, in return, Thibet would send into our territory, wood, cattle and sheep, and cloth." Therefore, "the sooner negotiations are opened up with the young Emperor of China the better." * Yarkund—now so famous for its Forsyth treaty, which is sure to give an impulse to British trade in the East—already forms a market for China teas and English piece goods, while percussion "caps and guns," we read, are easy of disposal. If we can only get the Thibetans to buy our Indian tea (the export of which from Calcutta in May, 1874, was some 23,000,000 pounds), and the English, as in duty bound, to use it more, the Indian tea-planters would be thankful. [By the mail from Calcutta, February 5th, we learn the export of tea from Calcutta in January, 1875, was larger by 200,000 lbs. than last year, and that "the quantity of Indian tea imported to England last year was 17,378,000 lbs., as compared with

Erratum: Page 251, fourth line from bottom, for "200,000 lbs.," read "£200,000."

the *Homeward Mail*, " is not decreasing in India, but other markets, besides those of England, are seeking for it."] With the now well-known Atalik Ghazi, or ruler of Eastern Turkestan, on the west, who will aid British commerce in that part of Asia (provided the Chinese let him alone), and the Kings of Burma and Siam on the east and south-east, with the young Chinese Emperor as a sort of guardian angel over trade throughout Upper Asia, there would be no cause for British merchants to fear ; and Russia is on too good terms with us now to require being warned, as we recently saw it stated, "in the matter of Afghan or *Chinese affairs*, against committing herself to any course of action hurtful to our interests in the East." For many years to come there will be no Eastern force or power nearly equal to ours ; the star of Albion is not yet going to decline ; so we may now safely employ our time in India and Chin-India in prosecuting works of utility, developing the resources of the countries we possess, and exercising our commercial tact in new regions. We have not only no desire to conquer lands beyond the Himalayas, but we conceive it to be madness to think of it : the days of annexation are fairly at an end. Nearly all sound Indian statesmen concur in this matter, and that no shot should be fired beyond Indian confines save in pursuit of the aggressor. We see every day, more and more, that the manners, the habits, the institutions of the people, "disqualify them for a struggle out of the territory to which they belong ;" and on this point, Colonel Stewart, A.D.C. to the great Marquis of Hastings, well remarks : " India has accordingly been many times conquered ; in the whole period of her history she never made a conquest."

Leaving such matters—to which a soldier naturally turns—we get back to a most peaceful and necessary action which has lately taken place—the British treaty with Siam. To make a good treaty with an intelligent Asiatic potentate is a great thing. Oriental princes occasionally seem, like ourselves, to be well aware of the fact that "Man is man, and master of his fate ;" and doubtless they think, like the old Elizabethan dramatist, that—

> " Our acts our angels are, or good or ill ;
> Our fatal shadows that walk by us still."

They believe in the necessity of ever doing something to be very great. Shakspeare has advice for them, which they seem very prone to follow :—

# APPENDIX. 253

> "If we shall stand still,
> In fear our motion will be mock'd or carp'd at
> We should take root here where we sit—or sit,
> State statues only."—*King Henry VIII.*

Siam* was formerly famous for learning and political power. Here Royal action has for some years been of a healthy nature. In 1871 the present king visited Batavia, Singapore, Calcutta, Bombay, and other places, being we are told, the first ruler of Siam "who had ever ventured so far from his own territory." The good effects of his trip have already appeared in many ways among his subjects, who now partially adopt European dress, and have a growing taste for European wines, provisions, carriages, and numerous other commodities, "until the last few years unheard of in Siam." Those who can afford it are sending their children to some European settlement for education. So much for the influence of the young King of many names, with whom, at the beginning of the present year, a treaty was concluded, and which, we believe, is now ratified. Ample provision is made for British subjects passing into Siamese territory, as also for Siamese traders in British; commercial intercourse with adjacent countries is to be encouraged, and crimes of a heinous nature—particularly the old one of dacoity—are to be vigorously grappled with. Timber from Siamese forests—to the British at Moulmein† a great commercial item—will now be under better management than formerly; and altogether the treaty between the Government of India and Siam may be considered an admirable one.‡ A commercial treaty was concluded between the British and Siamese Governments, A.D. 1827, by which all Asiatic subjects of Great Britain, "not being Burmese, Peguers, or descendants of Europeans," were allowed to travel through the interior of Siam from Tenasserim or other British provinces, and British subjects of all descriptions could proceed by sea to any Siamese port. For forty years the question of frontier between Siam and British territory had not been finally settled; till, in 1864, the zealous Commissioner of Tenasserim, General (then Colonel) Fytche induced the King to discuss the subject. The tribes on the upper course of the Salween River, and in the unknown countries beyond, require much attention. The chief are the Red Karens and the Zimmay Shans—both independent, although the Zimmay chief owes a nominal allegiance to the King of Siam.

* Population about 4,000,000.
† Tenasserim Provinces, British Burma.
‡ We have reason to believe that the Under Secretary of State for India (Lord George Hamilton, who succeeded Mr. Grant Duff) took a deep interest in this treaty.

Under Burmese rule these tribes were not well treated. The new route to South-West China, if successfully carried out, may bring us in contact with these remarkable tribes, who will, doubtless, be glad to see us as the pioneers of commerce and civilisation. It may here be remarked that a large number of the Laotian population (Shans) acknowledge themselves tributaries of the King of Siam. We believe that other Laotian states exist under Burmese authority. The civilising influence of Buddhism among the Laotians has had considerable effect, and, as in Burma, may pave the way for Christianity among them. With reference to Captain Sprye's route, the Burmese Embassy, in 1872, replied to the Halifax Chamber of Commerce: "As the line passes through an insignificant portion of the King of Burma's territory, the responsibility of opening it out cannot fairly be laid upon His Majesty." But still the Kings of Burma and Siam will be able to help in the great matter of opening up trade with South-West China. It would never do for us to behold the French (or it may be the Russians) getting a firm footing in Yun-nan or Sze-Chuen. The Golden Foot, who considers himself the greatest of Oriental potentates, "the Lord of Earth and Air," it is not at all probable (notwithstanding the rumour) would seek, for the sake of trade with Yun-nan, to become a vassal of the Emperor of China! The latter, too, the young "Vicegerent of all Heaven," has his own views on such matters. If the merchants of England are ever to found THE GREAT SOUTH-WEST CHINA TRADING COMPANY we formerly ventured to suggest,* the co-operation of China, Upper Burma, and Siam, will be absolutely necessary. Every route, therefore, available for trade, must be looked to.† With regard to how the Siamese look upon the French in Eastern Asia, we read that "the late King of Siam despatched an agent to England in 1865 for the purpose of making known his grievances in respect of the French encroachments upon an integral part of his dominions." Since this was written, the following important matter has been published:—"Admiral Dupré, the Governor of Cochin-China, has induced the Emperor of Annam to sign a treaty which is very advantageous to France. By this treaty three commercial centres are to be established in Tonquin, each with a French Consul and a garrison of 100 French soldiers. The whole of the empire is to be open to French

---

* See "Notes on Opening Trade with South-West China," p. 29.

† [In the *Illustrated London News*, 6th March, will be found a capital sketch map of some of the principal routes into South-West China, from Burma. The route from Assam to Sze-Chuen, strongly advocated by Sir George Balfour, K.C.B., M.P., is remarked on in the new edition of the present writer's "Notes."

traders, and no transit dues are to be charged for goods sent to the harbours from the southern provinces of China. In the event of disturbances arising, either at home or abroad, the Emperor of Annam is to apply to the French only for assistance."

THE ATALIK GHAZI, RUSSIA, AND CHINA.

To our brief record of a few recent important events in Eastern Asia may be added some remarks from a writer in the *Pall Mall Gazette* (July 15th), under the head of "Indian Affairs," June 15th, 1874. While recording "the march of events in Turkestan," which certainly make us feel that "coming events" are casting "their shadows before," he says:—

"The vigour and military talent by which the Atalik Ghazi wrenched Turkestan from the Chinese during the last decade, and consolidated it into a Mahomedan Power, have not yet had time to lose their force. But, on the other hand, there is the undoubted fact that the Chinese have lately managed to crush the other Mahomedan kingdom, which about the same time was established on its south-western frontier among the Panthays. There is, therefore, ample reason why the ruler of Turkestan should look about him for alliances of a closer sort than the Indian Government is willing to grant. A treaty of commerce, which is all that Mr. Forsyth was empowered to make in February last, is not worth the paper on which it is written in any of the real exigencies which befall an Asiatic State. So far as is known to the public, Mr. Forsyth still lingers within Turkestan, although in an advanced position, on his homeward route. But there is no chance of his being authorised to promise anything in the shape of an offensive or defensive alliance such as the Atalik Ghazi is said by Reuter to have obtained from Russia. If Russia has really stepped in, her path from St. Petersburg to Pekin is now open. India has not the command of European soldiers to render such a flight of ambition possible for her. The prevailing opinion here is that the wisest course for the Indian Government is to consolidate the vast possessions which it has already won, and by good internal management and a wise moderation towards her neighbours to render those possessions impregnable to foreign Powers."

THE CHINA TRADE ROUTE EXPEDITION.

The following extract is from the *Ceylon Times*, December 14, 1874; and, coupled with the more recent intelligence (*Times of India*, January 25th, 1875), that "the Burma Chinese expedition had arrived at Mandalay, and had met with a cordial reception from the King," is decidedly cheering] :—

"The *Pioneer* writes :—'The China Trade Route Expedition seems to have started with fair prospects of success. In the first place, its leader, Colonel H. Browne, is armed with passports from Pekin, and accompanied by two members of the British Embassy at the capital. Secondly, its chief members are men who have won their chief laurels as travellers and naturalists. Mr. Ney Elias, the R. G. S. gold medalist, is famed for his successful journey to Mongolia. Dr. Anderson, the scientific officer, is an old hand on the Bhamo-Yunan route, and wrote a book on the travels of the previous expedition. Colonel Browne and his companions will go to Momein, thence to Yunan—to the Viceroy of which they are accredited—and Talifoo. Sailing down the mighty Yang-tse, they may reach Shanghai.'"

Since the above was in type, the sad intelligence of the murder of Mr. Margary—the energetic and brave member of Her Majesty's Consulate in China, who, travelling by the Yang-Tse, had reached Bhamo, and thence was conducting the expedition to Talifoo and Shanghai—has been received in London (Thursday, 4th March). The telegram from Rangoon, 5th March, announced :—" The Western China Expedition has been attacked, and Mr. Margary murdered. Colonel Browne is retreating; "his baggage was lost, and three of his men were wounded."

This sad news reached us just before we learned that Sir Andrew Clarke's friendly intervention between the two Kings of Siam had been successful, and that trade at Bangkok had been actively resumed.

The Mission left Bhamo—about 250 miles from Mandalay—at the end of January, and Mr. Margery had been appointed interpreter. From Bhamo to Momein, the nearest frontier city, in Yun-nan, is only a distance of about 120 miles; so, after the travellers' daring and successful journey to Bhamo, it seemed there could be little or no difficulty in reaching Talifoo, the old Panthay capital. But, for the present at least, our advance in the cause of civilisation and commerce has been checked by a foul murder. Of course, under the circumstances, the cowardly deed will excite public indignation, and read us a lesson, in one particular at least, for the future. A London journal says :—" It seems not improbable that Colonel Browne's mission has been attacked much about the spot at which Major Sladen found obstacles too strong for him, and was forced to retreat."

Turning to the period of this last-mentioned event, or near the middle of May, 1868, we find that brigands killed two of the Panthay (Chin-Mahommedan) officers who were accompanying the Major to Momein. Indications of the insecurity of life and property in the neighbourhood of Momein were continually occurring, and the town itself was constantly "harassed by the forays of Chinese partisan bands;" which threatening aspect of affairs—although only 140 miles from Talifoo—compelled Sladen to renounce all intentions of proceeding to the Panthay capital. Still, he did much for the cause of opening trade with South-West China. The Imperialists gaining ascendancy over the Panthays appears not to have altered the state of affairs. Waiting further particulars, we cannot help agreeing with General Margary, R.E. (father of the deceased hero) that, had his son not been sent ahead of Colonel Browne's party and escort, " probably he would have escaped being murdered, as it seems three Europeans only of the party in the rear were wounded." (Letter to the *Times*, dated 4th March.)

Mr. Margary was probably a marked man through a large portion of Chinese territory, which his brilliant journey to Bhamo could not fail to make him. He may have been travelling in the wake of a Chinese army of observation; and hence the greater necessity for his not being detached from head-quarters, " accompanied by his servants only," *under any circumstances*. Perhaps it was his own wish to go ahead; but it looks as if he should have been restrained in such an unsettled region, where *isolated* cases of murder are by no means uncommon. However, the advocates of a China trade-route must not be disheartened by this calamity. We must try again, and feel our way more carefully. We lost Sir John Franklin and others; and yet we exhibit our pluck to the world by sending forth another Arctic Expedition !

Note.

LORD BYRON AND INDIA.

LORD BYRON has not much to say about India in his poems; so we cannot give him the place of even a *literary* connection. To a poet so fond of the " gorgeous East," there is much in the Indian land that might have been adorned by his pen. When he does allude to India it is in no very inviting colours. In " Don Juan," he mentions Nadir Shah, who built up " monuments defiled with gore," leaving " Hindustan a wild;"* and, again, in the " Curse of Minerva," he has some remarkable lines, written as if prophetic of the great mutiny of 1857 ! Minerva, with tears bedimming " her large blue eye," while

" Round the rent casque, her owlet circled slow,
    And mourn'd his mistress with a shriek of woe !"

* " And scarce to the Mogul a cup of coffee."—" Don Juan," Canto ix., stanza 33.

says, after making us feel pity for poor "lost Albion":—

> "Look to the East, where Ganges' swarthy race
> Shall shake your tyrant empire to its base;
> Lo! there Rebellion rears her ghastly head,
> And glares the Nemesis of native dead;
> Till Indus rolls a deep purpureal flood,
> And claims his long arrear of northern blood."*

On this attack from the pen of genius it may be said in defence, that whatever may have been our faults in wielding the sovereignty of India, we certainly do not deserve the reproach of "tyrant empire." To aid the weak and restrain the strong have been marked features in our policy. As to the Indus, with its prophetic bloody torrent, such a calamity might have been, had the Punjab, during the mutiny, not remained staunch to us under its able and energetic Governor. It may also be remarked that, as we had little or nothing to do with the Indus (called by the natives *Sind*, and by the Mahomedan writers *Hind*) in Lord Byron's time, he also prophesied the annexation of the country of the five rivers; for the "purpureal flood" alluded to could hardly have been possible without the annexation of the Punjab. Something of the same kind may be said of Sind. To muse over Lord Byron in the light of a *seer* regarding India, increases the interest we all feel in the great poet; and it may furnish an argument in favour of having brought forward his name (coupled with his faithful "Tita") in this little work.

* "Curse of Minerva." Edition of Byron in one vol., (1838), pp. 454, 455,

---

Erratum:—Page 194, line 23; for "1848," read "1844."

www.ingramcontent.com/pod-product-compliance
Lightning Source LLC
Chambersburg PA
CBHW031951230426
43672CB00010B/2124